UNIVERSITY COLLEGE DURHAM
A SOCIAL HISTORY

UNIVERSITY COLLEGE DURHAM

A SOCIAL HISTORY

Edgar Jones

First published in 1996
© Edgar Jones, Heddle, Llanbadarn Road, Aberystwyth

ISBN 0 9528264 0 2

Printed by Cambrian Printers Ltd, Aberystwyth

Contents

To

Ralph, and Duncan, and Harry

and all other fallen Comrades

CHAPTER 1

Before the Foundation

The history of Durham University has already been charted by two academics, and therefore it would be unreasonable to expect that a history of this, the University's first College, will not say anything that has been written before; but I believe that what repetitions occur will be brief, as I know they will be necessary.

The two histories of the University mentioned above are the old one of J.T. Fowler[1], which was published in 1904, and that of C.E. Whiting[2], which was published in 1932. Whiting was Professor of History in the University and Vice-Principal of St Chad's; while Fowler graduated from Hatfield in 1861 and ended up Vice-Principal of his College.

Durham seems to have been from the first inextricably associated with Oxford.

The first indication we have of a College in any real way associated with Durham comes as early as 1286, when Hugh of Darlington, Prior of Durham from 1286 to 1290, made provision for the education at Oxford of some of his younger monks. Even earlier, thirty seven years earlier, William of Durham, Rector of Wearmouth and Archbishop-elect of Rouen, had left a sum of 310 marks for the support of Masters of Arts in the University of Oxford, from which endowment arose University College.

Prior Richard of Houghton, Hugh of Darlington's successor, provided buildings for the eight designated Durham monks and is therefore regarded as the founder of Durham Hall, as it came to be known.

In 1380 Bishop Hatfield (1345-81) made an agreement with Prior Robert Berrington, by which the abbey should maintain four monks at Durham Hall, now really and truly a college, and the Bishop four others, as well as eight secular students.

In 1540 the last Prior of Durham, Hugh Whitehead, surrendered all the possessions of the abbey to the infamous eighth Henry, and became the first Dean of the new foundation; Edward Hyndmer, the last Warden of Durham College, became the first prebendary of the first stall.

The new Chapter received most of the property of the monastery as well as the estates belonging to Durham College. An attempt to carry on the College as a college failed; as did the attempt to continue it simply as a hall of residence for students paying their own expenses; and in 1544 the site and buildings were surrendered to the King. Henry, true to form, sold them in the following year: to Thomas Pope, who used them for his new foundation Trinity College.

After the failure of some abortive attempts under Cromwell to found a University of the North, nothing was heard of the idea until the early years of the Nineteenth Century. Then in the new post-Industrial Revolution and post-Agrarian Revolution world, two main impulses came together to resuscitate it: one was that interesting British impulse towards philanthropy, which could already boast of remarkable achievements in the field of primary education with the establishment of the monitorial schools; and the other was naked fear. The first needs little comment; the second calls for a bit more.

To deal with the first briefly, it was plain that the greatly increased and increasing populations of the northern industrial towns were badly served, so far as higher education was concerned, since the old universities, Oxford and Cambridge, were both remote from them and expensive. It could have been pointed out too - and often was - that the education Oxford and Cambridge provided was scarcely conducive to bringing about improvements in the world of manufactures and science; but there, the University of Durham, when it was established, itself did little to meet this particular need of the industrial north.

Philanthropy then certainly played its part, for these were times of great respect for education.

Fear however played a greater. For a long time now there had been a strident clamouring for parliamentary reform; for those very changes to the face of Britain which were referred to above, changes which converted many small towns into vast hideous sprawling conurbations, had left their new millions politically unrepresented.

The result was that for a hundred and fifty years a small class, the nobility and the greater gentry, had manipulated the system, with its rotten boroughs and its close corporations, in order to rule the country through the House of Commons. Now, as in pre-Revolution France, the affluent and influential middle class was clamouring for the power that it considered its status in society and its influence entitled it to; but such an upheaval as this promised, the abolition of the rotten boroughs and the close corporations, and the consequent transfer of power to the middle class, could not be effected without opening the floodgates of change, and admitting forces no-one could even begin to estimate.

The Bishops being Tories to a man, to a man were opposed to reform. Twice they refused to vote in the Lords for the Great Reform Bill, 'the Bill for giving everybody everything'. The part they played in the delaying of reform was known to everyone. But they were suspect for other reasons: for their supposed corruption, their certain scandalous amassing of plural livings, and their inordinate wealth. And none more so than the Bishop of Durham and his Chapter.

Everywhere it was believed that the result of Reform would be the Disestablishment of the Church of England; and it was the fear of this, and of wholesale sequestration of Church funds and Church property, that led to pleas within the Church for it to reform itself; and to demands from outside it (even from Prime Minister Grey) for the bishops to 'set their house in order'. The Radical Joseph Hume went so far as to hope in the Commons that 'the foolish ordinations' which were still going on would cease, as 'the young gentlemen' ought to be made to realise that there would be neither pension nor provision for them when the Church was 'abolished.'

The Chapter at Durham was one of the wealthiest in England. Most of the stalls were held in plurality. At the time of the founding of University College, the Bishop of St David's, in furthest Pembrokeshire, was Dean, while on the Chapter with him were three other Bishops: Gray of Bristol, Sumner of Chester, and Philpotts of Exeter. The Bishop of Durham himself had enormous revenues, many derived from coal; while the nine other canons on the Chapter drew large incomes. For these the future threatened, at the least, a wholesale distribution of Church property; at worst, wholesale confiscation. To forestall either, or both, of these contingencies the Chapter determined to use some of its wealth for a form of higher education irrevocably linked with religion.

The story is told in the Thorp Correspondence, which with some other papers fill five large volumes in the University Library. Archdeacon Thorp, of course, was the first Warden of the University of Durham, or, to put it another way, the first Warden, or Master, of University College.

What I give here is a brief summary.

The first mention we have of the projected University is in a letter written on July 20, 1831, by Dr Durell, a Prebendary of Durham, to his fellow Prebendary Charles Thorp. These two had clearly been discussing the possibility of establishing some sort of educational foundation in Durham, and Durell refers in the letter to his having written to Dr Prosser, yet another of the Prebendaries, and of his having 'struck with a heavy hammer the first stone of the foundation' – an unfortunate metaphor which could have been made only by an academic, and a non-mason at that, and one which later comes uncomfortably to mind when we read of the long early travails of what was from the start, by reason of its ecclesiastical origins, an ailing institution. Prebendary Durell goes on to urge Thorp to proceed actively; and as we read on we discover why there was this pressing need for urgency. He quotes from a letter he had written to the Bishop of Durham, Van Mildert:

> It appears to be morally certain that as soon as the Reform Bill is disposed of, an attack will be made on dean and chapters, and as certain that Durham will be the first object. It has occurred to us that it will be prudent, if possible, to ward off the blow, and that no plan is so likely to take as making the public partakers of our income by annexing an establishment of enlarged education to our college.

Van Mildert was clearly of like mind, and while advising Durell to 'open the matter to the Dean', he politicly advised that 'the university matter' should be kept quiet until it was 'in a producible shape, so as to anticipate . . . any fierce attack upon the Church dignitaries in the House of Commons.'

What Van Mildert's letter shows quite clearly is that the bishop owned to a moral dimension as well to one of hard nosed political acumen. Mention has been made of his wish to keep 'the university matter' quiet until a far more propitious time had arrived for making it public; to this must be added his objection to Prebendary Durell's suggestion that an Act of Parliament might be required, for if the 'matter' once got into the House of Commons 'Messrs. Hume and Co. would be for cutting up root and branch, not for lopping off portions.' At the higher level he takes Durell to task for his pusillanimity in promoting the scheme 'rather as a peace offering to the public than for its own sake', saying that he himself was inclined 'to view it in both lights'. And operating now on both parameters, he ends by expressing willingness to appropriate a portion of the episcopal revenues to the scheme, and to contribute as much as possible from his own means.

Not everyone in Chapter was in favour. While more far-sighted members, like Thorp, recognised that times were indeed ripe for the establishment of that long-needed institution, a University of the North, others, like Prebendary Gaisford, were daunted by the size of such an enterprise and expressed their doubts as to its feasibility. Gaisford's alternative proposition seems at this remove to be superciliousness personified, since he envisaged merely 'a superior school' for the poorer candidates for ordination. This is an appropriate point to quote Gaisford's celebrated remark, made from the pulpit of Christ Church, on the advantages accruing to the study of Greek Literature, 'which not only elevates above the vulgar herd, but leads not infrequently to positions of considerable emolument.' All those generations of Castlemen who have enjoyed the unique experience of living in Castle have cause to be grateful that Gaisford was overruled.

The first proposals were these. The Dean and Chapter were to be the directing body under the Bishop as Visitor. The new university would have a Principal, a Tutor who might also be Vice-Principal, and Professors of Divinity, Classics, Mathematics, Modern Languages, History, Natural Science, and Philosophy. There might be Readers later. The university would start off with twenty scholars and twenty paying students. To meet the cost of all this, one fifth of the income of the deanery and stalls should go to the funds as the offices were vacated, thus avoiding penalising present incumbents, and the £300 which the Chapter voted annually for educational purposes should be increased to £1,800.

A proposal to annex three stalls to the university, one for the Principal and two for professors, was greeted with some demur by the Bishop, who would have preferred that the Mastership of Sherburn Hospital was attached to one of the professorships instead of a Cathedral stall, but he expressed his willingness to go along with Chapter if it thought otherwise. To the Dean, the appropriation of the three stalls to three future professors was vital.

The Dean, the Rt Rev John Banks Jenkinson, D.D., Bishop of St David's, comes over to us as one of the prime and most forceful movers in the establishment of the university. He had already declared himself highly in favour of the university scheme; now he took a firm stand over the matter of the stalls, and insisted that the whole project be speedily - but silently - pushed forward.

> Timid and half measures will not meet the emergency of such a crisis. If it is pared down and frittered away it will degenerate into a milk and water measure, and instead of averting the meditated blow will rather exasperate than conciliate our enemies, and expose us to ridicule and contempt.

As with all committees, this of Chapter was ragged with dissention. Prebendary Durell considered the financial arrangements insufficient for the proposed university, and suggested that at least £6,000 be charged on the stalls instead of the proposed £1,800. Gaisford thought that a stall, which at that time was worth about £3,000 a year, was too generous an endowment for a professorship, although one might, he conceded without overmuch generosity, be given to a professor as a reward for long service.

Archbishop Howley of Canterbury, who had been consulted by Van Mildert, agreed. Gaisford went on to object to making the Principal a prebendary, holding that 'the regimen', as he put it, ought rather to be in the hands of the Dean or his deputy. Going farther than Van Mildert, he considered that the Principal (not, be it remembered, one of the professors) might be made Master of Sherburn Hospital. Fully the most horrendous of his proposals, to Castlemen, was to house the new university in the Hospital itself, since that was a more suitable situation for the college than any place in Durham. Gaisford was equally forthright about the proposed curriculum. Essentials, he stressed, should be attended to in the first place.

> Divinity, ancient languages, Mathematics and Natural Philosophy I consider essentials: the numerous tribe of medical sciences with names terminating in -ogy I consider non essentials and excrescences; they are amusing and to a certain degree instructive, but they are not wholesome discipline for the mind - are more suitable to the dilettante than the sober student.

Recalling the eccentricities of modern University curricula, one cannot at this point but feel some sneaking sympathy with Gaisford.

Happily, Van Mildert, not alone, was against the removal of the projected university to Sherburn Hospital. His objection to Thorp's proposal that
the Professorships of Divinity and Hebrew should each have a Reader paid
from their stalls sheds an interesting light on the times. It has already been
pointed out that most of the Cathedral stalls were held in plurality. Van
Mildert's opposition to Thorp's proposal was based on the fear that men
might be led to take the offices of Professor of Divinity and Hebrew for the
sake of the emoluments, paying their Readers to do their work while they
themselves drew the rest of the income as a sinecure, thus extending the
common scandalous practice whereby absentee holders of clerical livings
paid pittances to overworked, underfed, and over prolific curates to do
their parish work for them. A later letter from that Renaissance Man of the
early Nineteenth Century, one of those most active in promoting the Great
Reform Bill, the self-made man and workaholic Lord Brougham, also
sheds an interesting light, this time not on the age but rather on human
nature in general; for he considered that such a generous endowment of
the chairs might well deter their holders from over-exerting themselves.

In all this discussion, Dean Jenkinson and Bishop Van Mildert come to
the fore as men of both vision and a sense of realism. Van Mildert now, for
instance, expressed his unhappiness over the policy of appointing in the
first place only a limited number of Tutors, Readers and Scholars until
income became available, because of the adverse effect of such a move on
informed public opinion, which he correctly guessed would wonder at the
cheeseparing nature of the Chapter and depreciate the new university
accordingly.

The next active stage in the establishment of the University of the North
came on 31 August 1831, when Dean Jenkinson wrote to the Prebendaries,
Durell, Thorp and Archdeacon Prosser, announcing a threefold strategy.
He had in mind adopting some measure which would increase the efficiency of the new Collegiate body, give the public an interest in preserving
it, and support it under the attacks which he knew would be levelled
against it. As we shall see, the attacks he feared materialised; but while
prejudice, envy, and simple ignorance were the motivations behind some
of them, a very real suspicion of the new university rested on one sure
foundation: that Durham was essentially an ecclesiastical establishment
and therefore, to some extent, an anachronism in a post-Revolution world,
one in which anti-clericalism was a force to be reckoned with.

In another letter to Thorp, written on the same day, Dean Jenkinson happily expressed his agreement with Thorp that to site the university at Sherburn Hospital was out of the question.

Events now moved quickly - a sure sign of the urgency with which the establishment of the university was viewed, in face of the mounting opposition to the Church, and the Bishops in particular, over their stand on Reform. For on 28 September the Chapter unanimously resolved that an academic institution be established, to be called Durham College; and that its immediate upkeep should depend on an annual charge upon future incumbencies of one fifth of the value of the deanery and stalls, together with an annual vote of supply which should not exceed £2,000 - this until the money destined for its upkeep became available. It was also proposed that part of the income accruing from the Bishop's patronage should be deflected to the upkeep of the College. The Dean was to be instructed to put these proposals to the two Archbishops and the Prime Minister (Grey), either privately or officially, as he thought fit.

Thorp himself now drew up two draft schemes: the first, dated September 1831, concerned itself with the housing for the new College; while the second, drawn up in December, concerned itself with the staff. In the former Thorp says that there should be a building on Palace Green with rooms for a Vice Principal and forty students. The Chapel of the Nine Altars would serve as the College's Chapel, the Galilee Chapel for the Divinity School, the Dormitory for lecture rooms, the Crypt for a Hall, and the Exchequer for - a Museum. The Chapter House, when properly restored, could be used on public occasions.

Thorp put forward three names for consideration for first Principal.

The notable one is that of Keble. Since one must regretfully assume that not every reader of this history is au fait with the intricacies of nineteenth century theological disputation, it will be as well to point out here that John Keble was called by Newman 'the true and primary author of the Oxford movement.' An Oriel man himself, of which College he had been Fellow and Tutor, he was elected in this same year of 1831 Professor of Poetry at Oxford. Keble College, founded at Oxford in 1870, perpetuated his name.

The choice of Keble was significant for two reasons: as we shall see, in their search for staff, the founders of the new university consistently looked for the best; and their search fairly consistently rested on those of the High Church party. Keble, for instance, expressed 'the hope that if Oxford should fail in its maintenance of the Faith, Durham would still bear witness to the divine truth of the Catholic tradition.'

Thorp's draft scheme for staffing the new college, as it was called until the Act of Parliament explicitly referred to it as a university, took little account of Gaisford's objections. There would be four Professors: of Divinity and Oriental Literature, of Greek and Moral Philosophy, of Classical Literature, and of Mathematics and Natural Philosophy. Seven Readers would cover between them History, English Literature, Anatomy and Medicine, Law, Natural History, Chemistry and Geology. There were to be ordinary students and occasional students: and honorary members - these not exceeding one hundred.

Van Mildert, carrying out the wishes of the Chapter, in turn received the 'unqualified approbation' of Grey, the Whig Prime Minister. He was also told that the Duke of Northumberland highly approved. At this point he offered to appropriate three stalls to the officers of the university, and to give £1,000 to the university outright, and £1,000 and the use of a house near the Cathedral as long as he remained bishop. The Chapter thereupon decided to increase their £2,000 a year to £3,000 by enfranchising leasehold property known as the South Shields Estate to the amount of £80,000, in consideration of which increase they would relinquish the original plan of a tax on the stalls.

In the event the appropriation of the third stall to the new college, or university, as we shall call it from here, was unnecessary, for the newly appointed first Principal, or Warden, Archdeacon Thorp, held a stall already.

A printed sheet dated 9 December 1831, while announcing Thorp's appointment, also gave notice of intention to open the College or University in October 1832. It included a list of subjects of which there would be professors, readers or teachers, stated that the course of study would extend to four years, and announced that there would be foundation students, ordinary students, occasional students and - clearly a race apart - divinity students.

In February 1832 the Chapter decided that there should be twenty foundation scholars, who would receive £30 a year, with rooms, tuition and free admission to lectures. The candidates would be nominated by two members of the Chapter in rotation, the Dean having two nominations to each prebendary's one. The nominations, one is happy to add, were conditional on a certificate from the Warden and professors of the candidate's intellectual fitness, a limitation which must have cheered Van Mildert, who in a letter to Thorp of 14 January 1832 expressed his concern over standards, saying that nothing short of a university with the power of granting degrees would answer the expectations of the public, especially in the northern counties. If after four years they (i.e. the students) obtained no degree or ecclesiastical privileges, the northern gentry would refuse to send their sons to the college, and, in particular, candidates for the ministry would be no better off than students of places like St Bees, where they could only appeal to be ordained as literates. Chapter ought to decide as soon as possible which stalls were to be set aside, for a person appointed to office in the university would want to know his expectations.

February 1832 saw the plans being laid, as secretively and as exhaustively as if for a major military operation, for the getting of a bill through Parliament. Van Mildert, in a letter to Thorp, proposed that it should originate in the Lords, where he would introduce it, while Sir James Scarlett, the Attorney General of the Palatinate, would introduce it into the Commons. Sound and disinterested legal advice having been taken, the proposed bill should be immune against any foreseeable difficulties.

Only then would it be communicated to Grey and the Lord Chancellor, with the request that the Government support it in both Houses; and Van Mildert went on to list a number of people whose support it would be well to make sure of in order 'to guard against the incendiaries in the House of Commons.' If Van Mildert anticipated opposition from the radicals, he expected little beyond unenthusiastic acquiescence from the rest of the Whig administration.

It was on 22 May 1832 that the Bishop moved the second reading of the Durham University Bill, following which Lord Durham delivered a long, complicated, and decidedly rambling speech not, as he protested, for the purpose of offering any vexatious opposition to it, but simply so that he might understand the proposed arrangements, thereby enabling him to go into committee with a view to rendering the bill as perfect as possible. Whereupon he proceeded to attempt to alter it beyond recognition.

Lord Durham requested elucidation in two distinct areas: that of the disposal of Church lands in order to provide for the new university, the minutiae of which we need not here concern ourselves with; and the attitude of the new university toward Dissenters, those allies of the Whigs who had so greatly helped them into office.

The Dean and Chapter, said Lord Durham, were then to decide the different branches of education. This was important, as many Dissenters were likely to want to enter the new university. Was any regulation proposed to prevent their entry? If it was to be open to everyone, without a religious test, it would be beneficial; but if the Bishop and the Dean and Chapter chose to limit entrance to members of the Church of England, very few would present themselves. And he went on to paint a glum picture indeed of a University of Durham established under such a test: 'it would resolve itself into a mere manufactory for the lower members of the Church, for the creation of curates. A very useful branch of the Church, I would admit,' he retreats somewhat from the appalling brink, 'but in founding an institution of this description it ought to be done on a broad and liberal basis.'

Prime Minister Grey himself replied to Lord Durham's speech, saying that persons would be allowed to attend public lectures in science and literature at Durham without being subject to the discipline of the University - lectures which, incidentally, were a feature of the University from its inception - but that actual members of the University would be in the same position as members of the University of Cambridge: they would be subject to no test until they took their degree, though they would of course have to keep discipline and attend church. A parliamentary way this of affirming that the proposed new university would have religious tests in the same way as did Oxford and Cambridge. A movement for the abolition of religious tests at Cambridge did indeed begin in the early part of the century, but it was not until 1871 that these were finally abolished there.

Thus ended the second reading of the bill.

Not to be outdone the Dissenters now sought to cut the ground from under the Bishop's and the Dean and Chapter's feet. A meeting held in Newcastle decided to petition the House of Commons that provision be made in the Durham University Bill that persons of any denomination might have all the privileges of the university without any religious test.

It was an attempt that anyone with even a rudimentary knowledge of law would see was doomed to failure. For one thing, it would, if successful - and this was something the promoters of the amendment knew full well - exclude the rites and doctrines of the Church from the new university: the rites and doctrines, that is, of those who were actually paying for it.

The actual Act was entitled 'An Act to enable the Dean and Chapter of Durham to appropriate part of the property of their church to the establishment of a university in connection therewith.' It is noteworthy that it expressly calls the new institution a university: the previous reference to a 'college' has disappeared, never to surface again. The government of the university is vested in the Dean and Chapter, with the Bishop as Visitor. The Dean and Chapter have power to sell lands and to invest in others, and out of the proceeds of such sales to spend £2,000 in fitting up for temporary use any convenient buildings belonging to the Chapter, and a sum not exceeding £20,000 on other buildings. Any proceeds over and above these sums are to be held in trust for the university. The Dean and Chapter are to keep the university accounts, a copy of which is to be delivered annually to the Bishop. The Warden, or Principal, the professors and readers, tutors and students - all come under the jurisdiction of the Dean and Chapter, subject to the consent of the Bishop.

Dean Jenkinson now informed Earl Grey that the property which the Chapter proposed to appropriate to the university produced £2,986 18. 8 per annum, and that they had also laid out £5,000 on the purchase of new houses for professors and students. They had thus fulfilled their part of the bargain to give up £3,000 a year.

The new university was under way.

---

1) Fowler, J.T., *Durham University*, London, 1904
2) Whiting, C.E. *The University of Durham*, 1832-1932, London, 1932

CHAPTER 2

The Prebends

The University had as its Warden; and University College had as its first Master - Charles Thorp. Why, it may be asked, was Thorp chosen to be the first Warden: the most prestigious figure in a new university against whose future success all the chips were stacked, and whose struggle for recognition outside the close circle of Palace Green and the Bailey was to be such a long one?

The post of Warden had originally, and surprisingly, been offered to the Dean, who not surprisingly, in view of his already holding the bishopric of St David's as well as the deanery of Durham, refused it.

To answer our question we must interrupt our charting of the course of events in order to ask ourselves: what kind of Churchmen were those who founded the university and to whom we owe the existence of University College? For the most part they remain anonymous, those divines in their black and white and their clerical bands whose portraits look down on us from the walls of the Great Hall. But this history of the College is written on the principle that a College is not a building alone, nor the intentions of its founders; it is not the tutors who have buzzed down the years in its airless lecture-rooms, icy in winter, fly-blown in drowsy summer; it is not the undergraduates and the graduates who, down the years, twitter birds of passage in and out of its yellow limestone portals. It is all of these; and more. It is the buildings, and the vision of its founders. It is its tutors, and those who entered it as boys - to leave it as men. It is the god Youth itself. And as well as all these, it is that long procession of unsung and all-too-often anonymous servants who have grown old in its service and whose lives have been inextricably entwined with it.

I found it impossible to believe that those Churchmen were men of straw who merely rubber-stamped the decisions reached earlier, in book-lined studies over incense and sandwiches, by the Bishop and Charles Thorp. And yet one has to look to page 321, at the very end of Whiting's history, to see who the Dean was.

Let us start then with Dean Jenkinson: happily, for this writer who lives in the man's diocese - the Bishop of St David's. The future Dean was the second son of John Jenkinson, a colonel in the army, joint-secretary for Ireland, and a gentleman-usher to Queen Charlotte, wife of George 111. John Jenkinson was brother to Charles, the first Earl of Liverpool, who was twice Prime Minister: from 1812 to 1820, and from 1820 to 1827. So he was well-connected. Our Jenkinson was educated at Winchester and Christ Church, Oxford, where he graduated in 1804. His rise in the Church was swift, not to say meteoric. In 1808 he became prebendary of Worcester, in 1812 Rector of Leverington, Cambridge, in 1817 Dean of Worcester, and in the following year Master of St Oswald's, Worcester. This last meant that he was made Master of St Oswald's Hospital, or Alms House. On 23 July 1825 he became Bishop of St David's, and just over a fortnight later, on 4 August, he was appointed a canon of Durham. Two years later he became Dean of Durham, holding the deanery, then worth a solid £9,000 a year, together with his bishopric, for the remainder of his life. He died at Great Malvern in 1840, and was buried in Worcester Cathedral.

He married, and had two sons, the eldest of whom, George Samuel, succeeded his uncle Charles as 11th baronet in 1855.

Dean Jenkinson was, it seems, 'a man of amiable disposition'. Though he possessed a fine library, he was in no sense a literary man, as were many of his colleagues on Chapter, in his lifetime publishing only a few separate sermons. And this in an age which saw a never-ending torrent of sermons pouring from the presses. He seems to have been much more a practical man; and indeed his duties as dean would have demanded much of his time, as well of course as his duties as Bishop, however perfunctorily they may have been performed owing to the difficulties of commuting between Durham and the tiny remote village in rambling remote Pembrokeshire in which his cathedral is situated. St David's is indeed still notoriously hard to get to, even in the age of the motor-car. But he maintained a school for poor children in Carmarthen, and he achieved a certain degree of local fame by being the first to travel upon the new turnpike road between Llanbadarn, in Radnor, and Llanbister, which was opened in 1826. Arriving at Llanbister, he promptly confirmed 560 people.

Thomas Gisborne, who was born in 1758, was educated at Harrow and St John's, Cambridge. Though a political career was open to him, he preferred the quiet life of a country squire and clergyman, which was his when he was appointed in 1783 to the perpetual curacy of Barton-under-Needwood, a village about halfway between Alrewas and Burton upon Trent, a little way off the A38, and along the B5016. Needwood Forest, close by, and in his day unenclosed, was to Gisborne what Selborne was to Gilbert White, and he expressed his enjoyment of its natural beauty in poems, not without merit, which were modelled on those of Cowper.

Gisborne was an intimate friend of Wilberforce, whom he had met at College. He also counted among his friends Bishop Barrington, Van Mildert's predecessor at Durham, and the writer and humanitarian Hannah More. He was also a friend of most of the leading evangelicals.

Just as John Banks Jenkinson combined holding down the see of St David's with a canonry, and in a couple of years the deanery, of Durham, so John Bird Sumner combined the second prebendal stall in the Cathedral with being Bishop of Chester. He was born in 1780, and was educated at Eton and King's College, Cambridge. Interestingly, he seems to have been alone among the Durham prebends in having had any sort of schoolmastering career, for in 1802 he returned to Eton as an assistant master. Ordained in 1803, he was appointed in 1818 to the college living of Mapledurham. In 1820 he went to the ninth prebendal stall in Durham Cathedral, in 1826 moved up to the more financially rewarding fifth stall, and from 1827 to 1848 held the second, which was even better endowed. It was in the year which saw his last preferment at Durham, 1827, that Wellington himself nominated him Bishop of Chester. Sumner's elevation to the episcopal bench seems to have been due to a number of associated factors. From 1812 on he published a number of books on theological subjects which were held 'to reflect the best traits in the teaching of the evangelical party' within the Church of England. To these 'sound views' Sumner added equally sound scholarship and, what may whimsically be regarded as a further essential qualification for elevation to the bench of bishops - 'discretion in speech and action.'

He also saw eye to eye with Wellington on a number of issues, not least among which was strong opposition to making any concessions to the Roman Catholics, now agitating for emancipation. Yet in 1829, when Wellington himself saw the unavoidable necessity of surrendering over this highly contentious and emotive issue, Sumner joined the Prime Minister in voting for the Catholic Emancipation Act which, with a few exceptions, freed the service of the Crown, municipal office, and membership of Parliament, from religious disabilities. Typically, Sumner addressed a circular letter to his clergy after the vote, explaining his change of attitude and the stand he had taken.

He fell also out of line with his fellow Tory bishops, though not of course with the country as a whole, when he voted for the second reading of the Reform Bill in April 1832.

A man of such discretion must surely, one feels, have been marked for even greater preferment - and so Sumner was. Having been appointed by the arch-Tory Wellington to the see of Chester, in 1848 he was appointed by the *enfant terrible* of the Whigs, Lord John Russell, Archbishop of Canterbury.

Sumner had become known at Chester for his passion for erecting churches and schools. Indeed by 1847, just before he left Chester for Canterbury, he had consecrated more than two hundred new churches.

More contentious was his serving on the Poor Law Commission of 1834, that body which gave birth to 'the odious tyranny' of the New Poor Law. Sumner's Commission sought to amend the inequalities and injustices of the preceding, the Speenhamland, system by making life in the teeming workhouses less happy than employment in the field and the factory, even if this included the arbitrary separation of families. Dickens, in *Oliver Twist*, brought the system inaugurated by Sumner's New Poor Law into universal derision and disrepute.

Sumner's strong evangelicalism was tempered by that discretion which gave his rise the inevitability of a Greek tragedy, and he never, so it is said, on its account favoured his friends or allowed it to influence his appointments. Indeed, that discretion, called his 'moderation of tone', laid him open at times to a suspicion of want of strength. Samuel Wilberforce, for instance, Bishop of Oxford and third son of William Wilberforce, said of his speech at the Mansion House in favour of a church society that it was like the man himself: 'good, gentle, loving - and weak.'

Of the Venerable Richard Prosser, Rector of Easington, who resigned in 1839, of the Rev and Hon Gerald Valerian Wellesley, Rector of Monkwearmouth, who died in 1848, of the Rev David Durell, Rector of Crowmarsh-Gifford and Mongewell, who died in 1846, and of the Rev James Saville Ogle, Rector of Great Knoyle, who died in 1853, there is nothing to be said.

The Rev Samuel Smith, formerly Dean of Christ Church, Oxford, was the holder of the eleventh, or 'golden' stall in the Cathedral, the income from which, in 1832, was £3,367. As one-time Dean of Christ Church, he was expected to be *au fait* with matters of discipline, and is confidently believed to have played a leading role in drawing up the statutes of the University. He was known far and wide as 'Presence-of-Mind Smith', this on account of what it is hoped is an apocryphal story, invented perhaps by Oxford undergraduates but perhaps even by Samuel himself, for such eccentricities in academics have been known. Smith is supposed to have related how, as a young man, he was rowing with a fellow undergraduate on one of the Italian lakes when his friend fell overboard. His unfortunate companion made frantic efforts to clamber back into the boat. Smith saw in an instant that the boat was in imminent danger of capsizing, 'So,' he said, 'with great presence of mind I pushed him away with my oar and thus escaped with my life!'

Lack of information about some of these founders is more than made up for by what we know of the larger-than-life Henry Philpotts - the fiercely litigious and pugnacious Bishop of Exeter.

Philpotts was a Corpus Christi man, though he became a Fellow of Magdalen. His rise in the Church too was swift. Ordained in 1802, in 1805 he went to Stainton-le-Street, and a year later became one of the chaplains of Shute Barrington, Van Mildert's predecessor at Durham. In 1808 he was given the valuable living of Gateshead, in 1809 was promoted to the ninth prebendal stall in Durham Cathedral, and in 1810 was presented by the Dean and Chapter to the parish of St Margaret's, Durham, as well. The St Margaret's of the time was notorious for discord among its parishioners, but Philpotts earned a reputation there as a firm and, surprisingly, a tactful administrator and zealous parish priest. His next preferment, in 1815, was to the second prebendal stall, better endowed, as we saw with John Sumner, than the ninth.

It was at this time that Philpotts began to appear as a writer on public questions and an inflammatory Tory pamphleteer. One can barely imagine the fury Philpotts must have kindled with his pamphlet in vindication of the part played first by the magistrates and then by the government against the crowd which met, on 16 August 1819, in St Peter's Fields, Manchester, to demand reform: the Peterloo Massacre. The vastness of this orderly gathering of working-men and women thoroughly panicked the magistrates, who launched against them a charge of hussars which killed a dozen and seriously injured hundreds more. The Tory administration of Lord Liverpool (uncle it will be remembered to Dean Jenkinson) without waiting to enquire into the facts of the massacre publicly approved of this piece of craven idiocy. It outraged the rest of the nation.

Not surprisingly, after his cavalry charge to rescue a harassed and deeply unpopular government for whom almost everything that could go wrong was going wrong, Philpotts had further preferment. In 1820 Van Mildert collated this collector of plural livings to the rectory of Stanhope-on-the-Wear, one of the best livings in the country, which brought in the enormous sum, for those days, of £4,000 a year. On receiving this plum, Philpotts felt sufficiently financially secure to resign his stall in the Cathedral, spent the princely sum of £12,000 on building a handsome parsonage, and devoted himself to his duties as parish priest and his duties as magistrate, in that latter capacity disseminating no doubt the fear of God from his seat on the bench, while at the same time energetically continuing his career of fierce public controversialist. He was, of course, violently opposed to Catholic emancipation.

In 1828 Philpotts was rewarded by a grateful government headed by Wellington with the deanery of Chester. It would not be fair to put down his mellowing towards Catholic demands from that time to anything other than a facing of political realities. As we have seen, Wellington himself, once strongly opposed to it, had by now come to the conclusion that emancipation was not only not a threat to the state but also just and proper. Anyway, mellow towards Catholic claims Philpotts did, just as the Duke had done; and in 1830 he was made Bishop of Exeter.

When Exeter was offered to this interesting man, Philpotts replied that he couldn't afford to take it, with its income of a bare £3,000 a year, unless he retained Stanhope. To everyone's surprise and the outrage of most, the new Whig ministry of Grey agreed to Philpotts' condition. There was, predictably, vociferous opposition throughout the country. Shortly, however, a canon of Durham was induced to exchange his stall for Stanhope, and Philpotts took over the vacant stall to hold it *in absentia* for the rest of his life.

Philpotts' high-church beliefs stand in sharp contrast to the evangelicalism of Sumner. As I said, as a man he stands larger than life, somewhat of an intellectual, a forceful propagandist, a kind of latter-day Pope Julius 11, whose force of will and physical and moral courage are hardly approached let alone surpassed by churchmen of modern times.

I said earlier that he was fiercely litigious. Such a man could not be anything else. His son estimated that he had spent between £20,000 and £30,000 on litigation.

Henry Philpotts died in 1869. We shall hear more of him in a moment - but nothing to endear him to Castlemen.

Bishop Philpotts dwarfs all the others. Yet all these, Dean and Chapter, who played their part in founding the University, and our College, were men of note, men of interest as well as of interests, men not without stature or courage.

Of Robert Gray there is little to write - save that he distinguished himself, as Bishop of Bristol, during the Bristol riots which resulted from the defeat of the second Reform Bill in the Lords.

Born in 1762, and dying in 1834, Gray was educated at St Mary Hall, Oxford, a college unknown today for it was assimilated into Oriel in 1882.

A protégé of Shute Barrington, Gray was given by him in 1804 the seventh stall in Durham Cathedral. In the following year he was presented with the rectory of Bishopswearmouth, whereupon he resigned his previous living of Crayke, in Yorkshire, which had also been the gift of Barrington. In 1827 he became Bishop of Bristol.

He is little known, except for being an efficient and liberal man; and has few publications to his credit.

But on that memorable evening of 30 October, 1831, when Bristol erupted at the news that the Lords had rejected the second Reform Bill, the seventy year-old Bishop stood like a rock when one of his minor canons tremblingly suggested a postponement of divine service as the rioters were masters of the city. No, it was his duty, Gray said, to be at his post.

The service was held as usual: and Bishop Gray was the preacher. Before the end of the day his palace was burned to the ground, and he was £10,000 the poorer, to say nothing of the loser of all his papers.

William Stephen Gilly was one of those who champion the cause of the underdog. Was it, one inevitably wonders, because he was born in that mystical year 1789, the year of the Revolution, when

> Bliss was it in that dawn to be alive,
> But to be young was very heaven!

A boy when the Revolution still showed signs of the idealism which motivated it in the eyes of many, it may well have left its irremovable mark on him.

Gilly was educated at Christ's Hospital, London, that same Christ's Hospital at which only about seventeen years earlier Coleridge himself had been a pupil, and at Caius, Cambridge.

Gilly's, like Coleridge's, was the Romantic period; and his claim to fame is his championship of the cause of the Waldenses of Piedmont, that pitilessly persecuted sect judged to be equally heretical with the Cathars of Albi. The Holy Inquisition destroyed Catharism in Italy; but Waldensianism survived, and survives today. Entrenched in Savoy, the Waldenses were still subject, in Gilly's time, to disabilities, being unable to hold office or real estate, or to have physicians of their own faith.

It was to this interesting heretical community that Gilly in 1823 paid the first of his many visits, and in the following year he published the first of his many books on the sect: *A Narrative of an Excursion to the Mountains of Piemont* [sic], *and Researches among the Vaudois or Waldenses.* A swell of sympathy for this stubborn and independent-minded people was raised in England by Gilly's book, and a subscription, headed by the King and Bishop Barrington, was opened for their relief, the money contributed being devoted in part to the endowment of a college and a library at La Tour, in Piedmont. Colonel Beckwith, influenced by Gilly's book, later established as many as 120 schools among the Waldenses.

In 1826 Gilly was collated to a prebendal stall in Durham Cathedral. Up here in the north he took to championing other underdogs: the agricultural labourers of Northumberland. As determined to better their conditions as he had been to better those of the Waldenses, he wrote in 1841 *The Peasantry of the Border; an Appeal in their behalf,* in which he particularly called the attention of the landowners to the miserable condition of their labourers' cottages.

There may seem little need to include in this collection of biographical sketches one on Canon Gaisford, since he was not a party to the actual foundation, having exchanged in 1831 the stall that Van Mildert had collated him to two years earlier for the deanery of Christ Church, Oxford. Here, where his heart was, he spent the rest of his life. He took a part however, and an acerbic part, in the discussions leading up to the establishment of the University, and for this reason he deserves a mention.

Thomas Gaisford (1799 -1855) was one of the foremost Greek scholars of his time, being appointed Regius Professor of Greek as early as 1812, only eleven years after graduating from his college Christ Church. His view on the advantages of the study of Greek has been quoted already. Gaisford held the Regius Professorship for forty four years, during most of which time he was a canon of one cathedral after another, Durham as we have seen included, until he was appointed Dean of Christ Church.   Some explanation of this curious fact is necessary. The five Oxford Regius chairs had been founded by Henry VIII, who attached to each of them a stipend of £40 a year. The emoluments of Divinity, Civil Law, Medicine and Hebrew James I and Charles I had augmented by various canonries and sinecures. Only the Greek chair remained untouched, and stayed so indeed until 1865, when so great was the public scandal that Christ Church made the salary of the then Regius Professor, Jowett, up to £500.

Gaisford never once lectured, never took a class. His *forte* was Greek textual criticism, which he carried out in his room uninterrupted by unwelcome intruding undergraduates. His edition of the *Poetae Graeci Minores*, as his recensions of Stobaeus, Herodotus, Sophocles and Suidas, though now of course out of date, held some authority until quite late. They are now unknown.

Despite his weaknesses, some of which will shortly be further elaborated on, Gaisford comes across to us as a man of some intellectual honesty, common sense, and dry scholastic humour. The first two can be seen in an article in *The Gentleman's Magazine* of 1845, which gave an account of a conversation with him which took place in 1815. A regular feature of the *Gentleman's Magazine*, 'Extracts from the Portfolio of a Man of the World', a thoroughly misleading title if ever there was one, describes an interview with Gaisford at Christ Church over a passage in Agamemnon's speech in Euripides' *Iphigenia in Aulis*. Present at the interview was Professor Markland of Jena; before whom Gaisford complained that Markland's reading of the passage in question made much more of the words than they would bear, destroying its simplicity. It should be the established canon of criticism for all the writings of antiquity, Gaisford said, to give the simplest and most obvious meaning. If learning is used, the man of sense went on, as a finesse to draw out and torture and confuse the meaning, we would be better without it.

And he ends, with a dry laugh at his own labours: 'I often think, when I am reading a Greek proof, what the poor author would say to my emendations.'

Both Gaisford's common sense and his humour may be seen in the account of the note sent him on one occasion by Tyler, Dean of Oriel - an important office-holder in that college. No doubt much of the hilarity which convulsed the Christ Church Senior Common Room on that occasion will be hard to understand in today's blue jeans ambience. However . . . Tyler's pompous note began: 'The Dean of Oriel presents his compliments to the Dean of Christ Church.' Gaisford read this aloud before adding satirically: 'Alexander the copper-smith sendeth greetings to Alexander the Great.'

In Oxford a Gaisford prize still exists for Greek verse. It was won, it may be remembered, like everything else, by the omniscient Duke of Dorset in Max Beerbohm's engaging satire *Zuleika Dobson*.

If men like Philpotts of Exeter and Gray of Bristol were distinguished for courage of one kind and another, George Townsend can only be wondered at for a recklessness a hairsbreadth away from suicidal folly.

But first - he is listed, in the *Dictionary of National Biography* not as 'divine' but as 'author', a first step out of line for a prebendary of Durham. Or perhaps a second; for Townsend, who was ordained in 1813 after leaving Trinity College, Cambridge, was the son of an independent minister in Ramsgate.

A third untoward step was his first published work, which appeared in 1811, two years before his ordination, when he issued a reply to an eccentric and notorious publication by Sir William Drummond (1770 - 1828), *Oedipus Judaicus*, which put forward the ingenious theory that the greater part of the Old Testament was a solar allegory, and that the twelve patriarchs symbolised the signs of the zodiac. Townsend's reply, *Oedipus Romanus*, employed a similar ingenious technique to Drummond's to prove that the signs of the zodiac were represented by the twelve Caesars.

His great work was far removed from such esoteric comedy: *The Old Testament arranged in historical and chronological order* was published in 1821 and brought him to the notice of Bishop Shute Barrington, who in the following year made him his domestic chaplain. While enjoying this undemanding post, Townsend wrote his companion to the former book: *The New Testament arranged etc etc* . . .

It will be remembered that during these early years of the nineteenth century Catholic Emancipation was very much a political as well as a social and moral issue, and Barrington, no doubt drawing on his admiration of Townsend's successful squib against Drummond, now got him to write an anti-Catholic tract. As a reward, the Bishop gave him the tenth prebendal stall, which he held till his death in 1857. He was also given the Chapter living of Northallerton, though he exchanged this in 1839 for the perpetual curacy of St Margaret, Durham.

It was in 1850 that this perpetual anti-Catholic perpetual curate made his dramatic journey to Italy. Two versions of his assault on the Holy City exist. The first states that his object was to convert to the Church of England none other than - the Pope! The fact that the reigning Pope was no less a world figure than Pius IX makes Townsend's journey all the more remarkable; for this was the great *Pio Nono* whose historic Bull of 1854 promulgated the doctrine of the Immaculate Conception, and whose Vatican Council of 1869 imposed on the Church the doctrine of Papal Infallibility. The second version has it that, accompanied by his wife, he sought an interview with Pius IX in order to persuade him to summon a council of the Christian sects with the object of reuniting Christianity. Townsend spoke to the Pope in Latin, but his English pronunciation of the universal language was such that the Pope found him impossible to understand. The impasse was brought to an end by Mrs Townsend, an accomplished linguist, who translated her husband's Latin into Italian. If this latter version is the true one, one wonders why she did not translate Townsend's English direct. Wherever the truth lies George Townsend did not succeed.

Now what of the man whose perspicacity and assiduity carried the whole scheme of the new University through?

It is comforting, in these grey days, to learn that the bishop to whom University College owes its very existence shared with Nathaniel Lord Crewe that Magnificence proper to a Prince Bishop of Durham. For William Van Mildert, after whom first a prestigious society at University College, and then later a College itself was named, was the last Bishop of Durham 'to exercise the palatine dignities', as the *DNB* somewhat pompously expresses it. Not for him the championship of recalcitrant coal miners, the belabouring of Tory Governments in office, the infantile conception of the Christian Church as an extra if unpaid arm of the Social Services. Van Mildert carried on the magnificent tradition of Lord Crewe;

and the official world that with Victoria grew paler with every passing year was immeasurably the poorer for his passing.

William Van Mildert was born in 1765, of a family which originated in North Brabant (the Netherlands), and whose first immigrant came to England from Amsterdam about the year 1670. His father, Castlemen will be delighted to hear, was a distiller.

William went first to St Saviour's School, Southwark, then to Merchant Taylor's School. He first wanted to be apprenticed to the trade of chemist, but soon decided to be a clergyman. Thus it was that he went to Queen's College, Oxford.

The details of his career which are interesting date from 1795, when he was appointed Chaplain to the Grocers' Company. In the following year, at the Grocers' Company's nomination, he was given the Rectory of St-Mary-le-Bow, it being the Grocers' turn to enjoy the nomination.

Van Mildert's impressive gifts as a preacher and speaker got him elected to the preachership of Lincoln's Inn in 1812, a position he retained until he was made bishop. He was more than a preacher, however, being a formidable scholar, and it was his scholarship that got him appointed, in the following year, Bampton Lecturer at Oxford.

In 1819, in that age of plural livings which never ceases to amaze the modern reader, Van Mildert was appointed Bishop of Llandaff. Llandaff is a Welsh townlet situated on the right bank of the hideously polluted Taff. It is now incorporated into the administrative area of Cardiff. The foundation of the ancient bishopric, with a cathedral church, is said to go back to the days of St Dubricius in the early days of Celtic Christianity. Van Mildert was the first bishop for many years to live anywhere within his diocese. He took a house in the attractive market town of Abergavenny, which shows him to have been the possessor of some taste, despite what he did later to Auckland Castle.

In the following January, that is in 1820, he turned down the offer of the Archbishopric of Dublin, an action which will surprise a few but be approved of by many, and in the same year was nominated to the deanery of St Paul's - a progress which exactly paralleled that of the great Metaphysical poet John Donne, who before becoming Dean of St Paul's had also been Preacher at Lincoln's Inn.

In 1826 Van Mildert was translated to the see of Durham.

Durham was a rich see, scarcely any richer; and Van Mildert's income was princely, as was his generosity with it.

He made extensive alterations, not always as I said in the best taste, to the chapel at Auckland Castle: and, as we shall shortly hear, he gave Durham Castle to the University, as well as a yearly £2,000 out of his own income towards the University's upkeep.

It was at Durham that Van Mildert's flair for the princely came to the fore; and it scarcely needs pointing out that such aspects of character are rather innate than suddenly and contingently acquired. During assize week, for instance, he entertained at dinner at the Castle upwards of two hundred guests, and on his four public days at Auckland Castle he feasted nearly three hundred. The sumptuous banquet he gave at the Castle, on 3 October 1827, for the Duke of Wellington was graced by Sir Walter Scott and the painter Sir Thomas Lawrence, some hundred and fifty others turning up, and was described by Scott in his Diary. It is pleasant to note that the tables were laid out in Castle Hall then in exactly the same way as they are now for Reunion dinners.

Scott's description of the occasion runs:

> The dinner at Durham was one of the finest things I ever saw. It was in the old Castle Hall untouched since Anthony Beck for ought I know feasted Edward Longshanks there. The moon streamed through the high latticed windows as if she had been curious to see what was going on. There was a capital dinner all *hot* and excellent wines. The old prelate himself topd his part. Something between a baron and a bishop very well hit off.[1]

And he writes in his *Journal:*

> Amid the wellcome of a Count Palatine he did not for an instant forget the gravity of the Church dignitary. All his toasts were gracefully given, and his little speeches well made, and the more affecting that the failing voice sometimes reminded us that our aged Host laboured under the infirmities of advanced life.[2]

Van Mildert though was a man of his time, and subject to the limitations of vision his time imposed upon him. He spoke in the Lords, for instance, on 17 May 1825, against Catholic emancipation. This was a pungent attack, which he had printed later in the year; and he resisted Catholic claims to the last. He bowed to the inevitable in 1828 over the repeal of the Test Acts, seeing no doubt that Catholic emancipation must, later if not sooner, be an inevitable consequence of their repeal.

He is buried in front of the High Altar in the Cathedral; you will see a small slab there, with his initials on it. At the north end of the Nine Altars stands a full-sized statue of him by John Gibson, R.A., a lithograph of which, by R J Lane, was subsequently printed. The portrait of him by Sir Thomas Lawrence, who shared with Scott the Bishop's princely hospitality, hangs in the drawing-room at Auckland Castle.

Van Mildert was one of the great book collectors. An auction catalogue of his library was printed after his death in 1836, and the sale of his books that followed lasted ten days. *The Durham County Advertiser* notes, in the years between 1832 and 1836, continual presentations of his books to the Library of the new University. Perhaps his finest gift to it was a set of the St Maur Benedictine Fathers. He himself though wrote little. He was the author of a fair number of single sermons, as of course was virtually every other cleric of any standing in his generation and, indeed, subsequent generations. Perhaps his most notable work was that on the theologian Daniel Waterland (1683 -1740) which he spent the years 1823 to 1828 seeing through the Clarendon Press.

Looking back over the characters and careers of those prebends thumbnail sketches of whom have appeared above, one can understand how it was that, after the initial offer of the first Wardenship to Dean Jenkinson, it came to be offered to Charles Thorp. The disadvantages apart that were so plainly visible in other prebends - the negative factor - there was everything to be said in favour of Thorp. He was a local boy who had both a sentimental and a romantic attachment to the north-east; he was an efficient administrator, fore-sighted and far-sighted; he was generous; he was cultured; and, a feature which will endear him to readers of this history who look with horror on the mess that men in their criminal folly have made of their environment - like hoopoes fouling their own nest - he was a conservationist.

Charles Thorp was born on 13 October, 1783, at Gateshead Rectory, where his father Robert Thorp was rector. He went first to the Royal Grammar School, Newcastle-upon-Tyne, and afterwards to the Cathedral School at Durham. From here he went to University College, Oxford, where he graduated in 1803, and of which College he was elected Fellow and Tutor in 1806. He became a D.D. in 1835. In 1807 Shute Barrington appointed him Rector of Ryton, on the resignation of his father, who asked the Bishop to give the living to his fifth son Charles. Thorp's love of this place remained with him all his life; despite his further advancement, he remained Rector of Ryton until he died, and it was in Ryton Rectory, at once his home and the home of his father, that he died on 10 October, 1862.

In 1829 Van Mildert presented Thorp to the second prebendal stall in the Cathedral. Two years later, on the preferment of the imposing Philpotts to Exeter, Philpotts' valuable living of Stanhope-on-the-Wear, that 'Golden Rectory' mentioned in Trollope, was offered by Grey, now Prime Minister, to Thorp. Thorp, not wanting to leave his beloved Ryton, turned it down. Not long afterwards however, Archdeacon Prosser resigning, Thorp (who had been his assistant) was promoted to the archdeaconry, with the living of Easington attached.

How did Charles Thorp spend his time in his beloved parish? Well this was the age of the Sunday Schools, that movement which, started by Robert Raikes in the slums of the poor at Gloucester in 1780, spread rapidly after 1784. The Society for Bettering the Condition of the Poor, founded in 1796 by Shute Barrington, Wilberforce and others, and the Sunday School Union, founded in 1803, did a lot to increase the number and efficiency of these schools. They were at the start non-denominational, though it was not long before the Church moved in to annex them. Thorp played a significant part in establishing these schools, the one at Ryton being one of the very first to be brought under the control of, and into communion with, the Church of England.

More surprisingly, he established at Ryton the first savings bank in the north of England, and at Gateshead delivered a stirring sermon to the town's friendly society which led to the establishment of the much larger, and very flourishing, savings bank at Newcastle.

At Ryton too he showed that administrative ability which made his early tenure as Warden so successful. He visited every house in his very large parish, and compiled a record of every one, an exhaustive dossier which even at the time of his death was still extant and in use by his successors. The Rectory records state that under him, in 1812 'an enquiry was made throughout the parish to ascertain the want of Bibles and in families of members of the Church of England, of Prayer Books; when by means of a subscription by the assistance of SPCK, every home not before provided was supplied.' These records are today housed in the Records Office of Durham County Council.

Thorp built the school at Ryton, and the school in the neighbouring parish of Greenside. It is interesting - and touching - that elderly people in Ryton still call the local school 'the Thorp School'.

Thorp was a generous man. We shall hear how he gave out of his own resources to the new University; at Ryton he gave up £400 a year to endow the parish of Winlaton; and he also erected, at his own expense, a church at Greenside, in his day part of Ryton parish, to the memory of his father and mother. He also built churches in other parts of the parish which became parish churches as the old parish of Ryton was broken up.

If Philpotts was a collector of livings, Thorp was a collector of architectural bits and pieces. While he did not, of course, build Ryton Rectory - it was built by John Wynname, who was Rector in 1497 - he did, like others, make alterations to it. His jackdaw instinct can be seen locally. Some of the Rectory's distinctive chimney pots appeared on another building nearby that Thorp built as a family home. One of the stone pillars at the entrance to the drive of the Grammar School in Newcastle he had put into the wall of the garden of this home, as well as various other architectural features that he lifted from here and there, while a couple of purloined well-heads are built into the wall of the nearby lane.[3]

At about the time Thorp was appointed archdeacon, he was also elected one of Lord Crewe's Trustees, and it is in this capacity that he should endear himself to all those with Green leanings who read this account of the University's first Warden.

By his will this very amiable Bishop of Durham, who married the beautiful Dorothy Forster of Bamburgh when he was 67 and she was 27, gave a very large property to trustees to do what charitable work they liked with. These restored Bamburgh Castle, his property, and saw to the maintenance at Bamburgh of a surgery and dispensary for the poor, free schools, and so on. Other ways in which the Magnificent Lord Crewe's money was applied were in the rebuilding of churches, the helping of shipwrecked mariners (not uncommon along the north-east coast), and maintaining a lifeboat.

Thorp set himself to carrying out Lord Crewe's intentions with all the industry and imagination he had shown in his parish visiting at Ryton.

Overcoming the inevitable initial opposition he got the Convocation of York established on a firm and intelligible basis. He administered with efficiency those Bamburgh charities mentioned above. And Thorp's are the improvements in the village.

> The comforts of the cottagers, and those employed under the trustees, were always studied by him; and the washhouses and their appendages, with other conveniences to render the dwellings of the poor comfortable, are lasting records of the interest he felt for their welfare.

He was clearly a popular man at Bamburgh.

> His term of residence . . . was always looked forward to with feelings of pleasure by the villagers, for he never failed to discover something by which the place would be improved and the workmen kept employed.[4]

What warms those with aesthetic leanings to Thorp is his love of beauty - a quality not always to be found in busy administrators. For he contributed a lot to what the *Dictionary of National Biography* calls 'the embellishment' of the mainly thirteenth century church at Bamburgh, 'that fine church, St Aidan's'; and his hand is seen in the harmony of things in his own parish church of Ryton, as in the little XIV century church on Inner Farne, which he had restored at his own expense in 1848. To be seen there is the stone commemorating Grace Darling, who saved nine lives at the shipwreck of the *Forfarshire* one stormy September morning in 1838, and who died seven years later, at twenty-seven, of the consumption. The carved oak fittings of St Aidan's at one time formed part of Durham Cathedral. The jackdaw Thorp bought them and carried them over to that desolate island where Cuthbert had once lived and, with only a wooden spade, cultivated his patch of barley to make bread - bread which he shared with the eider ducks which had lived on the island long long before Cuthbert ever got there. Was this link in Thorp's mind, one wonders, when he made himself champion of the wild life on the Farnes?

Thorp's taste though was not limited to ecclesiastical art and architecture; he was a discriminating collector with a fine collection of paintings, housed both at Durham and Ryton, by old and - not surprisingly from what one knows of the man - modern painters, as well as some fine engravings. A private collection that, it was believed could scarcely be bettered in the north of England.

Thorp, as I said, became the champion - indeed the preserver - of the wild life of the Farnes, saving from destruction the wild fowl, some of which the idiocy and greed of man had almost exterminated as species. Not one of the brainless and acquisitive parties which visited the Islands, without restraint of any kind being placed on them, considered itself complete without its full complement of shot-guns; while especially during the breeding season a brisk trade was carried on in plundered eggs, which were carried off wholesale to be sold either for food or to lunatic collectors. French fishermen too, one reads without surprise, created havoc during the herring season. Thorp changed all this, keeping a watchman on the Islands all spring and summer; forbidding landing without an order; and prohibiting the shooting of the birds as well as the removal of their eggs.

Like Van Mildert, Thorp gave freely out of his own salary towards the upkeep of the University. He looked upon it, as I think he was entitled to look upon it, as *his* University; in the same way as other men of autocratic temperament, who have devoted their lives to an institution whose establishment and success have been intimately bound up with their own life and personality and effort, have looked upon that thoroughly individual creation as their own personal property. Like all of these men, Thorp kept the reins of government wholly, and firmly, in his hands; and with the passage of time he became, as was inevitable, more rather than less autocratic, more rather than less conservative, and more rather than less opposed to change.

Thorp's Wardenship of the University calls for another chapter, but before we leave this sketch of him a personal reminiscence of him as an old man will, I believe, bring him to life as no recital of his attainments as Archdeacon, Crewe Trustee or Warden of University College can.

In December 1918 the *Durham University Journal* published a thin but pleasant article, 'Reminiscences of Cosin's Hall'. Cosin's had come into existence as a College in 1851, but proved a failure and closed in 1864, when the building was taken over by University College. At the request of the editors of the *DUJ* in 1918, one of the very last of Cosin's Hall's students, Dr Scudamore Kydley Powell, M.D., sent in his reminiscences, mainly of Cosin's Hall of course, but including the following one on Thorp.

Scudamore Powell had entered the University in 1861 and remembered Thorp, then approaching eighty and in his last year as Warden, as 'a kindly old gentleman with . . . a lisping voice.' Thorp had several pretty daughters, but he was especially fond of the youngest, Jennie.

But let Scudamore Powell tell the story himself:

> I knew the Archdeacon, and with others often saw him with Miss Jennie on the Prebends' Bridge, both looking very happy. Miss Jennie was a great favourite with her father, who when he wished to correct her used to say: 'Now behave, Jennie, you know you were a mistake.' She came very late in the family.

1) *The Letters of Sir Walter Scott*, ed. H.J.G.Grierson, London, 1936, p.299
2) *The Journal of Sir Walter Scott*, ed. W.E.K. Anderson, London, 1972, pp.358-9
3) I am greatly indebted here to the Reverend S. Paul Toward, present incumbent of Ryton
4) *Dictionary of National Biography*

CHAPTER 3

The Search for Status

The two great concerns of Van Mildert and Thorp were first, that the University should be sufficiently endowed, and secondly, in some sort a corollary of the first, that the degrees of the new 'Church University' would be generally accepted. The significance of the term 'Church University' will be explained shortly. Viewing this latter concern from the vantage-point of the last decade of the twentieth century, we may feel that it was misplaced. It was however not. For while we have seen the mushrooming of new universities, the world of Van Mildert and Thorp knew only Oxford and Cambridge (as far as England and Wales were concerned), and one has only to look at the stunning ignorance of Durham shown by the non-academic public as the nineteenth century, and even the succeeding one, progressed, fully to understand Van Mildert's and Thorp's fears.

In 1880, for instance, nearly half a century after the University came into being, two gentlemen, one an undergraduate of Durham and blind, were dining at the house of 'a lady of considerable intelligence and position' in the West End. The hostess took an early opportunity of asking the sighted friend in a confidential undertone, 'Whether they were all blind at Durham?'

Twenty-two years later, the *Durham University Journal* was lamenting:

> We may search the London papers in vain for a word of Durham [University] news, and even a North-country paper, the Yorkshire Post, takes so little interest in our news that, giving the examiners for the First Year in Arts, it quotes the names of three fictitious personages.

On the occasion complained about, the *Yorkshire Post* had contrived the magnificent misprints of 'F.B. Jenans' instead of F.B. Jevons, and 'P.J. Hearwood' and 'J.H. Hews' instead of C.H. Herford and A.I. Carlyle. One wonders if the same cavalier attitude to typography would have been observed when reporting on Oxford or Cambridge affairs.

The same issue of the *DUJ* justifiably grumbled that, 'considering the importance of the Theological Faculty' it was surprising that 'the Church press . . . gives it so little attention.'

Part of this ignorance was, no doubt, due to bad or no advertising of the University by the authorities; but then, advertising as a medium of destruction was still in its infancy, and any academic worthy of the name would certainly have scouted the idea of stooping to make serious use of it. For all that, in the early years of the twentieth century, the *DUJ*, in advance of its time or at least keeping pace with it, suggested that advertising be made use of, and made use of efficiently.

> To the Spectator, for example, Owens College, Manchester, and the University of Birmingham, appear in very prominent columns, but Durham is in a back place, and is squeezed in between two provincial girls' schools. If advertisement is necessary, it should be well done.

That plea of all Castlemen from the inception of their College had, perhaps, been heard and acted upon by some astute sub-editor of the Spectator :

> Put me
> Among the girls!

That Durham was purely a theological seminary was a belief that seems to have died hard. The *DUJ*, which had a sensitive ear, as well as an eagle eye, for such irritant gossip, told how, in 1905,

> A lady in a southern county was on a recent occasion much interested in hearing about our women students and graduates from one who knew them, and could tell of their costume, their manners, their diligence in their studies, and so on. At last the lady asked, 'But how are they to get into the Church?

Perhaps the ignorance deepened the farther south one ventured.
In 1913 the *DUJ* printed an interesting letter from Iota (correspondence

to the *DUJ* often appeared under classical noms de plume) - interesting because it paralleled exactly my own experience of thirty-five years later:

One is appalled at the ignorance displayed by otherwise fairly well-educated persons, some of whom have never heard of Durham University, and others who think it is merely a university college (i.e. a sort of superior high school where young men and maidens *are prepared for London degrees.*[My italics]

It may be thought that misconceptions such as these must have died with the outbreak of the First War, and that the establishment of universities like those of London (1836), Manchester (1880), Birmingham (1900), Liverpool (1903), Leeds (1904), Sheffield (1905), Bristol (1909), and Reading (1926), would at least by the last quoted date have familiarised people of intelligence and education with the fact of a university system, spread more or less country-wide, and granting recognised degrees. It is a sad comment on the ignorance of even the intelligent and educated, however, that when in 1947 I came down to London for my first Long Vacation, and went to a party attended by my old Birkbeck College friends, one young lady said to me, 'So you've gone to Durham. They do external London degrees there, don't they?'

As we shall see in a moment, there was a certain amount of opposition to the new University from among those who, by reason of their position in the Church and their personal knowledge of the decadence into which the old universities had fallen, should have known better. But attacks appeared from perhaps unexpected quarters.

Two letters appeared in the *Durham Advertiser*, the one on 18 November 1835, and the other on 14 October 1836; both are worth quoting, afflicted though they are with the prevalent rash of underlinings. The first was written by a correspondent calling himself Dunelmensis.

Sir,

Some weeks ago, a letter appeared in the *York Herald* containing, no doubt, *very logical proofs,* that the University established in this city, was a deception on the country, that on her gates were inscribed promises *intended* to delude, and that her pale contained none but the *unwary* and *credulous*, whose feet were caught entangled in the net of Jesuitism and deceit.

The second referred to a far more serious attack, one made by the Editor of the *Atlas*, no doubt an early investigative journalist, for as we shall see from the succeeding pages, it had no vestige of truth in it. The correspondent (to the *Cambridge Chronicle*) had signed himself Rectus, 'Late Member of Durham University'. The *Advertiser* felt constrained to take up the cudgels on the University's behalf.

We copy from the *Cambridge Chronicle* of Friday last, the following reply to an angry, vulgar, and unfounded attack on the University of Durham,which lately appeared in the *Atlas* newspaper.

'To the Editor of the *Cambridge Chronicle*:

The attack to which I refer is in the columns of the *Atlas* of Sunday last, wherein the *worthy* editor *kindly* hopes that the "translation of Dr Maltby to the See of Durham will cause something to be done in behalf of its University." "Three years (says the *worthy* editor) have elapsed since an old building, scarcely large enough for the accommodation of a private gentleman, was, after some hasty repairs, pompously designated the 'Durham University'. This accommodation, let us observe, regards *tuition* only, for all the students live in the boarding houses of the place." Here the very outset carries with it the most palpable falsities. The *gentleman's house* has not, nor ever had it, one single room appropriated to tuition, nor is there one Undergraduate residing "in any boarding-house of the place". From the very commencement of the institution, distinct and convenient buildings have been made available for lectures and residence; and so anxious have the conductors ever been for the morality of the Undergraduates, that the most pressing applications for "living in the boarding houses of the place" have never yet met with a favourable consideration . . . succeeds the following question - "If morality, no less than literature, is to be enforced, the conduct must be watched with as much care as the principles of which it is the development; but how can this necessary surveillance be effected if its objects are not under the eye of their constituted guardians?" Next follows an attack upon the Tutors of the Institution. The miscalculating calumniator asserts that "they are miserably wanting, not one - no, not one - of them known to the public at all, or beyond the confines of the college at which he graduated", and that "some of them are far below mediocrity - little as is required either at Oxford or Cambridge to constitute a scholar." Untried men, he says, have been selected, because the remuneration is so niggardly . . . The article concludes with an unchristian-like attack upon the Dean and Chapter of Durham, and with the author's recommendation that Government immediately withdraw the funds, no less than the superintendence of the University, from the feeble and incompetent hands which now hold them.'

These experiences lasting over a century make it easier to understand the concern felt by Van Mildert and Thorp in the eighteen thirties.

What these two were particularly anxious to establish of course, at the very outset, was whether a man with a Durham qualification in Divinity would be accepted by the bishops for ordination. If he was not, there would be little point in his enrolling for the degree or the qualification at all, and consequently little point in the University's teaching him.

Van Mildert therefore sent a circular letter to all the bishops asking if they would accept for ordination 1) graduates of Oxford and Cambridge who had taken the theological course at Durham; 2) graduates of Durham who had taken the theological course; and 3) non-graduates who had taken simply the Durham theological course.

Most of Van Mildert's correspondents said 'yes' to the first two of his questions. Of the two who did not, the Bishop of Hereford said that he could not promise to receive Durham degrees and testimonials as if they were on a par with those of Oxford and Cambridge, while the Bishop of Rochester, Dr George Murray, a man far less politic, expanded on his refusal in terms which, even at this remove, are apt to make the sensitive cringe.

No, he could not, he replied to Van Mildert,[1] 'give any assurance of a general compliance with the propositions which have emanated from the Durham University.' First, it was difficult to find titles [places of work and sources of income as conditions for ordination] for all the candidates even from Oxford and Cambridge. This suggests of course that the Bishop of Rochester would give an Oxford or Cambridge man the preference, even though he had a markedly inferior degree to that of a contender from

Durham. If the Durham degrees were confined to the province of York, he continued from his see in the deep South, it might be advantageous to the Church; but - and here came the sting in the scorpion's tail - if they were to be accepted generally it would be difficult to reject applications from Dublin, St Bees, or even London! He did not think it desirable to encourage in the southern parts of the kingdom a cheaper mode of academic education than was supplied by the two universities.

No doubt a good part of the Bishop of Rochester's hostility can be put down to his patrician ancestry, for he was the second son (and therefore traditionally destined for the Church) of Lord George Murray, another bishop of St David's. 'Our' Murray had been educated at Harrow and Christ Church, Oxford. In 1808, at the advanced age of twenty-four, he was installed, like his father before him, archdeacon of Man, and three years later, Bishop of Sodor and Man. In 1827 he became Bishop of Rochester, and in the following year enjoyed the plurality of Dean of Gloucester. He wrote nothing. Nothing is known to his credit, for he attacked (if mildly) Newman's Tracts for the Times, especially Numbers 81 and 93, and he went to Hanover in 1838 to confirm the Crown Prince.

Murray's 'even London' tells us much about the odium in which that newest of new universities, on account of its 'godlessness', was held. St Bees deserves a word of explanation, for we have met it already in Van Mildert's strictures.

Situated in Cumberland, St Bees had been established in 1817, and partially endowed, by George Henry Law, who was at that time Bishop of the large and largely impoverished diocese of Chester, for the training of candidates for Holy Orders who were too poor to go to Oxford or Cambridge. Inevitably, in a clerical world dominated by these two universities, St Bees' licentiates in theology were clearly doomed to labour in the very poorest curacies, often perpetual ones at that, for a pittance that was scarcely at subsistence level. Knowing this from the start, a candidate for ordination who entered St Bees must be motivated by either the direst necessity to earn his crust, or be filled with a real sense of vocation.

Van Mildert, always stung by comparisons of Durham University with St Bees, sharply replied that neither the Chapter nor himself would have made the sacrifices they had done for an institution such as St Bees. Durham had been established as a university, to provide nothing less than a university education. He and his co-founders had had in mind the needs of the Church in the north - higher education was, as will be seen later, still regarded as essentially clerical, and those who profited by it were in the main ordinands - but if Durham degrees were not regarded as equal to those of Oxford and Cambridge, Durham graduates would sink to the level of an inferior caste. Van Mildert, who it will be remembered was himself not only not a patrician but the son of a father 'in trade', took Murray to task for that superciliousness which had led him to disapprove of a policy of encouraging the inferior orders to aspire to stations in life for which there were already too many candidates from the classes above them. In the north - Van Mildert's inference was that the north to Bishop Murray was 'another country' – candidates for Holy Orders existed who were not of the inferior orders but men of real respectability, to whom what Durham offered was eminently adaptable. He concluded:

> I . . . think that the object of increasing the respectability of the clergy will even be more attained by countenancing such a plan as ours than by throwing it in the shade.[2]

Thankfully, not everybody was of George Murray's kidney. The Bishop of Norwich went so far as to say that Durham seemed likely to give a better training than Oxford or Cambridge - why, we shall see shortly - and that he would help in every way; and the Bishop of Chichester said much the same. Predictably, and understandably, most of the bishops in their replies avoided saying that they would accept non-graduates who had simply acquired a Durham qualification.

That problem being settled more or less to Van Mildert's and Thorp's satisfaction, the seemingly intractable one of remunerating the Warden and the Professors of Divinity and Greek remained. There is no need, in a history of University College, to go over in all their tedious wealth of irritating detail the arguments over the assignment of Cathedral stalls to the holders of these posts, a solution which Thorp strongly advocated and in which Van Mildert concurred. Time and again agreement over this thorny question seemed on the point of being reached, only for someone or other to exocet it at the point of launch.

Interested objections were of course raised from inside Chapter itself over the wisdom of attaching stalls to the professorships; but of more moment was the argument devolving on that close relationship between

Church and State, the Crown (that is the Prime Minister) having the predominant say in the more senior ecclesiastical appointments.

While Van Mildert naturally wanted to keep the patronage of Durham University's offices exclusively in the hands of the Bishop, circumstances could be foreseen in which there might be interference from the Crown, were it only given a toehold; yet to bar the Crown's prerogative, as had been done in respect of some Oxford offices, might in the end only result in blocking the way to any further advancement by the holders of the chairs, thus putting off the best men from applying for them. Put simply, as I hope has been done, it was a problem admitting of swift solution; but the matter dragged on for years. It was further complicated by the death, on 21 February 1836, of Van Mildert, whose wishes over the disposition of the stalls, as well as whose intention regarding the nature of Durham, were now called in question and made the subjects of endless argument, some of which, as we shall see, were less than creditable on the part of a few of the principals concerned. The matter of the stalls was finally settled only in August 1840.

A survey of the financial problems facing the new University will illustrate both the self-generating complexity that seems to be inherent in such problems, as well as, sadly, the predictable unpredictability of human nature.

The abuses existing in the Church were well known, and by now had become a public scandal. A few entertaining examples will suffice. Bishop Sparke of Ely, a most notorious nepotist, and his son and son-in-law enjoyed more than £30,000 a year of church endowments; while Archbishop Manners-Sutton presented seven of his relations to sixteen benefices. Manners-Sutton's predecessor at Canterbury, who is said to have left a million pounds, provided his elder son with £12,000 a year and his younger son with £3,000 a year from benefices and other well-paid offices.

In February 1835 Peel's first short-lived Cabinet set up a Commission, the Church Commissioners, to consider the state of the several dioceses in England and Wales, with reference to ecclesiastical duties and revenues, and other matters. The first report of these Commissioners, issued in March 1835, suggested large reductions in the incomes of the richer sees, and the cutting of Durham's revenue of between £17,000 and £20,000 to £7,000. Peel fell in April, to be succeeded by Melbourne, who formed the

Commissioners into a permanent 'body politic and corporate' under the name, 'Ecclesiastical Commissioners for England'.

It was to the earlier body, under the chairmanship of the Archbishop of Canterbury, that Thorp wrote, in February 1835, setting out the financial position of the University. He said that the first intention of the Dean and Chapter had been to allocate to it £7,500 a year and three stalls; but the immediate endowment had been the inadequate one of only £3,000 a year together with the stalls. If it was left in its present state of poverty and dependence, Thorp argued, the University must sink to the level of a theological seminary. He had in mind, no doubt, the ever-recurring spectre of the unfortunate St Bees. Durham's future therefore depended on positive measures being taken, with of course the advice of the Church Commissioners; and on 10 April 1835 he gave evidence before them.

Some interesting facts came to light. There were, in 1836, about sixty students at University College. The Professor of Divinity was getting £600 a year and fees, and the Professor of Greek £500 and fees.

Thorp himself, being a prebendary of Durham, received nothing for being the University's Warden. As far as the non-endowment finances were concerned, Bishop Van Mildert's £2,000 a year was his personal gift, and would therefore end with his death. Van Mildert had also bought and given to the University three houses, as well as contributing generously in other ways. Clearly this was not a satisfactory basis on which to build a hopefully expanding University.

Among the disagreeable wrangling that went on over the perpetually recurring issue of the 'University stalls', some surprising admissions were made. First, Dean Jenkinson wrote to the Commissioners, in February 1836, with an amended scheme of his own for the disposition of the stalls. This concluded with the realistic observation that even the £10,000 a year which would accrue to the University if his plan were carried out would not be sufficient to put the University on a satisfactory footing. Then - but here, I feel, a whole new paragraph is called for!

For, 'I was against the scheme from the first,' the Dean continued, 'and thought the Chapter money might be more usefully employed. Now,' he added forcefully, 'either make it what it professes to be, a real university, or abolish it, and put the money to a more useful purpose.'

It is difficult to take this, which Whiting modestly describes as a 'surprising statement',at its face value, for we have seen how the Dean was one of the foremost in the setting up of the University. There are, I think three possible interpretations.

First, one can argue that, by 1836, the physical dangers of wholesale confiscation and sequestration that had been so fearfully expected before the passing of the Reform Bill had receded so far as to take on the remote and hallucinatory appearance of a dream, and that actions taken to forestall the anticipated catastrophe would, when the catastrophe did not take place, have been stuffed into the recesses of Jenkinson's unconscious mind.

Secondly, in the meantime two other deadly foes had appeared, both equally alarming to religious men. On the one flank there was a growing rationalism, and as if this foe were not enough, another was girding its loins for the fray in the shape of the Tractarian Movement. From 1833 on, the Movement engaged itself in a punishing programme of learning and argument in which the whole of the Church was involved; and the possibility must exist that disclaimers of support for the establishment of the University made in 1836, by those who had supported it in 1832, may well be due to the fact that, compared with this increasingly savage internecine war, Durham University was small beer indeed.

But there is a third possibility. This is that Dean Jenkinson was playing the politic Machiavel, presenting the extreme case, brandishing the ultimate deterrent, at whose prospective use every one of the Commissioners would shy; for it would have been inconceivable that a University, founded only three years before and given the Royal Warrant, should after so much expense of spirit be so casually eliminated owing to a piddling dispute over its funds, with the consequent humiliation to the Dean himself and his Chapter, to say nothing of the legal redress that would have had to be made to the teachers, who had accepted their positions in good faith, and the sixty undergraduates *in statu pupillari*.

If this last reading of the Dean's testimony is the correct one, the key to his intention is to be found in the first words of that veiled threat:

either make it what it professes to be, a real university . . .

His subsequent championship of the University before the Commissioners seems to bear out this interpretation, and indeed Dean Jenkinson's proposal it had been in the first place to hand over the Castle to the University - to University College - a stroke, by any standards, of genius. [3]

This proposal of the Dean's the Commissioners agreed to. The gift would, of course, relieve the Bishop of a heavy charge; although that charge, ever-increasing, and a matter of constant concern to the present day, would be simply transferred to the University. This was bound to hit hard, even in 1836 when, already in dire need of increased funds owing to its initial inadequate underfunding, it had just lost £2,000 a year with the death of Van Mildert. To make matters worse, the University had lost, with the Bishop's £2,000, the three houses which went with the gift, for Van Mildert had unfortunately omitted to convey them to it. The castle, while a very substantial gift, and one which would answer, as nothing else in Durham would, the needs of both undergraduates and teachers, would be expensive to run and to maintain; and a number of other buildings, which it was suggested could be made over to the University, on their falling vacant through the abolition of the Bishop's civil jurisdiction and the new regulations for ecclesiastical courts, would also become a charge.

Next, in April 1836, two of the original prebendaries who had sanctioned the establishment of the University gave some surprising evidence to the Commissioners. These were Bishop Philpotts of Exeter, and Dr Gilly, whose heart, it will be remembered, was given first to the Waldenses of Piedmont and then to the agricultural labourers of Northumberland.

Philpotts' extraordinary disclaimer is worth spending some time over, if only as an illustration of that infirmity of the human mind and friability of the human intellect which have been persistently lamented above. And this story of University College is, after all, as was said earlier, about people. Worth quoting also is the equally forceful rebuttal of Philpotts by both the Dean and Thorp, a rebuttal which goes some way towards bearing out that interpretation of the Dean's 'surprising statement' which I have spent a little time over.

For Philpotts wrote to the Commission that he had been against the idea of the University from the beginning, feeling that a theological seminary was much more needed. This, of course, with the Marley's ghost of St Bees, together with the equally depressed spectres of its non-graduate licensees in Theology, capering before him. However, 'finding that the resolution for undertaking this University was acquiesced in rather than approved, I gave my acquiescence, but on the understanding' that the Chapter should give £2,000 a year. The Bishop had wanted the sum given to be £3,000, and had himself promised £2,000. Most of the Chapter, Philpotts wrote, would have preferred the money to be given to the improvement of poor livings! No doubt those whose incumbents had come from St Bees!

The Bishop of Exeter now went from bad to worse. He didn't think, he said, that there would be any breach of faith if the Commissioners did not make over the stalls to the University, since no pledge had been given - that is, nothing existed in writing that would legally force the gift to be made. He knew that Bishop Van Mildert had been against lumping the income of the three stalls together for the endowment. At this point it appears that the pre-Reform Bill Tory controversialist in Philpotts ran away with the rest of him, for he forecast that if the University attracted students it would only increase the discontent in the country, for there were already more educated men in it than positions for them to fill - a variation on the theme already sounded by the aristocratic Bishop of Rochester. It would be different if Durham, like Oxford and Cambridge, could have provided endowed livings for its graduates. Philpotts was here lauding the deplorable system which existed at the older Universities and which was the cause of untold misery among the clergy of his time.

> The livings of which a College was the patron were offered in rotation, as they fell vacant, to its members; and many a man, waiting to marry but without the means to do so, lingered on as a College tutor, year after year, eating his heart out and weary of his office, until opportunity at last came his way.[4]

Philpotts thought that the best thing that could be done now was to turn the University into a theological institution. It would be much cheaper - just as, of course, its students would be inferior. If Philpotts' diatribe up to now had failed to raise the hackles of the Dean, Thorp, and (Gilly excepted) the rest of Chapter, his peroration must certainly have done the trick, for he concluded that the consent to establish the University in the first place was all due to everybody's deference to and respect for Van Mildert; and now that he was gone, the implication was - that was that! For the University was utterly unlikely to succeed.

One understands, particularly in view of the responses to all this, how it came about that Philpotts spent a fortune on litigation costs.

Both Dean Jenkinson and Thorp now went on to the attack, the Dean in a long letter dated 17 October to Dr Blomfield, the Bishop of London and one of the Commissioners; and Thorp in a letter dated 13 May to the Archbishop of Canterbury. Jenkinson was vitriolic. There was not a single statement in the Bishop of Exeter's evidence which could not be disproved. Worse (as far as Philpotts was concerned, and a revelation to us who read this today), the Bishop of Exeter, who it will be remembered held the sixth stall in the Cathedral, had never resided in Durham and had, *mirabile dictu* never once attended a meeting of Chapter! The Defence could of course have rested its case here. However, the Dean went on, the Bishop of Exeter's opinion had been asked by letter, and he had said not a single word of disapproval, either then or later, until the Bill to establish it was actually before the House of Lords, when he had told him, the Dean, that he considered it a foolish venture. By that time it was too late to do anything about it.

Dean Jenkinson did not elaborate on the absurdity of abandoning a great educational venture on account of the opinion of one man, and that one an absentee pluralist. Philpotts, even on that occasion, the Dean said, had suggested nothing else. At this point, the Dean comes out once again with that 'surprising statement', his disclaimer of having been in the forefront of the move to establish a University; and one feels, given the context of the disclaimer, and the terms in which it was couched, that the Dean was, certainly here if he had not been earlier, playing the politic Machiavel for all the role was worth; for he confesses, first, that he agreed with Philpotts over the foolishness of the whole affair, and secondly, that he agreed with him that, if it were possible to turn the University into a theological seminary he would concur. But - and here he was on unassailable ground, and knew that he was - the University was actually in existence, the students were in residence, the teachers were teaching, and, all these apart, it would be a daunting task to appropriate the University's funds to something quite else.

Gilly was pessimistic about the future of the University, rather than antagonistic to it, and his evidence points to faint-heartedness rather than anything more sinister. Meanwhile, his evidence is interesting for revealing, as well as the character of the man, something of the condition of the University getting on for four years after its establishment. Up to 22 April 1836, the date when he gave his testimony, 'only' 96 students had been admitted. Most of these intended to take Holy Orders. Contrary to expectations, no contributions had been received from wealthy patrons in the north. On the other hand, the University had so far managed to pay its way, the receipts for 1833 to 1835 having amounted to about £21,500, and the expenses to about £20,500.

The Ecclesiastical Commissioners had been less than helpful over the financing of the University in general, and the matter of the stalls in particular, and Dean Jenkinson's letter of 17 October, as well as taking the Bishop of Exeter apart, did not spare the Commissioners either. Nor, it is pleasant to report, did Van Mildert's successor Dr Maltby, who had been appointed Bishop of Durham in the summer of 1836, and who wrote to the Ecclesiastical Commissioners on 3 December. The telling point Maltby made was that the Commissioners knew next to nothing of the north and its needs, understood less, and had no expectation of ever going up there to find out.

It will not come amiss here to enquire into why Oxford and Cambridge were so expensive, as well as into why the need was urgent for the establishment of another University, and I can suggest no better source-book for the interested reader than Thomas Hughes' *Tom Brown at Oxford*,[5] in which Hughes describes at length the chronic inadequacies, inequalities and general corruption of an Oxford almost exactly contemporaneous with the Durham we have been describing.

His spokesman is in the main the servitor Hardy, up on a beggarly sixty-five pounds a year and despised by the tufts and the gentleman-commoners. Tom, while still a freshman, is 'being driven more and more to the conclusion that the worship of the golden calf was verily and indeed rampant in Oxford.'[5] Much later in his first year, he has advanced so far in radical - or rather reformist - opinions as to ask Hardy rhetorically: 'How can a place be a university where no one can come up who hasn't two hundred a year to live on?'[6]

But one has to look at Hardy's outburst against Oxford's decadence to catch the full flavour of the institution that such men as Philpotts wished to be preserved undiluted by an upstart University in the north. The occasion is when the wealthy cad Chanter has just attempted to bribe a junior servitor a tenner to prick him in at chapel.

And who are they, I should like to know, these fellows who offer bribes to gentlemen? How do they live? What do they do for themselves or for this University? By heaven, they are ruining themselves body and soul, and making this place, which was meant for the training of learned and brave and righteous Englishmen, a lie and a snare. And who tries to stop them?[7]

It was then a combination of the overt bad influence on young men of the 'Fast Set' together with their tolerance by the authorities, and the covert pernicious influence of the Oxford tradesmen, who plied the same wealthy idlers with unlimited credit - knowing that the fathers of those young men would in the end pay up - that made residence at Oxford so very expensive. And all too often a travail of misery.

It was this double-headed monster that Thorp above all wished to exclude from his University; and to this end he bent all his efforts.

Even the getting to Oxford or Cambridge in itself was not easy. The intending undergraduate had to wait until a vacancy came his way, sometimes, as with the young Mark Pattison, for two years.

Bearing in mind all these factors, it is difficult to understand the obstructionist attitude of some of the higher clergy towards any expansion of the Universities. Maltby, Van Mildert's successor, put the new University in a much more pleasing, and indeed optimistic, light than they. A letter to the Secretary of the Commission, dated 3 December 1836, ends:

> I ought not to conclude this statement respecting the University of Durham without doing it bare justice, when I express my belief that it is working extremely well. The professors are men of worth and talent, and appear to labour in their several duties with a zeal and agreement amongst themselves that promise the fairest fruits of a well-ordered society, trained with all due regard to economy in a soundly practical and religious course of learning.

For all that the University was working well, it was still very insufficiently endowed; and if further endowment was not forthcoming, teachers as good as those already in the University would not be attracted to it, while neither would undergraduates, without inducements such as scholarships and fellowships. A rational observer might have drawn the conclusion from the first of these contingencies, that the resulting inferior teaching by second-rate men would itself be a deterrent to both teachers and undergraduates who were considering applying to Durham.

Thorp laboured tirelessly for further endowment. He brought up again his old argument that moneys had long since been set aside, long before the Dissolution of the Monasteries, for liberal education at Durham College at Oxford, even though by now the moneys that had then been set aside were negligible.

A consequence of the underfunding was that, at the time when Thorp was writing, the Divinity chair was vacant, the teaching being done by the Professor of Greek; while there were only ten teachers in the University, including those who, while resident elsewhere, turned up to give only occasional lectures. Thorp wanted £7,500 a year, and that, he declared, would not be too much.

In the end, the original wishes of Bishop Van Mildert and the Chapter became the basis of an Act which was drawn up by the Ecclesiastical Commissioners, put before Convocation, approved on 22 May 1841, and put into effect by an Order in Council of 4 June.

The main items of the settlement were these. The Wardenship should, on the resignation or death of Thorp, become attached to the Deanery, and when this should come about, the Warden's salary of £500 was to be used to fund a chair in Hebrew and Oriental Languages. The Professor of Mathematics was to be appointed Professor of Mathematics and Astronomy, at a salary of £700 a year. It's interesting to note that, as at Oxford, Mathematics was the only subject with Classics which was on offer in the Schools. Eighteen new Fellowships were to be founded, bringing the total up to twenty-four. The annual value of these was to be £120, though ten Senior Fellows were to get £150. Only eight of the Fellows over twenty-five years of age were to be laymen. The lay Fellowships were to be held for eight years, the clerical ones for ten, unless of course they were vacated by marriage or preferment. These last clauses should put an end to the puzzlement of generations of Castlemen who, knowing that behind the wall lies a Secret Garden, the Fellows' Garden, know of no Fellows ever to saunter in it.

To provide the money for these changes, the lands belonging to the deanery and the eleventh canonry were to go to the University. Henry Jenkyns, at the time Professor of Greek, held the third stall; this was to be permanently attached to the professorship of Divinity. At this time Jenkyns was also doing the work of the Divinity Professor. In time, when the eleventh stall became vacant, that would be permanently assigned to the

Professor of Greek.

So much for the endowment. There remain to be mentioned the arrangements for the governing of the University. On 15 February 1834 Chapter instructed Thorp to draw up a set of statutes for these. The Rev Samuel Smith, who held the eleventh stall, played a large part in this compilation, drawing no doubt from his former experience as Dean of Christ Church, Oxford. These Statutes were put before Chapter on 21 November. They covered of course the rules relating to the keeping of terms, the conduct of examinations, the granting of degrees, and the duties of the professors. What is interesting to us is the wording of the minutes of that fateful Chapter meeting, for it certainly envisages University College as a separate entity to the University. Chapter is spoken of as having founded the University and partly endowed a college within the same while reference is made to 'the Warden of the College and Vice-Chancellor of the University.'

It is impossible of course, at this remove, to come to any hard and fast conclusions about what precisely was in the minds of Chapter; but it would be doing an injustice to the prebends to assume that they looked no farther than the day, or the decade. They were, after all, as we have seen, men of distinction in academic life: scholars. The alma mater of most of them, Oxford, itself had had similar small beginnings. Not one of the Durham prebends can have been unaware of the humble, and indeed obscure, beginnings of their University, even if those precise beginnings had yet to be properly charted.

Being versed then to some degree in the logic of events, they must have reckoned on the University's either expanding or dying-off, since the truth that no organism stands still is not an amazing discovery of the twentieth century. The notion of its dying-off seems to have been confined to the absentee Philpotts down at Exeter, from which remove he could hardly have been the best judge.

William Gilly's pessimism over its future seems to have been rather idiosyncratic. His gloomy fear over another issue speaks volumes: this was that, if the Commissioners abolished some of the stalls, when the houses that were attached to them would fall vacant and therefore become of use to the University, the Chapter would be greatly inconvenienced by having young men about the premises.

A truly shocking thought!

To return, if the University were to follow the universal law and expand, it could not possibly be confined to one College, and it would be reasonable to expect that that happy expansion would not take place overnight, nor indeed in the roughly one year that had elapsed since its foundation. Events were to bring about the expansion sooner than one might have supposed, for it was only twelve years after this meeting that the second College, Bishop Hatfield's Hall, was founded - in 1846. And in only another five years, in 1851, was founded a third, the short-lived Bishop Cosin's Hall.

A later Act of Chapter, that of 4 April 1834, formally appointed Charles Thorp as Warden, the Rev Henry Jenkyns as Professor of Greek and Classical Literature, the Rev Temple Chevallier as Professor of Mathematics, and the Rev C.T. Whitley and the Rev T.W. Peile as Proctors. I shall have more to say about these in a moment, as well as about the Rev Hugh James Rose, who was appointed the first Professor of Divinity.

Meanwhile - the Rules and Regulations.

On 20 July 1835 Chapter formally passed that the University would confer degrees, and instructed its first Warden to join with the Bishop in applying to the Crown for a Charter. The list of University officials above was repeated, and the University was declared to consist of the Warden, professors, teachers, graduates, scholars and other members.

In brief, the constitution of the University was as follows: with the Bishop as Visitor, and the Dean and Chapter governors, the University's affairs were to be managed by the Warden, and a Senate and Convocation. The ordinary discipline of the University should of course be in the charge of the Warden.

The Senate should transact the ordinary business of the University, and should be empowered to originate regulations and other measures relating to it, though these were to be confirmed by Convocation. Convocation itself could confirm or reject any submission by Senate; but they had no power to originate or amend. Senate was to consist of the Warden, the Professors of Divinity, Greek and Mathematics, the two Proctors, and one member of Convocation to be nominated annually by the Dean and Chapter, and of 'such other persons as might hereafter be appointed.' The present Convocation was to consist of the Warden, and of Doctors in any of the three Faculties, or of Masters of Arts of Oxford, Cambridge or Durham who were members of the University of Durham; while future

Convocations, besides containing these original members, should consist of all persons admitted to the degrees of Doctor of Divinity, Civil Law or Medicine, and Masters of Arts of the University of Durham. Noone might be admitted to a Durham degree without the assent of the Dean and Chapter, and of Senate and Convocation, nor without keeping the requisite residence and going through the requisite exercises and examinations, or without subscribing to the three Articles of the Thirty-Sixth Canon. These last were: recognition of the King's supremacy, and assent to the Book of Common Prayer and the Thirty-nine Articles.

The regulations of the University were issued in March 1836, by which time of course teaching was getting into gear. They make interesting reading, not least that regulation which required the intending student to have passed an examination in the rudiments of the Christian religion.

Let us look finally at the 'Regulations of Discipline, &c., for the Students at Durham', signed as they were by 'C. Thorp, Warden.'

What is particularly interesting about them, apart from the religious test above-mentioned, is the serious attempt made to curb that extravagance among undergraduates, and their exploitation by unscrupulous tradesmen, which was so bedevilling Oxford.

1) Applicants for admission must present to the Warden a certificate of their age; the ordinary age for admission being from sixteen to twenty-one. They must also bring Testimonials to their character and conduct during the two previous years.

2) No one will be admitted until he has passed an Examination. The Examination usually extends to construing Greek and Latin, writing Latin - Arithmetic - the Elements of Geometry and Algebra - History (particularly that of the Old Testament) and Geography - the Evidences and Doctrines of Christianity.

3) At the time of entering, the Applicant is required to subscribe his name to a declaration of obedience, adding his age - the address of his Parent or Guardian, and the date of his admission. He is required at the same time to pay twelve pounds as Caution-money to the Treasurer. This money is returned whenever he ceases to be a member of the College,

4) Immediately after admission, the new Student is shewn the Rooms assigned him by the Warden. The Furniture of the Rooms is supplied by the Establishment, and charged to the Student. No Student is suffered to furnish his own Rooms, nor to add any thing to the Regulation Furniture, without permission of the Censor.

5) The Students are required to be present
At Breakfast in Hall,
At Chapel Prayers, or at Cathedral Service, at the times appointed,
At Dinner in Hall,

At Prayers in the Evening.

They are also required to attend such Lectures of the Professors and Tutors, and such other Lectures as the Authorities may direct.

6) No day will count as a day of Residence, unless the Student has been present on all the occasions required; and if he absents himself on more than one occasion, he will be liable to lose a day for each non-appearance. The Censor, or other Officer under whose notice the irregularity has come, will signify the loss of the day by a cross in the Butler's Book. Ten such crosses will lose the Term.

1) Yet the Warden, Professors, Tutors, and other officers will, in certain cases, give permission to be absent from Chapel, Lectures, &c., and the day will then reckon. They will also remit crosses on a satisfactory explanation being given.

2) Also, any one wishing to absent himself from Hall may make an entry in the Butler's Book of the person he is going to visit, or the place he is going to, and the reason of his absence. If the cause be approved, the day will reckon, but if disallowed, or if no entry has been made, the day is lost.

3) In cases of aegrotat, the day will always be crossed, but with a distinct (a red) cross. The Censors will judge, at the end of the week, from the medical certificates, and from their own knowledge of the Patient, how far such crosses should or should not be counted against the Term.

7) Students are expected to be in College before the gates are closed at night; a report of all those who come in afterwards is delivered to the Censor.

8) Any Stranger going out of College after the gates are shut, will be required to give the name of the Student from whose Rooms he comes. All Strangers must leave the College before Prayers at night.

9) At twelve o'clock the Servants will go round (and occasionally the Censor with them) to see that all lights are extinguished.

10) The Academical Dress is always to be worn in public except

1) On the River; and then the Cap and Gown must be worn down to the boat house. In the boat, either the Academical Cap or a boating-cap may be used, but no hat.

2) In going to a gentleman's house more than two miles distant from Durham; and of this notice must always be given beforehand, by entry in the Butler's Book. On any other reasonable occasion, a similar entry may be made, subject to the discretion of the Censor to disallow or approve.

11) All play with Dice and Cards, and generally all Betting and Gambling are strictly prohibited.

12) Students must not hire any Room or House in the Town, nor frequent Inns, Public-Houses, Cooks' or Confectioners' Shops.

13) It is forbidden to Students to go to the neighbouring Towns, (as Sunderland, Newcastle, &c), or to hire Horses, Gigs, Chaises, or other Vehicles, without reasonable cause assigned, and notice given to the Censor, either verbally or by entry beforehand in the Butler's Book.

14) The Parent or Guardian of every Student will have the option of putting his Bills contracted out of College, under the control of the Tutor. In that case, the Bills must be made up and sent in by his Tradesmen to the Tutor three days before the end of each Term. The Tutor will then forward them to the Parent or Guardian, and, if desired, will transmit the money to the Tradesmen. The Student will be expected to give his Tradesmen notice to send in their Bills, and will be held responsible if they are not delivered to the Tutor in proper time; or if they do not contain the whole amount of debt. If the Tradesman also shall appear to be in fault, all Students will be forbidden to deal with him.

1) *Thorp Letters*, 19 February, 1834
2) *Ibid.*, 22 February, 1834
3) *Ibid.*, 26 February, 1836
4) Geoffrey Faber, *Oxford Apostles*, London, 1954, p.54
5) Thomas Hughes, *Tom Brown at Oxford* , London, 1880, p.54
6) *Ibid.*, p.242
7) *Ibid.*, p.68

Chapter 4

Teachers

What now about the University's first teachers? Certainly noone can say that Van Mildert looked for second-raters, let alone nonentities.

The Chair of Divinity was, of course, considered the most important, and a look at the candidates canvassed in Van Mildert's mind shows us the calibre of the men he was after. He first offered the chair to John James Blunt, Fellow of St John's College, Cambridge. Blunt had written a popular *History of the Reformation* for the *Family Library*, had given Hulsean Lectures which Van Mildert thought highly of, and had contributed three articles to the *Quarterly Review* which he considered masterly. Blunt however turned down the offer. Van Mildert next considered Edward Parr Greswell, Fellow of Corpus Christi College, Oxford, Greswell having written *Harmonia Evangelica*. Against Greswell was the fact that his bent was towards Classics rather than Divinity; and, even more decisive, he had a reputation for being a recluse, which would hardly make him the ideal choice to lecture to undergraduates - especially in a new university which would have to make its way. Van Mildert finally offered the chair to Hugh James Rose.

Rose is now known only to a few specialists, but in his time he was a man of great influence in the Church of England. A sizable section of Dean Burgon's book, *Lives of Twelve Good Men*, one hundred and sixty-seven pages in fact, is given up to him under the title 'The Restorer of the Old Paths'. Even when the book was written however, in 1888, Burgon could start his essay:

> The name above written, besides being a boast and a praise, was reckoned a tower of strength by Churchmen of a generation which has already well-nigh passed away. Pronounced now in the hearing of those who have been in the Ministry ten, fifteen, twenty years, it is discovered to be unknown to them.[1]

This History of the College is no place to give a one hundred and sixty seven page biography of Rose, but a word or two about him and his all-too-short tenure of the Divinity Chair at Durham will go some way towards fulfilling one of the chief aims of this History, which is to put before today's Castlemen their predecessors, and those to whom the Castle itself owes its being.

Rose was born in 1795, the son of the Rev William Rose, of Little Horsted, in Sussex. Those who have toiled across the arid deserts of Latin accidence and syntax will relish the following anecdote.

> For a prolonged period his father took him into his school to keep him out of the way of mischief. When I [Rose's mother] proposed to take him again, - 'No,' (said Mr Rose) 'he is learning the Latin grammar. He wanted to read so much English every day, that, not having time to hear him, I gave him a Latin grammar to employ him.' Before he was four years old he had mastered it.[2]

It was well known that Rose's health was poor. Van Mildert certainly knew before he invited him to Durham, and it must be confessed that the Bishop was not over-inclined to make allowances for it when Rose was safely installed; but Rose's reputation was such that it over-rode that consideration. Indeed, after the collapse of his tenure of the Chair at Durham, he was invited to succeed Bishop Otter, newly translated to the see of Chichester, as Principal of King's College, London. This was in 1836 - but three years after his leaving Durham.

The calamitous state of Rose's health dated from an attack of croup suffered when he was five years old. This left him 'liable to frequent inflammation of the lungs'.[3] This was that wasting and debilitating scourge - asthma.

By 1827 (Rose had left Trinity College, Cambridge, in 1818 and had been presented to the living of Horsham, in Sussex, in 1821) he was considered the recognized English authority on German Protestantism, having published discourses on the state of German Protestantism two years earlier. From this time on, Rose was regarded as a prominent champion of the English Catholic tradition and of the Apostolic Order. Inevitably, he came to be in the forefront of the Oxford Movement.

'Solemn' is the word again and again used of Rose's bearing, his preaching, even his conversation. Someone who had long before heard him read 'but once', that once which he would 'never forget . . . as long as I live', was the Rev Henry Low, one of the Fellows of Exeter, who told an Exeter College Common Room how he had heard Rose read the Ten Commandments: 'it was as if Mr Rose had been personally commissioned to deliver the decalogue to the congregation.'[4]

In 1830 Rose was appointed vicar of Hadleigh, in Suffolk. In two years he had founded the *British Magazine*, a monthly organ for 'the dissemination of sound Church views', whose main object was to be 'the defence of the Church, her institutions, her doctrines',[5] in the face of the scepticism, the unbelief, the irreverence, and the apathy of the times, times in which the Church's fortunes 'had sunk to the lowest ebb.'[6]

William Palmer, the liturgiologist, of Trinity College, Dublin, and Worcester College, Oxford - not to be confused with the William Palmer (*infra*) who became a tutor at Durham - gives a brief but vivid word-picture of Rose as he was in about 1832:

> his tall, bending, and attenuated form, and aquiline features - which, amidst their intellectual and commanding character, gave evidences of deep suffering - indicated but too truly the sad presence of decline.[7]

In society, however, that grave, and even sad and solemn expression, 'gave way at once to the radiance of intellect, benevolence, and wit.'

Such a man inevitably came to the fore of Newman's Oxford Movement. But his health was failing. Hadleigh, of which he had grown fond, clearly did not agree with him, and he sadly left it for two small cures: that of Fairstead, in Essex, and that of St Thomas's, in Southwark. It was at this time that Van Mildert made him the offer of the Divinity Chair at Durham at £500 a year:

> the one man in England who was fittest by his sound theological learning and orthodoxy, - the breadth of his views and the ardour of his disposition, - to set an impress on Durham as a School of Divinity, if he might be persuaded to become the first to occupy the professorial Chair.[8]

Rose himself, while fearing that his health would not enable him to do justice to Van Mildert's hopes, was enthusiastic about the challenge. 'I have views which, if they could be realized, would make Durham a stronghold for the Church,' he wrote to Newman on October 1, 1833.[9] Not for Rose at Durham, any more than Newman at Oriel, the heresy that the tutor's concern with his pupils did not extend to their religious views. He held to the view that the tutor should be 'a moral and religious guardian of the youths committed to him.'

Rose arrived in Durham towards the end of October, in order to keep the Michaelmas Term. The house he occupied was that adjoining to the gateway of the College – elsewhere called 'the Close' – on the north side; and his study was the room on the right of the entrance-hall. His lectures to the students in Divinity were given in private, catechetically, day by day - on the exegesis of the New Testament. On Sunday evenings Rose gave a general lecture addressed to the whole University. He received his pupils after these Sunday evening lectures in his drawing-room, which was also to the right of the entrance-hall.

The Dean and Chapter having decided that each Professor should also deliver a Public Lecture every term, Rose delivered his first, on 'An Apology for the Study of Divinity', in Bishop Cosin's Library. His second terminal Divinity lecture, for the Lent Term, also delivered in Bishop Cosin's Library, was a very much more brilliant affair, and one very much to the minds of the Tractarians, being on 'The Study of Church History Recommended'.

This, given before an impressive audience, received a fulsome mention in the *Advertiser* of March 21, 1834. 'The Lecture,' the *Advertiser* reported dauntingly, 'which was most learned, eloquent, and interesting, seemed to rivet the attention of the entire auditory, during its delivery, which occupied about an hour and a half.'

There can be no doubt that what was in Van Mildert's mind in appointing such a formidable man as Rose was that the appointment must make acceptance of Durham degrees an absolute certainty. After all, even parasitic nonentities like Murray of Rochester could hardly fail to accept a man trained in Divinity by Rose, among the first in the country. Writing at the end of February 1834, Rose himself indicates the way the wind was blowing:

I have been here nearly six months, and have now so arranged matters as to courses of lectures, etc., that twenty-four out of the twenty-six Prelates have agreed to accept the full education here, (i.e. three years before B.A., and two at Divinity) or a B.A. degree from the older Universities with our Divinity lectures.[10]

It was not the bracing Durham air which put paid to Rose's career up in the north, for contrary to expectation the air of Durham agreed with him at least as well as any other he had breathed, but the work-load. He wrote of this, in February 1834, to Joshua Watson:

They overwork me here, for while my brother Professor has two lectures a week, I have seven days' lectures, and the Sunday evening lecture is a very distressing and weary one.[11]

Rose consequently urged the Bishop and Thorp to find an assistant for him, and this was agreed to on consideration of one third of Rose's stipend, with the fees, and some moneys to come out of Van Mildert's gift, being made over to him.

The Thorp Correspondence, however, makes it clear that Rose's ill-health, and his requests for concessions on account of it, made for some ill-feeling - naturally enough, since the newness of the University made it all the more important that it get off to a good start. 'I certainly should not incline to any further concessions,' Thorp told Van Mildert in a letter of 5 July, 1834.

The new professor can hardly have been an easy man to live and work with. Thorp continues:

Though I have done everything for Mr Rose, and always consulted his wishes and his comfort, I suppose I am to be subjected to his hard sayings, as the Bishop of London was last year, unless I go into controversy, which I am loath to do. . . But I am quite ready to defend myself.

However, Rose's health deteriorated rapidly. In February 1834 he broke his journey south, to visit a friend, and was forced to spend the whole night sitting bolt upright in a chair - utterly unable to lie down in bed.

By March, Durham was unbearable. 'I leave this beautiful place,' he wrote to Newman, on March 10, 1834 from 'College, Durham,' 'with great regret; uncertain as it is whether I shall ever return.'[12]

Return he did not, giving up the Professorship to his brother, the Rev Henry John Rose, who was then Fellow of St John's College, Cambridge.

To sum up the man's unhappy story, he was, as I said earlier, appointed Principal of King's College, London, in October, 1836; but his health gave way in the following January, and he never recovered.

Rose died on his way south to winter at Rome - in Florence, in November, 1836. He was buried in the protestant cemetery at Fiesole.

Deserving a word are four others on the teaching staff of what I shall now, following the example of A.A. Macfarlane-Grieve, Master from 1939 to 1953, call University College. These are Henry Jenkyns, the Professor of Greek; Thomas Williamson Peile, Senior Fellow, Senior Tutor, and Censor; William Palmer, the second Senior Fellow; and Temple Chevallier, Professor of Mathematics.

But first . . . Durham did not, with Rose's departure, get off to a better start. To plunge the College into deeper gloom, the Rev John Carr, formerly Fellow of Trinity College, Cambridge, and Headmaster of Durham School since 1811, who had been appointed Professor of Mathematics on 20 June, 1833, died in the October of the same year, two days after the opening of term. The College went into mourning for fourteen days.

R.S. Surtees, the historian of Durham, described the general gloom cast by this untoward blow in a letter to J.G. Nichols:

> The new University is hailed by all parties as a rising star (a northern light, may I say?) of bright and unsullied lustre. Everything seems propitious, and the wealthy cathedral church of Durham has devoted a large portion of its revenues to the new institution: but the death of Carr has thrown a gloom on the general feeling . . .[13]

A thin 'Calendar' of twenty pages is in existence. This, though usually referred to as the first 'Calendar', is a bit of a misnomer, since the actual first Calendar did not come out until 1836. It merits mention, since it bears out what was said earlier about the intentions of the founders to include in the curriculum subjects other than Classics and Mathematics, the staple of the older Universities, and particularly science, even if most of the teaching in these subjects was done on a general or part-time basis.

Besides the Professors and Senior Fellows, the 'Calendar' mentions six Junior Fellows, five of whom are Readers. William Gray, of Christ Church, Oxford, was Reader in Law; William Cooke Reader in Medicine; Thomas Greenwood, of St John's, Cambridge, Reader in Philosophy; the Rev James Miller Reader in Moral Philosophy; Charles Whitley, Fellow of St John's, Reader in Natural Philosophy; while the Rev Luke Ripley, then a master at Durham School, was Bursar. Two Lecturers are mentioned: J.F.W. Johnston was Lecturer in Chemistry and Mineralogy; and James Hamilton was Lecturer in Modern Languages. The Rev P. George was Librarian.

A word about the scientists among these will not come amiss, since we shall now be looking at the very forward-looking policy with regard to an expanded curriculum which distinguished the early founders of the College.

Charles Thomas Whitley was another Cambridge man, being Senior Wrangler in 1830, and subsequently Fellow of St John's. He was Reader in Natural Philosophy at Durham from 1833 to 1855, during which time he held the offices of Librarian, Tutor, Proctor, and Vice-Master of University College. He too of course was an ordained priest, and in 1849 was made an honorary canon of the Cathedral, before being offered the vicarage of Bedlington in 1854. The University conferred on him the honorary degree of D.D. in 1884. He was very popular with his undergraduates, by whom he was called 'the Brick'.

James Finlay Weir Johnston was born at Paisley, and educated at the University of Glasgow. In 1825 he opened a school at Durham, but being fortunate enough to make a wealthy marriage in 1830, he went off to Switzerland to study under Berzelius. As well as being Reader in Chemistry and Mineralogy at Durham, he was also Chemist to the Agricultural Society of Scotland, which meant that during term time he lived in Durham while his vacations were spent in Edinburgh - until, that is, the Society was dissolved.

Johnston was a Fellow of the Royal Society, as well as of the Geological Society. As keen as Temple Chevallier (*vide infra*) for the advancement of science, he had a finger in almost everything at Durham that promised to promote the cause. As early as 1841 he proposed the establishment of an agricultural school at Durham, but his plans were not approved by Senate. It was at his instigation, however, that Chemistry was made an optional subject in second year Arts! Like one of the first of Castle's undergraduates, Matthias Stephenson, Junior, about whom more will be said in the next chapter, Johnston seems to have been something of a Renaissance Man, for in 1850, when there were no engineering students, Johnston was asked to give a course of not less than twelve lectures to students in Arts on a subject decided by the Warden and Senate.

From 1848 to 1852 Johnston taught agricultural chemistry at Bede. Indeed, agriculture seems to have been his speciality. He published a lot, and his *Chemistry of Common Life* was particularly popular in his day. When he died, in 1855, he bequeathed the residue of his estate after the death of his wife to such literary, scientific or educational objects as his executors decided upon; and it is to this bequest that the foundation of the Johnston School in South Street, Durham, is due. The Johnston Chemical Laboratory in what was formerly Armstrong College, and is now the University of Newcastle, also derives from him. A bust of him graces the Castle.

It is clear that the College intended to take the broadening of the curriculum seriously. The *Durham Advertiser* carried all the necessary inducements. The Reader in Natural Philosophy, C.T. Whitley, was scheduled to deliver in the Michaelmas term of 1833 a course of lectures on

> the History and Objects of the Various Sciences . . . in the public Lecture Room on the Palace Green, to commence on Monday, 11th November, and to be continued on alternate days at 12 o'clock. The lectures will comprise: A general survey of the Modes in which one enquires into the Laws of Nature - Sketches of the lives of the principal Contributors to Science - a detailed account of the past history and present state of the several branches of Natural Philosophy, with consideration on the peculiar objects of each and on their mutual connection.

The Reader in Medicine was to be kept as busy, delivering

> the first part of a course of lectures on Anatomy and Physiology ... in the Public Lecture Room, College Green. These will commence on Tuesday the 11th November and be continued on alternate days, at one o'clock.
>
> Each Saturday will be more particularly devoted to Anatomical Demonstrations, in allusion to the previous lectures, explaining the

application of Anatomy to the practice of Surgery and Pathology, generally, and intended more especially for the Benefit of the Professional Bodies.

These Lectures will be illustrated by a series of Wax Preparations, modelled from actual Dissection, and representing the minutest details of the structure of the Human Frame; also by Engravings, Obstrological Specimens in Human and Comparative Anatomy.

The modest cost of this macabre feast was one guinea and a half.

Inevitably, public lectures of this sort brought problems in their train. 'Wm Cooke, M.D.' was obliged on the very same day as this advertisement was published to issue a public statement:

Enquiries have been made, from various quarters, whether Certificates for Attendance upon Lectures delivered at this University, on the different branches of Medical Science, would be accepted at Apothecaries' Hall, London; it is hereby published, for the information of those interested in the subject, that as soon as the different Courses of Lectures required have been delivered, the recognition of Durham, as a School of Medicine, will take place.

Dr Cooke's Terminal Lecture, given at 12 o'clock on 10 June in Bishop Cosin's Library, promised more palatable fare, being on 'the Application of Anatomy to the Arts of Sculpture and Painting.'

The Reader in Modern Languages delivered in the Epiphany term of 1834 'a Popular Course of Lectures on the History of the Literature of Germany. Terms - one guinea.'

Charles Whitley was as hard worked as Wm Cooke. An advertisement in the *Advertiser* of February 7, 1834, gave notice that the Reader in Natural Philosophy 'will deliver his Principal Course during the present and following Terms.'

The lectures will commence on Monday February 9th at 12 o'clock, and will be continued on Mondays, Wednesdays, and Fridays at the same hour.

Subjects for the Present Term: Mechanics, Hydrostatics, Pneumatics.

For the Easter Term: Optics, Astronomy.

Whitley delivered another 'Popular Course of Lectures', this time on the Application of Science to Manufactures - a course that must have been thought particularly appropriate to the North-East - in the Easter Term. This, commencing on Tuesday April 29 at 12 o'clock, was to be continued on alternate days.

J.F.W. Johnston, the Lecturer in Chemistry and Mineralogy, likewise delivered a 'Course of Popular Elementary Lectures on Chemistry' during the Epiphany Term, 1834; and followed this up in the same Term with a 'Course of Experimental Lectures on Practical Chemistry'. Each course cost two guineas, but anyone attending both obtained a reduction to three guineas. At 2 p.m. on November 3, he began a further 'Course of Popular Lectures', this time on 'Mineralogy, including the Geological Relations and Economical Applications of Mineral Substances'. This continued twice a week throughout the Term, and must have been a success for he followed it with another on Geology during the Easter Term, 1835.

Wm Cooke's Course of Lectures of 1833 on Anatomy and Physiology must also have been a success, for he followed it up with another on the same subjects, beginning on Tuesday 4 November 1834, at the unnatural hour of one o'clock, and continuing every Tuesday and Thursday during the Michaelmas Term. The Course was opened by an 'introductory Lecture on the Origin, Phenomena, and Laws of Human Life, to which,' so the advertisement in the *Advertiser* engagingly runs, 'any Gentleman may be admitted.'

Charles Whitley's '12 Popular and Elementary Lectures' on Science also carried on in 1836.

The Engineering course, which opened in 1838, with Professor Chevallier (*vide infra*), Charles Whitley and J.F.W. Johnston as tutors, had petered out by 1852. It must certainly have been a serious undertaking, with two such dedicated proselytisers for Science as Temple Chevallier and Johnston not only framing the regulations but also doing the bulk of the teaching. It failed largely because of the system of apprenticeship of the day, gradually declined in numbers, and came to a virtual end in six or seven years - a virtual end, because though there was no candidate from 1844 on, in 1852 a J.S. Worsley is said to have passed, though nothing is said about his class, if indeed he was put in any.

The course is certainly not without interest. It covered three years, there was an examination at the end of each year, and two languages, ancient or modern, were required. Shockingly, the course continued during the Easter vacation. Various prizes were awarded to those undertaking the course: for an English essay, for an essay in French or German, for Chemistry and Geology, and for engineering drawing. In 1838, for instance, a certain G.B. Read gained the prize for the best set of architectural drawings of the new London Bridge, and a W. Taylor for the best plan of Kepier College from a personal survey. Finals consisted of three sections: Mathematical, Physical and Practical Science; Chemistry, Mineralogy and Geology; and Languages. There were four classes under each section.

One Castleman who took his finals in 1840 possessed the delightful name of Arthur Beanlands. We shall hear a very little about him in a moment. Beanlands took a first in the mathematical section, a second in the chemical, and a fourth in languages. He was one of those fortunate Castlemen who returned to teach at his old College. Later he became University Treasurer.

One of the Engineering students was Charles Grey Grey, who entered on the course in 1842, and is one of those few invaluable creatures who have left some record of the ephemeral years of their university life. This he did in a privately printed document somewhat grandiosely entitled *The Story of His Official Life*. 'I was in the engineer class,' he wrote,

and I have a note that in January, 1843, Mr Beanlands took us out and taught us levelling and laying down sections . . . From the 13th to the 19th February was a very hard frost, thermometer 25 degrees, and we skated every day. The term ended the 22nd March . . . I went up again on the 22nd April. In that term I took levels and plans from Mungywell to the Castle, and drew plans and sections which I was required to show to, and explain to, the Warden and Senate on the 9th May, for the purpose of laying water pipes. I don't know if ever they were laid. I spent the month of September with the Reverend John Gibson at Bedlington, who coached for exam.

Clearly, reverend crammers were as evident at Durham in the eighteen forties as they had been for generations at Oxford.

Grey tells a simple yet graphic story of the dramatic night of 19 April, 1846, when 'there was a fire in the buildings where the laboratory was, and an Irishman called Fitzpatrick sat across on the roof with the hose to keep the fire from the chemicals. We got it out at 2 a.m., and were treated to a glass of ale at the buttery.'

Four other men on the teaching staff of University College call, as I said, for mention: Henry Jenkyns, Thomas Peile, William Palmer, and Temple Chevallier. Though none was so considerable a figure as the austere and formidable Hugh James Rose, Chevallier at least was a scholar of renown.

Of Jenkyns there is little to say. It will be remembered that he had been appointed Professor of Greek; but owing to Rose's precipitate exit from Durham through ill-health, and the inadequate funding of the Chairs, Jenkyns for a time coupled the Professorship of Greek with that of Divinity.

Jenkyns was the younger brother of Richard Jenkyns, the great Master of Balliol from 1813 to 1854, and was a powerful Oriel man. Our Jenkyns' claim to memory is a strange one. The young Pusey had been preparing feverishly for the Fellowship examination at Oriel in the Easter of 1823. Pusey was a desperate worker, and had put in as much as sixteen or seventeen hours' reading for his degree. Now he all but collapsed during the Fellowship examination. On the first day he tore up his essay; on the second he 'wrote a letter begging to retire from the examination and left the hall.' Jenkyns, a *deus ex machina,* if ever there was one, now stepped in. He picked up the pieces of Pusey's essay and laboriously pieced them together. The result was that Pusey was recalled; and he was elected to the Fellowship. With far-reaching results for the High Church movement in the Church of England and the future of the Church in general.

Thomas Williamson Peile was born in 1806 in Whitehaven. He was educated under the redoubtable Dr Butler of Shrewsbury . In 1824 he entered Trinity College, Cambridge. After gaining in his freshman's year the Davies Scholarship, for Classics, Peile graduated B.A. in 1828 as eighteenth wrangler, and was bracketed second in the first class of the classical tripos. He was also second Chancellor's Medallist. In 1829 he was elected Fellow of his College, and proceeded M.A. in 1831 and D.D. in 1843.

In 1829 Peile was appointed headmaster of the Liverpool Collegiate School, and in the same year was ordained by Bishop Sumner - of Chester, it will be remembered, and Durham. In 1831 he became perpetual curate of St Catherine's, Liverpool. He went to Durham in 1834, to hold a tutorship, and in 1836 was given the perpetual curacy of Croxdale.

Peile was at Durham only five years, for in 1841 he accepted the headmastership of Repton, where he stayed until 1854. He died in 1882.

A scholar by any standards, Peile's knowledge of the classics, especially of Thucydides, and of the Greek Testament, was held in his day to be remarkable. He published a number of works, of which the principal ones are the Editions of the *Agamemnon* of Aeschylus (1839), and the *Choephori* (1840). A portrait of him hangs in Repton School.

William Palmer was born in 1811, the eldest son of William Jocelyn Palmer, Rector of Mixbury in Oxfordshire. He is listed in the *DNB* as 'theologian and archaeologist'.

Palmer was another of those educated at Rugby, that school of enormous influence during the nineteenth century, but before Arnold went there as headmaster in 1828, when it was still a relatively undistinguished school, peopled by Flashmans as well as Arthurs and Easts. He went on to Oxford, where he was elected to a Demiship at Magdalen. In 1830 he obtained the Chancellor's prize with a Latin poem, 'Tyrus', and a first in the classical schools. A year after graduating he took deacon's orders, and was elected to a Magdalen Fellowship. In 1833 he proceeded M.A., and gained the Chancellor's prize with a Latin *Oratio de Comoedia Atticorum*, which was printed later in the same year. Palmer's next three years were spent as a tutor at Durham, but in 1837 he returned to Oxford as examiner in the classical schools before, in the following year, becoming tutor at Magdalen.

Palmer was a very high churchman. In an unpublished Latin introduction to the Thirty-nine Articles written for the use of his Oxford pupils in 1839, he anticipated the ingenious argument of Newman's famous Tract XC. Surprisingly, in view of all this, he took little part in the Movement itself; preferring to strike out his own path to spiritual peace. This was not easy for him: for he tried first, unsuccessfully, to find himself a place in the Greek Church, before going over to Rome in 1855.

Temple Chevallier, 'the Great Professor', unlike those others we have briefly looked at, spent his life at Durham. He was also, without question, the most interesting of those first tutors.

He was born in 1794, the youngest son of the Rev Temple Chevallier, and was educated at home by his father, and then at the two grammar schools of Bury St Edmunds and Ipswich. He went up to Pembroke, Cambridge, in 1813; obtained one of the Bell Scholarships in the following year; and graduated in 1817 as second wrangler and second Smith's prizeman. He was elected Fellow of his College, and afterwards Fellow and tutor of St

Catherine's Hall (now St Catherine's College).

In 1818 Chevallier was ordained by the Bishop of Ely, and three years later was given the living of St Andrew the Great, Cambridge, a place he held until he went up to Durham in 1835. He proceeded M.A. in 1820, and B.D. in 1825. Like many another parson of his time he published sermons - two volumes in all.

In 1826 and 1827 he was Hulsean Lecturer, later publishing his lectures in two volumes, the second being called 'Of the Proofs of Divine Power and Wisdom derived from the Study of Astronomy, and on the Evidence, Doctrines, and Precepts of Revealed Religion.'

Like Peile, Chevallier was not only a mathematician; he was also a classical scholar, if not one of Peile's rank. For instance, at Cambridge he acted as moderator in 1821 and in 1826 in the classical tripos. He migrated to Durham in 1835 as Professor of Mathematics, and from 1841 until he retired in 1871 he doubled as Professor of Astronomy. During most of this time Chevallier was also Reader in Hebrew!

In 1835 he was given the perpetual curacy of Esh, close by Durham, and shortly afterwards was made an honorary canon of the Cathedral; thereafter he became Sub-Warden under Thorp, rural dean, and at last, in 1865, a canon proper of the Cathedral.

Chevallier was a man of diverse interests; with of course science, and particularly astronomy, predominating. He published eighteen papers, for instance, in the journals of the Astronomical Society, thirteen of which were the results of his own observations; the remaining five dealing with physics. He also collaborated with a fellow-astronomer, Rumker, on three papers, and with another colleague, Thompson, on a further two, one of these being on the planet close to his heart - Neptune. The titles of some of his papers are daunting to the non-scientist: 'Observations of the Planets Flora, Isis, and Neptune'; 'Diameters of the Sun'; 'On a Method of finding the Effect of Parallax at different places, upon the time of disappearance and reappearance of a Star occulted by the Moon'. Less remotely - if only to some of us - he published translations of the 'Epistles' of Clement of Rome, Polycarp, and Ignatius; and the 'Apologies' of Justin Martyr and Tertullian. He also found time to edit an edition of 'Pearson on the Creed', and produce - rather amazingly for the SPCK of all people! - Easy Lessons on Mechanics.

As might be expected, Chevallier was all in favour of the efforts the

College made to broaden the curriculum by introducing into it scientific studies. As we saw above, his Engineering and Mining class came to a somewhat inglorious end after a somewhat inglorious start; but in 1865 the now 71-year old Professor saw his hopes once again rekindled, when the University tried to set up a School of Physical Science, the subjects to be taught being Physics, Pure and Applied Mathematics, Chemistry, Mining and Engineering. This too, to 'Chev's' disappointment, was abandoned quite soon. Arthur Beanlands was appointed to teach for three years all of Civil Engineering - including Mechanics, Hydrostatics, Hydraulics and Mining - but when his term was up no further appointment was made and the School fizzled out, though Arthur Beanlands himself was giving a few sporadic lectures as late as 1870. At least though, Chevallier saw the College of Science opened at Newcastle in 1871: some small compensation perhaps for his having to resign in that year, on account of ill-health and the general infirmities of age, not only his Professorships but all his other appointments as well.

Temple Chevallier is described, somewhat euphemistically, as being 'rather under the middle size'. That means - he was short. And like many short men, he abounded in compensatory energy. His kindness and benevolence come in for continual comment. Scudamore Powell, who it will be remembered told that delightful story about the Warden and Jennie Thorp, knew him well; and I let him have the last word on this man of many talents and interests:

> Chevallier was a fine specimen of a University Don of the old time, very much wrapped in astronomy and abstruse calculations, and quite unable to impart much elementary knowledge. In the winter I used to see the great Professor, i.e., 'Chev', skating on the river below the bridge like a young man, and he must have been well over seventy then. I think he held a living somewhere near Durham, as I often saw him on market days talking to some of the country folk, men and women, as if they knew him very well and were proud to be seen talking to the kindly old man, for I am sure he must have been much beloved by all who knew him.[14]

1) Dean J.W. Burgon, *Lives of Twelve Good Men*, London, 1888, p.116
2) *Ibid.*, p.119
3) *Ibid.*, p.121
4) *Ibid.*, pp.143-4
5) *Ibid.*, pp.145-6
6) *Ibid.*, p.151
7) *Ibid.*, p.161
8) *Ibid.*, p.181
9) *Ibid.*, p.184
10) *Ibid.*, p.187
11) *Ibid.*, pp.187-8
12) *Ibid.*, p.188
13) *Memoirs of Robert Surtees*, Surtees Society, p.439
14) *DUJ*, December, 1918

Chapter 5

Undergraduates

Sadly, almost no personal testimony exists as to day-to-day academic life in Durham in the decades from the eighteen thirties to the eighteen fifties, testimony such as exists, for instance, in the Rev William Tuckwell's *Reminiscences of Oxford* which, published just after the turn of the century, painted an unforgettable picture of the Oxford of the Eighteen Forties - the Oxford of less than a decade after Durham was founded.

Durham, or rather University College, had to wait until much later - until 1965, when C.F.Turnbull put down his reminiscences of life at the Castle in the Eighteen Nineties; and to wait moreover until 1981 before these same reminiscences appeared edited in *Castellum*, in the year of the University's one hundred and fiftieth anniversary. Few men from any university have taken the trouble - or thought it worth while - to put down their account of what was, in every case, their formative years; and when they have done so it has mainly been in a spirit of denigration and protest.

Only a few domestic details about Castle life remain extant, so if one wants to know what University College life was like in those early days one must have recourse to external evidence and inference. Some of our knowledge of the lighter side of undergraduate life it is possible to reconstruct *via* Edward Bradley's (Cuthbert Bede's) *Verdant Green*, a book as perennially amusing as *Charley's Aunt*.

Durham and the older Universities being ecclesiastical foundations, they were, legally and actually, clerical incubators. One can confidently assume therefore that the issues discussed in the clerical incubator of Durham in the eighteen thirties, forties and fifties were the same as those which were discussed at Oxford and Cambridge. And there can be no doubt that the arguments among the clerical teachers in the new University, in the main Oxford men, were the same as those which rent the Senior Common Rooms elsewhere. Namely: the present situation and the future of the Church of England, torn as it was between High Church Tractarianism and Evangelicalism on the one hand, and threatened by secularism on the other.

It is difficult, in this secular age, to understand what all the fuss was about; why Common Rooms both Senior and Junior were rent apart by theological disputation. And Newman's going over to Rome in 1845 made matters for many virtually intolerable.

The whole period, Dean Burgon wrote, was one 'which I can never recall without anguish and heartache.'

That the absorption with Tractarianism was not confined to the Senior Common Rooms is shown in that invaluable book *Tom Brown at Oxford*. For Tom finds it even in his 'fast' College, St Ambrose's, where 'The best men amongst them (the quiet and studious men) . . . were diligent readers of the Tracts for the Times, and followers of the High Church party, which was then a growing one . . .' [1]

During these early years then of the new University, these theological and ecclesiastical matters must have been the all-absorbing interests of thoughtful young men. At Oxford and Cambridge the great majority of the abler undergraduates were sons of clergymen, and there is no reason to suppose that the same did not hold true for Durham. And the great majority of these were themselves destined for the Church. No doubt prayer-meetings and Bible-readings flourished among the undergraduates at Durham; and no doubt worthy senior scholars existed who made it a point of duty, as they did at Oxford, to get hold of the more promising freshmen to prevent their falling into a bad set.

The phenomenal advance of the railways must also have been a talking-point. The Liverpool and Manchester Railway was opened in 1830 - a memorable occasion this when 'tall, slovenly, and ignoble-looking' Secretary of State Huskisson was knocked down by a locomotive and killed. Certainly cheap railways had an unfortunate result on recruitment to Durham, for almost at a stroke the argument that fathers resident in the north would balk at sending their sons the long slow coach-journey to Oxford and Cambridge, and send them instead to Durham, was rendered null and void.

It is inconceivable too that Durham, despite the high seriousness of its undergraduate and Senior Common Room wrangling, should not, like the rest of England, have fallen under the spell of *The Pickwick Papers*, which took the country by storm. This was published by instalments from the April of 1836 to the November of 1837. And we can deduce from Turnbull's memories of University College in the 1890's (*vide infra*) that there was no lack of interest in serious - indeed very serious - literature.

We can find out a great deal about the more joyous world of those early days by following the career of young Verdant Green who, one imagines, went up to 'Brazenface', Oxford, at the same hour as his creator Edward Bradley ('Cuthbert Bede') went up to University College - that is in 1845. Many Castlemen will have read too much already about Cuthbert Bede, and about 'Gig-lamps' Verdant, to bear with further tedious repetition; but one can, judiciously reading, piece together out of the adventures enough to give us some idea of undergraduate life at the time - always taking care that what we read in Verdant Green is corroborated elsewhere.

The first thing one notices is Mr Green Senior's dismissal of Durham as a proper place for young Verdant to receive a University education 'on account of its infancy, and its wanting the prestige that attaches to the names of the two great Universities'; which is of course Bradley's own perfectly valid excuse for sending Verdant to Oxford, which everybody knew about, even wandering Bedouin on the desert sands, instead of to Durham, which very few knew about and even fewer knew anything accurate about, and with a resulting guarantee of greatly increased sales.

The second thing is that, when Verdant goes up to Brazenface to matriculate, his father travels with him: an unheard-of occurrence today, unless freshmen's fathers are pressed into service as chauffeurs and baggage porters. But, as Geoffrey Faber points out,

> Being entered at Oxford - and presumably at Cambridge too - was a serious business in those days. Fathers made it an excuse to escape from the cares of business, the exigencies of matrimony, or the tedium of country parishes, and set out by road, with their sons beside them, and their own youth temporarily renewed.[2]

The Greens, father and son, are if not quite asphyxiated certainly thoroughly fumigated on the journey, by the clouds of smoke from their undergraduate travelling companions' pipes and cigars. Tobacco clearly had an important place in undergraduate life. The view from Verdant's rooms was

> pleasanter than the stale odours of the Virginian weed that rose from the faded green window-curtains, and from the old Kidderminster carpet that had been charred and burnt into holes with the fag-ends of cigars.[3]

The interminable procession of rags perpetrated against Verdant begins with Smalls' suggestion to him that he go to the Vice-Chancellor 'as soon as possible, and ask him for an order for some weeds. He'd be delighted to think you are beginning to set to work so soon!' This since 'The Germans, you know, would never be the deep readers that they are, unless they smoked.'[4]

Smalls should know, for at his wine, to which Verdant is invited, 'a great consumption of tobacco [was] going on, not only through the medium of cigars, but also of meerschaums, short "dhudheens" of envied colour, and the genuine yard of clay.' Verdant soon finds himself, to his great amazement, with a real cigar in his mouth; a none-too-pleasing experience, but one he consoles himself upon with the reflection that

> on the homoeopathic principle of 'likes cure likes,' a cigar was the best preventive against any ill-effects arising from the combination of the thirty gentlemen who were generating smoke with all the ardour of lime-kilns or young volcanoes, and filling Mr. Smalls' small room with an atmosphere that was of the smoke, smoky.[5]

Wines were a popular form of entertainment. Tom Brown attends so many that one feels he must have been in a near-permanent state of intoxication. The cost must have been enormous, and bears further witness to the expense of being up at Oxford. While the staple drinks of Verdant's friends seem to have been Bass, Guinness and porter (a dark brown bitter beer brewed from charred or browned malt and now, in the 1990's, coming back into fashion), College wines offered guests a variety of drinks: cup, punch, milk-punch, egg-flip, sherry cobblers, 'and other liquids' - perhaps spirits. Bishop (mulled and spiced wine) was popular, and indeed Verdant, on the first evening of his vacation, boasts to his proud Mama, and his trembling sisters, that Oxford has taught him not only how to 'smoke a weed - a cigar, you know,' but also how 'to make shandy-gaff, sherry cobbler, and brew bishop and egg-flip.'[6]

Wines at Tom Brown's St Ambrose's seem altogether more splendid affairs than those at Brazenface (Bradley's University College, Durham), with sherry, port and claret predominant, and biscuits and a plate or two of nuts and dried fruits on the tables.

An interesting feature of St Ambrose's is that men did not give wines in their first term; and bearing in mind the rigorous discipline imposed on freshmen by their elders at Durham, something we shall be looking at later, this may very well have been a University College tradition too. Owing to this custom, Tom Brown has to wait until his second term before giving his wine, for which occasion he brings back up with him from his father's cellars a quantity of port which had been more than twelve years in bottle, the social cachet of providing good wine being enormous. Competition of this sort cannot but have been endemic. Interestingly too, manners had changed somewhat by 1845 from what they were when Tom's father was up, since Squire Brown recalls giving his first wine, when 'eleven men came . . . and he had opened nineteen bottles of port for them.'

Cards were played at these wines, principally loo (a round card-game with penalties paid to the pool) and Van John, (Vingt et un: a variety of pontoon), which was Verdant's favourite game; while a fair amount of singing seems to have gone on - of a seemly as well as, no doubt, of an unseemly character. Charles Larkyns, for instance, Verdant's mentor, 'trolled out [at Smalls' wine] in a rich, manly voice, old Cowley's anacreontic'

> Fill up the bowl then, fill it high!
> Fill all the glasses there! For why
> Should every creature drink but I?
> Why, man of mortals, tell me why?[7]

While the Innocent Verdant, when it comes to his turn, trills back, 'I dreamt that I dwe-elt in mar-arble halls.'

As is only to be expected from those whose education has been so severely classical, the undergraduates are liberal quoters of Latin and Greek - not always with accuracy. Linguistic jokes abound. Verdant, at Smalls' wine,

> from the unusual combination of the smoke and liquids, was beginning to feel extremely amiable and talkative, - [and] made a reflective observation (addressed to the company generally) which sounded like the words 'Nunc vino pellite curas, Cras ingens, which calls forth an amiable rebuke from the amiable Mr Bouncer: 'Who's that talking shop about engines?'[8]

Undergraduate rooms in the eighteen forties were markedly different, as far as personal effects were concerned, from those of the nineteen forties. Some things of course stayed the same. Verdant's bed was 'very hard, and so small, that, had it not been for the wall, our hero's legs would have been (literally) at the foot!'[9] It will be recalled that Archdeacon Thorp's Rules for Undergraduates expressly state that

> The Furniture of the Rooms is supplied by the Establishment, and charged to the Student. No Student is suffered to furnish his own Rooms, nor to add any thing to the Regulation Furniture, without permission of the Censor.

An attempt, no doubt, to impose economy on a class notoriously incapacitated to exercise it, and to avoid Durham's going the way of spendthrift Oxford.

Bradley has more than one description of such rooms. There is Charles Larkyns': and it is quite impossible that Bradley was not calling on his memories of his own set, or a friend's, at Castle.

> The walls of the room were decorated with engravings in gilt frames, their variety of subject denoting the catholic taste of their proprietor. 'The Start for the Derby,' and other coloured hunting prints, showed his taste for the field and horse-flesh; Landseer's 'Distinguished Member of the Humane Society,' 'Dignity and Impudence,' and others, displayed his fondness for dog flesh; while Byron beauties, 'Amy Robsart,' and some extremely *au naturel* pets of the ballet, proclaimed his passion for the fair sex in general. Over the fireplace was a mirror . . . its frame stuck full of tradesmen's cards and (unpaid) bills, invites, 'bits of pasteboard' pencilled with a mystic 'wine', and other odds and ends: no private letters though. Mr Larkyns was too wary to leave his 'family secrets' for the delectation of his scout. Over the mirror was displayed a fox's mask, gazing vacantly from between two brushes.[10]

There was also a list of hunting appointments pinned up on the walls over a list of lectures, tabular views of prophesies, kings of Israel and Judah, and the Thirty-nine Articles.

The 'pets of the ballet' referred to by Bradley no doubt included the great ballerinas Marie Taglioni and Fanny Cerrito, who are both to be found hanging on the walls of the undergraduate Drysdale's set in St Ambrose's, for, as Ivor Guest puts it about Cerrito in his biography of the great artist, 'There were few young men about town that summer (1841) who would not cheerfully have become her slave.'[11]

Indeed, a very little earlier, after her success in the *Teatro Olimpico* in Vicenza, an enterprising barber is supposed to have been selling small phials of Cerrito's bath water to her admirers!

It is perhaps not without significance that Drysdale's lists of meets are for the current week; Charles Larkyns' list of hunting appointments is specifically stated to be 'of the past season'. Perhaps Thorp's discipline was not without its effect.

A quaint description of 'An Undergraduate's "Digs" Sixty Years Ago' appeared in the D*urham University Journal* in November, 1912, the writer signing himself 'Jyrollam'. This, if the article were a serious account and not just a piece of contemporary satire, would take us back to 1852, a little later than the period we are dealing with. However, if Jyrollam were writing such a description of his own set of sixty years ago in 1912, he would of course be at that time in his nineties. Not an altogether improbable circumstance, of course. But the 'Dr Eeg' whose portrait most improbably hangs on the wall of the undergraduate's room is clearly intended to be Dr Henry Gee, who became Master of University College in 1902, following the retirement of Dr Plummer. The Professor Ykroc (presumably Corky), whose portrait also hangs there I have failed to identify. Jyrollam's is clearly a grumble at the antiquated accommodation and furniture in the Castle between 1902 and 1912, more likely closer to the latter date, since Jyrollam would hardly have waited ten years to launch this rather feeble squib. Castlemen today will be unfamiliar with such laments.

The general air of dilapidation is disquieting. The walls are covered with

a dirty yellow paper, on which green and blue flowers alternate in diagonal lines. Now and then, where the paper has been torn, another piece of the same pattern has been pasted on upside down, probably for the sake of procuring a pleasing variety; while in other cases the damage has not been repaired, and an earlier wall decoration, in orange and black, is apparent in patches.

Evidences of tobacco, cards and drink abound. Jyrollam gives an interesting inventory of his furniture.

1. A small mirror in a polished wooden frame, - the glass consisting of two sections, each of a different colour. .

2. A mahogany secretaire, which has no other defects than that the lower drawer will not shut, that one of the hinges of the flap is loose, and that one of the feet has long ago declined further service, and preferred a horizontal to an upright position. . .

3. A wooden tub containing coals, with a poker and tongs. The latter cannot be handled without pinching the skin of one's forefinger, and the legs slip across each other as soon as one tries to pick up anything with them.

4. An arm-chair, and six chairs with plush seats, showing their stuffing through numerous wounds - all venerable invalids, and especially weak in the back.

5. A square table, in the middle of which stands a lamp; further, a wooden tobacco-box, and an inkstand.

Round this table sit several students, kicking up a tremendous din, and all 'leer[ing] through a thick, smoky atmosphere at the remains (a negligible quantity) of a bowl of punch.'

Clearly little had changed between 1834 and 1912, save perhaps that at the earlier date the tongs performed more efficiently and humanely.

There remains another area which must inevitably be conjectural, and that is our undergraduates' behaviour to their dons.

The Eighteen Thirties and Forties were not polite days. Lectures, by all accounts, must have called for some mild form of antidote to alleviate the excruciating tedium, one common to Oxford and Cambridge as well as Durham, the classical texts having been gone through over and over by the undergraduates while they were at their public schools.

Bradley has something to say about the teaching, as well as about the undergraduates' responses to it.

The dryness of the daily routine of lectures, which varied about as much as the steak-and-chop, chop-and-steak dinners of ancient taverns, was occasionally relieved by episodes, which, though not witty in themselves, were yet the cause of wit in others; for it takes but little to cause amusement in a lecture-room, where a bad construe; or the imaginative excuses of late-comers; or the confusion of some young gentleman who has to turn over the leaf of his Greek play and finds it uncut; or the pounding of the same gentleman in the middle of the first chorus; or his offensive extrication therefrom through the medium of some Cumberland barbarian; or the officiousness of the same barbarian to pursue the lecture when everyone else has, with singular unanimity, 'read no farther'; - all these circumstances, although perhaps dull enough in themselves, are nevertheless productive of some mirth in a lecture-room.[12]

We have already heard from Scudamore Powell that 'the great Professor', Temple Chevallier, was 'quite unable to impart much elementary knowledge.'

Verdant 'has the privilege of attending' the lectures of the eccentric Reverend Richard Harmony:

Much learning, though it had not made Mr Harmony mad, had, at least in conjunction with his natural tendencies, contributed to make him extremely eccentric; while to much perusal of Greek and Hebrew MSS., he probably owed his defective vision. These infirmities, instead of being regarded with sympathy, as wounds received by Mr Harmony in the classical engagements in the various fields of literature, were, to Mr Verdant Green's surprise, much imposed upon; for it was a favourite pastime with the gentlemen who attended Mr Harmony's lectures, to gradually raise up the lecture-table by a concerted action, and when Mr Harmony's book had nearly reached to the level of his nose, to then suddenly drop the table to its original level; upon which Mr Harmony, to the immense gratification of all concerned, would rub his eyes, wipe his glasses, and murmur, 'Dear me! dear me! how my head swims this morning!' And then he would perhaps ring for his servant, and order his usual remedy, an orange, at which he would suck abstractedly, nor discover any difference in the flavour even when a lemon was surreptitiously substituted.[13]

We close this account of the College's early history with a look at the invaluable Bursar's Memorandum Book of the Rev Luke Ripley, the first Bursar of University College. This, his 'Waste Book', as he called it, records the Bursar's memoranda of payments, receipts, and 'things done or to be done', from 2 September, 1833, down to 1840. A. A. Macfarlane-Grieve first drew attention to this 'Waste Book' in an article published in the *Durham University Journal*, in March, 1925. It gives the day-to-day domestic details of the first term, the Michaelmas Term of 1833, when undergraduates first came into residence.

The term began on October 28 and ended on December 18, a short one indeed of seven weeks. Forty-two students were in residence, though one, W.C. Maclaurin, although he paid his registration fee, does not seem to have come up.

Clearly, Ripley's first task was to appoint his staff, as well as generally prepare for the reception of the undergraduates. University College was not as yet, of course, housed in the Castle, but in what was then known as Archdeacon's Inn, on Palace Green; was later known both as University House and Bishop Cosin's Hall; and is now known only as Cosin's Hall. What undergraduates could not be accommodated there were lodged in adjacent houses.

Ripley himself, as has been said, had been a master at Durham School. In January, 1833, he was presented to the livings of Ilderton and Alnham by the Duke of Northumberland, in whose gift these were. Whether the Bursar managed satisfactorily to run his two livings in Northumberland as well as the complex and touchy domestic side of University College is a question that admits of no answer.

Ripley's first appointment was, of course, that of Housekeeper.

Sept. 18th:- Agreed to give Mary Roach as Housekeeper £18 per Ann. Wages to commence when services are required. Character to be sent.

At a later date he records of Mary Roach: 'Commenced Oct. 10th 1833.' The following appointments were also made.

Sept. 19th:- Appointed John Grainger waiter at 7s. per week with board, these wages not agreed to be paid during Long Vacation: he engages to make himself useful in any way he may be called on.

Sept. 21st:- Matthw. Herbert applied for a situation as waiter, recommended by Mr Maynard, 7 child., a Painter, principal drum in the Durham Militia eleven years, age 48, S. Street.

Sept. 24th:- Alexander Mitchell applies for waiter's place: has lived all his life as a Gentleman's Servant, and is now with Mr Bowlby as Groom. Calls himself fifty years of age: is I think more. Recommended by Mr T. R. Shepperdson: I have desired his register to be sent.

Sept. 28th:- Hired Eliz. Coxon (age 25) at £7 7s. per Ann. to be House-maid: character from Mrs Treacy.

Sept. 30th:- Michael Richardson to be Brewer at 5s per head, no perquisites, yeast and grains to be accounted for. 4 Bush. = 54 Galls.

The Brew-house was, of course, a vital part of any large residence, or institution, in those days, and Ripley goes into its management in some detail. One J. Wright was appointed to look after it, and arrangements were made to brew elsewhere, should the Brew-house not be ready in time. Michael Richardson was required to brew 4 half barrels of beer from 6 bushels of malt and 3 lbs. hops, and the following utensils were bought for the brewing: 'Copper, Cooler, Working Tub, Poker and Coal Rake, 2 Pails and Handies, Funnel Tub, Bungs and Taps, Mash Tub, Mash Stick, Drainer Hair Cloth, Mops, Spouts, Shovel, Brooms, 12 Half Barrels, Brass Taps and Mallet for Tapping.'

The recipe given is an astonishing one for the College brew - for any College brew; and one wonders if an error has not crept into it. Certainly Ripley has often been found to be not infallible. Mr Richard Guinness, of the brewing family, to whom the amounts were submitted, kindly wrote that: '6 bushels of malt to 4 half barrels would give an OG [Original Gravity] of 1,126 [degrees]. This would be excessively sweet and would rival the strongest beer mentioned in the *Guinness Book of Records*.' He continues: '6 bushels of malt to 4 barrels would give an OG of 1056, about the same as Fuller's ESB, or 50% stronger than an average bitter.' He gives a table of beers for comparison, the highest in OG being Carlsberg Special at 1090, and Barleywines at about 1100.

Ripley goes on:

Oct. 9th:- Fran. Cashew applies for washing: washed for Mr Shafto

26 years, Mr Wooler, Lord Barrington. Husband Beadle at the Market Place.

There are further entries regarding the engagement of servants, including that of Ann Prudhoe as 'Sempstress to the University', but by October 28 Ripley's staff seems to have been complete. As with domestics down the ages, Ripley found the going anything but smooth, his Housekeeper, Mrs Roach, being particularly trying. At the start she was dissatisfied with her bed, and on November 1 Ripley records:

> Mr Caldcleugh ordered to make a bed for the Housekeeper, width of bedstead 3.3 in., 6.1 in. length, 1¾ feathers at 35s. per stone: will give in weight of tick. This bed he considers in all respects sufficient.

Caldcleugh was a prominent local ironmonger, with a business up the Claypath.

It was not however sufficient for Mrs Roach, who expressed her dissatisfaction anything but genteely, for

> Nov. 30th:- Mrs Roach says her bolster is nothing but rubbish, and she believes the bed to be the same. Mr Caldcleugh complains of this statement, and wishes to have bed, bolster and pillows examined.

She remained a demanding thorn in Ripley's flesh, and true again to Housekeeper form throughout the ages, she took a high hand with servants, dismissing them in droves. The Bursar clearly found her a handful, and when unable to cope, pusillanimously passed her on to Mrs Ripley.

Mrs Roach, true again to form, clearly thought her position entitled her to special consideration, for Ripley notes at one exasperated point that she had been out three times after locking-up. She survived only until December 6th when, Ripley records, and one can almost hear his sigh of relief:

> Mrs Roach quitted the house.

The Fran Cashew who applied to do the washing presumably had an idle husband, which would account for her lifetime of slavery in the suds, for on November 4 a James Kashew is recorded as having given notice to quit at the end of term: 'he cannot stand the work.'

Furniture and utensils seem to have been bought, sensibly, as the need arose. On September 2 Wm Wright, a Cooper, sent in 2 pails and a handy [sic], and one John Oliver delivered 1 long duster, 1 short duster, 1 dust pan, 2 black lead brushes, 1 scrubbing brush and - a daunting item - 3 lbs. black lead for grates; and there are numerous other references to such purchases. Chairs, tables, bedsteads and so on are continually being added to, and there is a charming purchase of '40 tin candlesticks, complete with sockets and extinguishers.' On September 21 Ripley's purchase of fire fenders involved 'expenses at Newcastle and coach 13. 6d.' The coach was no doubt The True Briton, which left Thwaites' Waterloo Inn at half past nine every morning for Newcastle, to return at six in the evening - Sundays excepted.

Ripley began his Bursarship by setting all the kitchen needs out in detail, but before long he was content to leave the ordering of these to the formidable Mrs Roach. The Housekeeper also undertook to make sheets at 1s. the pair, material provided. One cannot but feel that Mrs Roach cut off her nose to spite her face, for she held down a job of considerable responsibility, and there were doubtless, apart from such opportunities for making extra money by knocking up sheets at 1s. the pair, sundry others - perhaps less official.

When one reads Ripley's arrangements for feeding his undergraduates, one tends to shake one's head in disbelief.

But first, before ever the students came up, on September 11, Ripley wrote off to Cambridge, perhaps to his old College, St John's, for a buttery price list. One Jos Wilkinson, of the Folley, was appointed to supply milk at 13 pints for 1s. On September 20 we find Ripley buying 1½ pecks of preserved gooseberries for 5s. 3d. and 14 lbs. of sugar for 8s. 2d., to which he adds, cryptically, 'woman preserving 2s.' Coals for the rooms were to cost 21s. per term; and on October 27, the day before term began, Ripley memo's:- 'Speak to the Warden about a supply of candles for the Students and whether to be allowed from a Chandler or from Housekeeper.' A 'Hair dresser or Barber' was also laid on.

As soon as term begins, the entries concern themselves most interestingly with food. On October 28, for instance, the first day of term, Ripley writes: 'The Warden wishes to have for dinner: Fish, Boiled Mutton,

Chicken, Tart, Ham, Pudding, Goose, Roast Beef, Fish, Roast Mutton, Boiled Beef.' Even allowing for the gigantic dinners of the day, these could hardly have been intended for one sitting; and faulty punctuation cannot be blamed for reading as one meal what was intended for two or more. Moreover, 'Fish' appearing twice suggests an error of Ripley's. Clearly, the Warden had laid down his undergraduates' menus in general terms, and Ripley had recorded his wishes as he recalled them.

Further illuminating references to the food of the day abound. On 30 October Ripley reminds himself to get Mrs Roach to send up the pickles. On the same date also he shows himself as concerned with the servants' predilections for dining in style as every other employer of domestics throughout the century. 'Enquire of the Warden,' Ripley glumly notes, 'whether servants are necessarily to have meat hashes when there is plenty of cold meat.' The abundance of meat in nineteenth century menus meant that there was always a plentiful supply of it cold, and Ripley dutifully records, after the previous reference, 'Let there always be plenty of cold meat.'

Interestingly, Ripley seems to have considered accommodating the menus to the wishes of the undergraduates, if we are to go by the entry: 'If we are to battle, would it not be best that each young gentleman, the day before, should put down or name to the Butler what he would have for dinner?' This goes some way towards explaining the previous longish list of items the Warden communicated to Ripley, as well as the following order of his to the butcher, dated November 8: 'Loin & neck of veal, hind-quarter of pork, 4 sirloins of beef, 3 fore crops of beef, 4 rounds of beef, 2 briskets, 10 legs of mutton & 6 necks of mutton', an order which was to last eight days. It also, of course, bears out what has already been said about the plethora of cold viands in nineteenth century England.

An equally interesting item is Ripley's breaking down the cost of a day's meals. The date is November 10.

Breakfast	*Dinner*
Bread, 1½ d.	Meat, 9d.
Milk per pint, 1½ d.	Veget., 1d.
Butter, 1½ d.	Bread, 1d.
	Ale.
	Puddings, 4d.
	Tart, 4d.
	Cheese.
	Celery.
Lunch	
Cold Meat, 4 ½ d.	
Bread, ½d.	
Cheese, 1d.	
Ale, 1d.	
Soup, 3d.	
Butter.	Tea or Supper as for Breakfast

The Bursar's entries concerning his correspondence over the twenty Foundation Students make equally interesting reading. One can see that the first intake drew heavily from the north-east. Ripley's first note, on September 11, records that Mrs Surtees of Mainsforth wanted a Mr Ra Robinson to be admitted an ordinary student, to which he added a later note: 'Give him a good room.' Clearly Surtees was a name to conjure with in Durham. On 23 September Dr Cook engages the South East Room for his nephew Mr St Claire Raymond, No. 10. There follow:

September 26th:- Mr Thomas Mansfield wishes to become a Divinity Student here. He has no knowledge of Latin or Greek, but is disposed to read very hard and considers in two years he may qualify himself for orders: directed to see the Warden.

September 27th:- Wrote to Mr Thomas Mansfield advising him to commence Classics immediately either at Ryton or with some private tutor for a year.

Several inquirers wrote to Ripley asking the expenses of a student at University College. Ripley wrote back that they should be £50 per annum, or at the outside £60.

On 4 October he announces having written to the twenty prospective Foundation Students of the College: 'Wrote to the 20 Foundation Students announcing examination Oct. 28th, 10 a.m. precisely, mentioning that Blankets, Sheets, and Quilt and Pillow cases with towels will be required, and if they choose we can supply them.'

Oct. 6th:- Mr Burrell applies for Prospectus and Information respecting the admission of Mr Creighton's son of S. Shields. The youth's age between 14 and 15. Write to the Warden. Wrote to Mr Creighton with Prospectus.

Oct. 10th:- Letter from Rev A. Watson, H. Island who wishes his son to be furnished with Sheets, Rug, Blankets and P. Cases: he brings his own towels.

In the event, the number of Foundation Students was reduced by one to nineteen, for a Septimus Fairles defected to Cambridge at the last moment.

On their arrival, the undergraduates were fitted out with caps and gowns. On October 29 the Bursar took their Caution Money of £10, Admission Fee of £2, £1 to the University Chest, and 2s. 6d. Registration Fee.

Mention has already been made of their staying, in the main, in Archdeacon's Inn. There were some however less fortunate, and of these on 31 October Ripley wrote: 'Mr H. White would take Students and give them two Rooms, Fire, Candle, Board, Shoe-cleaning and everything complete for £7 7s. per month. Mr White can accommodate 4, each having two Rooms. He has a large dining Room. If the students have each a Room and sit in the dining as a Common Room, he would find Lodgings, Fire, Candle, etc. for 10s. each per week.'

Grace was of course formally read at the foundation, for a somewhat cryptic entry reads:

Mr Cundill to read Grace this week and the next to instruct him.

Ripley's entries are all too often lacking in lucidity.

Mrs Roach seems not to have been alone in being touchy about her bed. Ripley writes of two undergraduates who caused him minor problems with bedding. Of one who felt the cold he writes with some amazement:

Nov. 12th:- Mr Francis Thompson wishes to have another blanket.
He has already had three. 3 large blankets.

And he takes a strong line on the 30th with a fastidious Mr Legard, who
'returned his blankets on October [he must mean November] 27th after
having used them one month. They must be returned to him again.
Mention this to his Bed-maker.'

Sundry other problems, perennial to undergraduates, find entry in the
Bursar's Book. There was clearly, even at this early date in the College's
history, a tendency to stay out late, for another entry of 12th November
memo's: 'A bill of students entering after 10 o'clock to be sent in every
morning to Mr Palmer.' This of course was William Palmer, one of the
Senior Fellows. One assumes that these gentlemen incurred a gate fine, for
mention of fines is frequent.

Fire was, as throughout the College's history, a hazard. Twenty-eight
students are listed as having coal fires, and on November 30th Ripley
records, again with comic ambiguity: 'The house was accidentally pre-
vented from being set on fire. Remedy this,' he adds determinedly.

On the same day he notes that a couple of undergraduates have
exchanged rooms. 'Mr Wright and Mr G. Marshall have exchanged Rooms,
no permission asked: can this be permitted?' he asks, this frightful contin-
gency not having been covered in the Warden's otherwise meticulously
detailed rules for College governance.

His charges were likewise lax about marking their linen:

Dec. 14th:- Every Student must have every article to be sent to the
Laundry marked with his name in full, otherwise they will be sent to
the Sempstress and charged.

What became of these Foundation Scholars - these first men of
University College, Castlemen after 1837? Surprisingly, we know something of one of them; and it is a good note on which to end this chapter.

In the Parish of Farnworth, near Widnes in Lancashire, there was in existence until the turn of the century an old Grammar School, which had been
founded about the year 1500 by William Smyth, later Bishop of Lincoln
and founder of Brasenose College, Oxford. In 1838 the three Trustees of the
school advertised for a new headmaster. Seventeen gentlemen applied for

the post, among whom was a certain Matthias Stephenson, Junior, who must have been one of those first students at University College. His application is worth quoting in full.

Egremont, Novr. 26th, 1838

Sir,

I was favoured with your note on Saturday, in reply to which I beg leave to make the following statements.

I am not a clergyman, or a Master of Arts: I consider myself a Master of Grammar, if it means a proficient in Grammar.

I am happy to say that I have been brought up and educated in the religious principles of the Church of England; to the fundamental doctrines of which, as they are set forth in the Liturgy and the Thirty-nine Articles I conscientiously give my decided approbation and assent. I am as much opposed to the erroneous theological dogmas, to the intolerant bigotry, and to the absurd superstition of the Romanists on the one hand, as I am to the undefined sectarian tenets, to the whimsical fanaticism, and to the apparently zealous but preposterous enthusiasm of the dissenter, on the other.

I consider myself qualified to teach Writing, Arithmetic, Book-Keeping, Geography and the use of the Globes, Mensuration, the Latin and Greek Languages, the Mathematics, pure and mixed together with other higher branches, viz.: Algebra, Euclid's Elements of Geometry, Plain and Spherical Trigonometry, Navigation, Analytical Geometry, Conic Sections, Mechanics, Differential and Integral Calculus, Astronomy, Newton's Principia, Logic and Ethics, a regular course of which I studied at the University of Durham.

As regards my political opinions, or convictions, I have no hesitation in avowing myself to be a conservative. With the crude speculations, and visionary theories of the reckless agitator, and unprincipled demagogue, I have no sympathy: I am a staunch advocate of the stability of our excellent constitution in Church and State, the pride of

Britain, and the envy of Europe. Church and Constitution is on the banner under which I take my station.

I am not married, but, on that account, let me not be considered as advocating the principles of celibacy, on the contrary if I had any favourable prospect of permanently settling in life, it would not be long before I should enroll myself amongst the votaries of Hymen.[14]

Regrettably, this delightful letter from one of University College's first Renaissance men, who could also boast of being a True-Blue Conservative, was not sufficient to get him the job.

Let us all, especially those of us at Castle Reunions, drink a bumper in his memory!

1) Thomas Hughes, pp.4-5
2) Geoffrey Faber, p.49
3) Cuthbert Bede, *The Adventures of Mr. Verdant Green*, p.39
4) *Ibid.*, p.60
5) *Ibid.*, p.67
6) *Ibid.*, p.109
7) *Ibid.*, p.69
8) *Ibid.*, p.68
9) *Ibid.*, p.52
10) *Ibid.*, p.57
11) Ivor Guest, *Fanny Cerrito*, London, 1956, p.36
12) Cuthbert Bede, pp.78-9
13) *Ibid.*, p.79
14) *DUJ*, June, 1935

Archdeacon Thorp, the first Warden.

Top:
The Castle
Courtyard

Left:
Tunstal Chapel

99

Top:
The Great Hall

Right:
The Keep

CHAPTER 6

Warden Thorp

With some Observations on the Keep, the Choral Society, and 'Keeping Day'

The Castle then was made over to University College in 1837. Its passage was, like everything else in the College's early history, a difficult one. Thorp had proposed to Bishop Maltby, shortly after his appointment as Van Mildert's successor, that he hand over the Castle to the College. Maltby, who seems to have had the welfare of the University very much at heart, though he was unable to transfer the Castle at once, nevertheless took a step towards it by allowing the College in the Michaelmas Term to take possession of the Hall, the kitchen, the Chapel, and a further room for use as a council or common room.

There were difficulties, both real and practical, about making the Castle over entirely. The Bishop, for instance, had to retain the right to lodge in the Castle on the admittedly infrequent occasions when he needed to. Before 1837 was over Maltby had overcome this particular problem by selecting a small suite, consisting of a sitting-room, a bedroom, an antechamber, and servants' quarters, which would be retained for him and his successors. He would also have on the Green a coach-house for two carriages and stabling for six horses.

The Judges' needs were a different matter, though Baron Parkes, one of the Judges, had at the summer Assizes of 1836 let it be known that he thought his brethren would be satisfied with the same accommodation as they enjoyed at Trinity College, Cambridge, where four bedrooms were provided for them. In June of the following year the Home Office decided that it was the responsibility of the High Sheriff of Durham to provide suitable apartments for the visiting Judges, as was the practice elsewhere, and that the High Sheriff would then be reimbursed by the Treasury. At this, that aging *enfant terrible* of the Whigs, Lord John Russell, declared that he did not propose that the High Sheriff should take the charge of the Judges' accommodation on himself, and furthermore he had no intention of recommending that it fall on the Government.[1] The situation seemed incapable of resolution but before long, in true English fashion, an accommodation was arrived at. The Judges were to continue to be lodged in the Castle, thus upholding tradition, and a house in Queen Street was to be furnished for their retinue; for these privileges the High Sheriff would pay the University £70 a year.

There were though looming problems which would, in the none too distant future, dwarf all others.

Despite its vast size, the Castle would hold nothing like the number of undergraduates that might be expected when the University really took wing. It was impossible for Thorp, or Maltby, or anyone else for that matter, to foresee that for many years to come the number of undergraduates housed in the Castle, as in the other Colleges that were later founded, would be pitifully small; it was also beyond the bounds of imagination that, in the second half of the twentieth century, Durham would be one of the most sought-after Universities, and University College in particular the jewel in her crown.

What was certainly realised, even at that early date, was that the cost of maintaining the Castle was enormous and could not but grow. When Van Mildert died, the cost of putting right the dilapidations in the Castle was greater than that of putting right all the dilapidations in the rest of the see. The money for this maintenance could not possibly come from the undergraduates, who could never be expected to pay an economic rent. It was felt that the Government could certainly pay its mite by compensating the College for the loss of some of its precious rooms to the Judges; and it was also felt that the Ecclesiastical Commissioners, who had just taken great slices off the income of the Cathedral and the see, ought to contribute to the upkeep of the Castle. The first of these hoped-for contributions would of course go nowhere; the second might well be substantial.

On 19 July, 1837, the accommodation problem was found a temporary solution when the recommendations of the Commissioners were embodied in an Order in Council. The Bishop of Durham was henceforth to hold the Castle and all its precincts in trust for the University. The clergy of the diocese were to continue to have right of access to Bishop Cosin's Library, which had been left by Bishop Cosin for the use of the clergy in the diocese. The Bishop would have the right to his chosen apartments in the Castle, on his giving three days' notice. And the University was to be responsible for all repairs.

A few of the other provisions will be of interest to readers of this history, since they have a bearing on the College as well as show quite clearly that Palace Green was envisaged as the University's centre.

Van Mildert had assigned the lower apartments of the old Exchequer building, now the old University Library, to the University. Some of the officials of the see and the palatinate retained their offices in the rest of it; and the inconveniences to which these officials were put were aggravated by the fact that some of them did private business as lawyers, and their clients of course had to call on them there. Later a building was put up in North Bailey, and in 1855 assigned to these officials in lieu of the Exchequer. On the east side of Palace Green stood the old Song School and the Writing School, foundations of Cardinal Langley, with the old alms-houses for the bedesmen between them. Since the two old schools had not been occupied for years, Van Mildert had given these to the University. Now the intervening alms-houses were also acquired by the University, the bedesmen being provided with houses at the north-east angle of Palace Green. The old stables on Palace Green were pulled down, to make way for a lecture room, the bishop being provided with stabling elsewhere. The Master's House was one of those bought for the University by Van Mildert before his death, and through an oversight not made over; now it had to be bought from his representatives by the Dean and Chapter, and held in trust by the University until such time as they handed all the property over to it.

The Keep was at this time (1837) in ruins, and the possibility was that it might be rebuilt as an observatory. It was clearly a splendid site for a tele-scope, and Temple Chevallier for one would have been behind its being rebuilt for this purpose. The plan envisaged also the siting of the museum (for which exhibits were coming in from all quarters) on the lower floors. In the event of course, when it was rebuilt in 1840 it was to provide rooms for undergraduates.

A word here upon how it came about that the Keep had fallen into such disrepair. When the necessity for maintaining the Keep as a defensive structure had ceased to exist, the maintenance of such a huge, uninhabited and now useless building became a burden few bishops wanted to be sad-dled with. Bishop Morton indeed, in 1650, obtained a decree discharging him from future dilapidations. Some of his successors, considering the Keep as something of an ornament, did make small repairs; but the cost of putting the building on a permanently secure footing would, in any day, have been enormous. It is not known whether Bishop Cosin, who did such a lot to the Castle itself, also touched the Keep; but Nathaniel Lord Crewe apparently did so, for his arms were placed on the east side with the following inscription underneath:

HAEC DIU RUITURI CASTELLI LATERA CU'
VETUSTATE TANDEM UTRINDE EXESA NEC NON COLLAPSA
DE NOVO NUPERRIME EXTRUXIT AC CITO CITIUS FIRMIORA
EREXIT
NATH D'NUS CREWE DUNELM EP'US ET BARO DE STANE COM.
NORTHAM.
ANNIS CONSECR. 45, TRANSL. 40, SALUTIS 1714.

A picture of what the unfortunate Keep had sunk to by 1750 is conveyed by correspondence unearthed and copied by that Master of University College, the Rev Henry Gee. On the death of Bishop Chandler, a disagreement broke out between a Mr Course, a London surveyor representing Bishop Butler, and a Mr Shirley, representing the executors. Mr Shirley raised an objection to the following charge for dilapidations:

clear the rubbish away so as to come at and secure the foundations of the great octagon tower, make good the inner walls, and arch it over, so as to make a surface capable of carrying the weather that falls into it, and repair the breaches of the inner part of the walls to preserve it from ruin . . . £229 5s.

Mr Course cryptically replied:

To the Tower - Mr Shirley allows his refusal to view it, though I often pressed him, there is nothing left but outside walls, which are so much impaired that in many places where it is presumed formerly were chimneys and towers, for want of care being taken as the parts have fallen down, insomuch that in many parts of it the walls are nearly perished through. I am very certain that the best that can be done is what is now proposed to make the building safe, carry off the water and preserve it from ruin.

Mr Shirley remained obdurate:

> As to this article I did refuse to go to the inside to view as knowing it has been disused ever since Bishop Fox's time which is 250 years or thereabouts.
>
> Thomas Shirley
>
> Durham, 1st Jany., 1750-1.[1]

Bishop Egerton in 1773 had some repair in mind, as a drawing of the tower and the south screen wall was prepared for him. This drawing shows the original height of the wall. The Keep must have been in a depressingly dilapidated condition at this time, as Bishop Thurlow had the upper stories pulled down in 1789 lest they fall. During the half century that elapsed before it was rebuilt, in 1840, under the direction of Mr Anthony Salvin, the years and the weather must have taken an even savager toll.

As was mentioned earlier, there were, when the University began, nine Fellows - three Senior and six Junior. All these held some other office, and the intention seems to have been to get rid of these official fellowships as they fell vacant and have instead prize fellowships, which was of course the Oxford custom. In November 1839, the two chaplains who had been appointed the previous year were made Fellows, with an annual stipend of £50, and three fellowships were established, also worth £50 and tenable for six years; the first to be filled in 1839, the second in 1841, and the third in 1843. Luke Ripley, the Bursar, resigned in May 1841, whereupon it was decided that in future the Bursar should be elected annually, at a salary of £75, and that the fellowship attached to the office should hereafter become an open one. A further step towards the Oxford model was taken in March 1841, when the three Tutors were deprived of the title of Fellow and were given £100 a year to compensate.

Another fellowship was founded in 1844 by Mrs John Pemberton of Sherburn Hill, whose husband had been one of the first members of the College. Under the terms of his will a fellowship was founded worth £100 for ten years, as well as two scholarships worth £30 a year. The right of nomination for the fellowship was reserved to Mrs Pemberton for her life; but the qualifications for it make interesting reading. The candidate had to be at least of B.A. standing, a churchman, a member of University College and, other things being equal, a native of Durham. The fellowship would be vacated by marriage, accession to a fortune, or preferment to a benefice worth £200 or more a year.

The first Pemberton Fellow was William Greenwell, who was elected in 1844. To Greenwell we owe a graphic picture of Bishop Van Mildert driving in his coach-and-six with outriders from the Castle to the Cathedral. He was a Fellow of the Royal Society; his book British Barrows was an important contribution to archaeology. His permanent great claim to fame, however, was his invention of the 'fly' 'Greenwell's Glory', he being a dedicated fisherman.

I have already mentioned the somewhat cumbrous system by which young men were nominated to foundation scholarships - the candidates being nominated by the members of Chapter in turn and the Dean having two nominations to each prebendary's one. In 1840 a new arrangement allowed the Dean the right of nomination to two such scholarships, but now gave every prebendary one. One was allotted to the Grammar School, and was awarded on the nomination of the Headmaster; the other five were for undergraduates who had been recommended by the examiners for their work in the first and second year Arts examinations. Scholarships in the nomination of the Archbishop of Canterbury (Canon John Bird Sumner of the second stall), and of the Rev and Hon Gerald Valerian Wellesley, were thrown open in 1848. It took another eight years before the prebendaries agreed to make open the scholarships attached to suspended canonries, and yet another six before all were thrown open to undergraduates reading or entering on the Arts course.

Sad to say, after the initial eventful years, and after showing so much promise, the University (and inevitably the College with it) fell into decline; until the Royal Commission of 1862 put an end to Thorp's Wardenship and, at the same time, to the old man's life.

The history of the University during those twenty-odd years makes sorry reading, for it went into such a palpable decline that there was serious talk of closing it. It must be remembered that the University consisted now not only of the College but also of Hatfield, which had been founded in 1846, as well as Bishop Cosin's Hall, which was founded in 1851. Inevitably this possibility led to a deal of concern among past graduates, who now saw their degrees and licences about to be rendered worthless as having been granted by a flash-in-the-pan and now quite fizzled-out institution, and their career prospects accordingly blighted. Letters to the *Record* and the *Guardian* from these worried unfortunates put forward the suggestion that, if the worst came to the worst, the owners might be granted *ad eundem* degrees at Oxford - a less than likely possibility. Indeed, things had come to such a pass by 1861, the year of its greatest misery, that only nineteen degrees and licences were conferred.

Statistics tell baldly the painful story. In the Easter Term of 1840, there were 31 students in Arts, 30 in Theology, and 21 in Engineering. In the corresponding term of 1850 there were 73 in Arts and 41 in Theology - something of an improvement, but not one that a young and thrusting University could congratulate itself upon. In 1860 the numbers had dropped dramatically to 30 in Arts, 20 in Theology, and 1 in Medicine. While in February 1862, the nadir of the University's fortunes, there were only 46 students all told. The greatest number in residence at any one time in these twenty and more years had been 130. The pass lists tell as miserable a story. In 1839-40, 4 had passed B.A. and 4 Civil Engineering. In 1849-50 17 passed B.A. In 1859-60 - only 9.

Clearly noone could allow the downward spiral to continue, and in 1861, without waiting to set up a preliminary commission of enquiry, Parliament passed a Durham University Act to provide for the better government and extension of the University. Under this Act a Royal Commission was appointed in 1862 to look into the state of its affairs and make provision for its future. The big gun among the Commissioners, under the Bishop of Durham as Chairman, was Robert Lowe, at this date Vice-President of the Committee of Privy Council on Education, and the man responsible in the previous year for introducing into elementary education the immediately disastrous practice of 'Payment by Results'. There were three other Members of Parliament, all with local connections, Adderley, Liddell and Ingham; and the Rev Charles John Vaughan, D.D., a man of most suspect reputation when headmaster at Harrow. Among those who appeared before these Commissioners were Chevallier, Henry Jenkyns, Arthur Beanlands, and the 'great' Jowett of Balliol.

The Bishop of Durham who presided over the Commission was the newly appointed Charles Thomas Baring, one of the banking Barings, who on account of the rank and opulence he exuded was generally known as 'Overbaring'.

Anyone who has read thus far in this history would, if asked to do so, be able to put his finger on the instant on the fundamental weakness in the University's structure. It was hopelessly underfunded; and the wealthy men in the north who had confidently been expected to contribute to it had given it little or nothing. True, a stream of donors had presented books to the Library - issue after issue of the *Advertiser* records the gifts - and a subsidiary stream had given birds' eggs and stuffed creatures and fossils and shells galore to the Museum; but these in no way made up for the lack of hard cash. There was a deficit in the University's revenue, even after receipt of the income from the estates, and this, especially in recent years when the number of undergraduates had so declined, had not been made up by fees or the rent from rooms. Cosin's Hall indeed had gone down so far as to be at this date almost entirely a part of University College.

The second great weakness lay in the power of the Warden, which was both absolute and capricious. It is difficult to see that any great harm was done by Thorp's authoritarianism in the early days of the University, when indeed it may well have been a blessing; but times had changed. One of the grievances aired at the enquiry of 1862 was that the Warden had the power of veto at Convocation, and Members would not attend when they knew that Warden Thorp might well exercise it in order to prevent discussion, even though, in fairness to Thorp, he had done so on only one occasion. One result of this particular power of the Warden was that graduates of the University tended to have little interest in it.

Again, Thorp was strongly opposed to any innovations, and his power was such that he was able to exert a great deal of pressure on those who advocated them. Chevallier perhaps summed up this particular weakness of the University when he described its government as 'very monarchical'. Among the Warden's other powers, those which apply to University College, of which of course he was Master, are particularly interesting. The Council of College officials met once a week, but again the Master presided and was of course absolute. Nothing could ever be done without him, and the fact that he still lived at Ryton made it impossible both for him to know properly all the day-to-day workings of the College, and to carry on such an absolute rule efficiently. Worse still, and a sad reflection on an old man who had given such service to the place, men were admitted to the College when the examiners had recommended the contrary.

One inevitably wonders whether the traditional friction between Hatfield and University College does not stem not from mere tribal partisanship but from some ancient memory of what was said at this Commission of Enquiry, for the Principal of Hatfield's evidence was such that no man against whom it was directed could ever forgive either the words or the man who uttered them.

The Principal was the Rev David Melville, who had been Tutor from 1842 to 1846, before being made Principal of the new Hall.

> If you could imagine a Chancellor, a Vice-Chancellor, and a Hebdomadal Board rolled into one man, that is the constitution of the University of Durham, and if you could think of not merely a number of colleges swamping the University, but one college swamping the University, that is the Durham system: and the same man presides at both 'boards.' . . . During the whole of my experience there [Melville had left Hatfield in 1851, after five years as Principal], I should say the Dean and Chapter were simply managed, the Convocation was simply dictated to, and the Senate simply checkmated: that is the constitution of the University of Durham.

Melville also said that, when he had been at Durham, it had been a common saying: 'You can do nothing till the Warden goes.' The University and Thorp had become 'convertible terms', and the great evils at Durham were the small, jealous, narrow constitution, and the private and close patronage.

However much one would like to, one cannot dismiss Melville's evidence as simply the rancorous outpourings of an aggrieved man. There is, too, ample evidence that the animosity between him and Thorp went beyond the bounds of one man's resentment of another and older man's absolute and by now inefficient rule.

For in Melville's last year as Tutor, 1846, Hatfield Hall came into being, and Melville was invited to take charge of it. Thorp at first proposed that he himself should be Principal, and Melville Vice-Principal, but when this invidious offer was declined, Thorp submitted, though one cannot say with much grace. For he attached two conditions to the appointment: one, that the Principal should not hold church preferment, and the other that he should not marry. Both were particularly unkind impositions, since they were dictated by a happily married family man who had long enjoyed, and was still enjoying, the living of Ryton. Melville, true to the discreditable system of absentee livings of those days, held a living in Worcestershire; and it is difficult to believe that this condition was arrived at by Thorp fortuitously. Melville was also a young man and might well be expected to desire to marry. At the time of his appointment, Melville reminded Thorp of his Worcestershire living, but the Warden said that the condition did not apply in his case. As time went on however, the success of the new Hall clearly caused the Warden unease, for when in 1848 it was proposed to enlarge it, Thorp declared that had he foreseen that it would grow to such proportions he would never have allowed it in the first place.

Matters came to a head in 1850. Three years earlier Melville had told Thorp that he wanted to marry, and Thorp had answered in the friendliest possible way that he might do so and remain as Principal. Melville duly married in the following year. In 1850 however Thorp declared that the unfortunate man's licence was at an end because he had violated the terms of his appointment both by marrying and by retaining his non-residential preferment in Worcestershire. The harassed Melville, who could hardly have got over his honeymoon, offered to resign his Worcestershire living, and indeed the Bishop of Durham offered him a Durham one in compensation. It is only fair to point out here that, unlike the prebends of whom we read earlier, poor (in every sense) Melville was getting only about £100 a year for being Principal - though of course he had free accommodation, and there was also a little extra money coming in by virtue of his Tutorship. Thorp, who really comes out of this sorry saga very badly, now said that he had no objection to Melville's accepting a Durham living; whereupon the Principal of Hatfield resigned his Worcestershire one. This drastic step having been taken, the Warden then withheld his permission for Melville to stay on as head of Hatfield - on the ground that he was married!

It is hardly surprising that, following Melville's relinquishing the Principalship in 1851, he was followed by no fewer than three different Principals in as many years!

At the Commission, the decline in Durham's fortunes was attributed to a number of factors, but interestingly none of those who expressed an opinion considered that the expansion of the railways had anything to do with it. One argument was that there was no increased demand for university education. The theological students had decreased in numbers partly because they had found facilities elsewhere, but partly because some of the bishops still persisted in their refusal to accept the Durham L.Th. as a qualification for ordination.

David Melville very interestingly thought that the reason for the decline was Durham's slavish imitation of Oxford and Cambridge; though it is difficult to imagine what other models at the time the university could possibly have been founded on. It seems likely that Melville's experience of Durham under Thorp had soured him, for he was convinced that the feeling in the country against Durham was so strong that it was past ever attracting sufficient numbers.

Among the suggestions for reform, some are interesting. The 'great' Jowett recklessly suggested transferring the whole University to Newcastle, and there re-fashioning it after the Scottish model, only Theology being allowed to remain at Durham.

Inevitably, the old chestnut, that of turning Durham into a theological college, turned up once again; and Hornby, who was in favour of this, suggested that an Arts course might then be retained so that the prospective parsons would be better educated than those who emerged from the perennially maligned St Bees. Jenkyns, to his great credit, referred back to the high intentions of Thorp and Van Mildert: Durham was intended for a place of liberal education; a purely theological institution would not be in accord with the purposes of either its founders or its charter, would be an injury to the present students and to its private benefactors, and what is more, would be, he was perspicacious enough to see, highly unlikely to succeed.

On 30 June 1862 the Commissioners issued a set of Ordinances, under the Durham University Act. Sweeping, indeed revolutionary, changes were to be set in motion. Most of these need not concern us here, particularly since they came to nothing; but a couple do. In future, the Dean was to be Warden, and a pension of £400 a year was to be paid to Thorp - provided he resign the Wardenship forthwith.

Such a storm of angry protest was aroused at the proposed changes that both the Chapter and the University petitioned against them, and they were in due course disallowed by the Privy Council.

In a couple of years an Act of Parliament known as the 'Durham University Act' received the Royal Assent.

There is little in this Act specifically to interest Castlemen. In the main it abolished a number of the twenty-four fellowships, the proceeds being applied to the School of Theology and to 'the school of Physical Science' which the Dean and Chapter proposed to establish in the Faculty of Arts - a School which in the event was a failure.

As of course had been the Commission itself, its failure in some sort vindicating Charles Thorp's refusal to appear before it. And that being so, the Dean and Chapter resolved to proceed with reforms off their own bat. An Act of Chapter of 11 February 1865 made for some extensive changes.

No longer were nonconformist students obliged to attend cathedral or chapel. Also in future only candidates for the Licence, or for the Degree, in Theology, as well as members of the Senate or Convocation, were obliged to declare in writing that they were members of the Church of England.

A Professor of Hebrew was to be appointed as soon as the money was forthcoming. The School of Physical Science was to be opened in the Michaelmas Term, 1865, the subjects taught in it including Physics, Pure and Applied Mathematics, Chemistry, Engineering and Mining.

But the most revolutionary change instituted by the Dean and Chapter was, in the very nature of things, bound to be disastrous. This enabled a man to take the B.A. degree after only two years' residence. The terms for Arts and Science, though significantly not for that Queen of Sciences Theology, were lengthened to extend over eight months in the year; though Senate was empowered to shorten these if it found them inconveniently long. The change was apparently made on the hopelessly unworldly assumption by the Dean and Chapter that, while it was aimed at only those who could not afford more than the minimum residence, those who could afford to stay up longer would altruistically do so. As 'The Student's Guide to the University of Durham' naively put it, in 1897, 'Those who have their own interests as students, and the interests of the University as a centre of education, at heart, will make a point of residing more than the actual minimum required.'

Inevitably, some more men did come up; though whether the quality was maintained is open to doubt, for Durham as inevitably won the unenviable reputation of being an institution at which a man could get a degree easier than at any other university. And of course, since there was a shorter time at the men's disposal before examinations, there was an inordinate amount of cramming, and consequently of 'plucking' or 'ploughing'.

Since the Commission had, most surprisingly in view of the evidence, decided that the extremely moderate charges at Durham were 'excessive', another Act of Chapter, in 1865, decreed that Senate should take steps to reduce them.

Perhaps as a result of this latter, or of the shortening of the time needed to take the B.A. degree, or maybe through a combination of both, the number of students did increase, rising from the 41 on the books in 1861 to 119 in 1891. More promisingly, students began to come again from other parts of the country than the north east. About ninety per cent of these were ordinands, who tended to take the B.A. and the Licence in Theology.

It is time now to catch up on the day-to-day life of the time, which it is possible to do from references to it in the Memoirs and Lives of men who were up at University College in those relatively uneventful, yet profoundly important, years.

At first the undergraduate gown was the short one, the 'bum-freezer', as worn at Oxford; but the men petitioned the Senate for something more dignified - or more suited to the bleaker northern climate! - and the longer gown was substituted.

Walter Augustus Shirley, who was Bishop of Sodor and Man from 1846 to 1847, was very favourably impressed by the Castlemen he saw when he was examiner. He wrote to a correspondent:

> At Durham, I examined into the new university, which seems to be very well conducted. The young men had, on the whole, a very gentlemanly appearance: all the appointments seemed to be extremely comfortable, and the education, especially the theological department, of a superior character. It is a charming situation, in the keep of that fine old castle with the river and the cathedral, etc., all round. What a beautiful place it is![2]

Charles Grey Grey's reminiscences (*vide supra* Chapter 4) tell us something of life at Castle in the mid Eighteen Forties. Despite the stringency of Thorp's regulations for governing the College, the keeping of terms was somewhat more flexible than it is today. It is to be noted too that the social background of the undergraduates seems little different from that of those at Oxford; and immediate parallels can be seen between Grey's pursuits and those of Charles Larkyns in the '30's. For Grey did not go up for the Epiphany term in 1845, 'professing to read at home, as I was changing from Engineering to Classics, though I spent much time hunting and otherwise amusing myself.' The explanation for this seemingly cavalier attitude to terms is that, though a man could not take his degree until after twelve terms, he was only obliged to keep nine. Grey, who kept eleven, took his finals in the Easter term of 1846, then stayed on for three more terms for his M.A. He was examined for the M.A. in June of '47, but 'was taken ill and allowed Aegrotat degree, though I had to go in, ill as I was, for one or two papers, which I suppose I passed.'

Grey refers to the clapping of a fellow undergraduate, one Philip Rudd, by the 'men in the gallery' at the degree Convocation on 4 May, and of the Warden's telling them to be quiet. This manifestation of high emotion becomes, as we shall see, something of a problem as the century progresses, and degree Convocations later become a byword not only for the applause given to deserving (and undeserving) friends but also for the downright rudeness to, and catcalled abuse of, the dons.

Grey's description of his time in the Keep is interesting. One of his friends was 'Bell that Cat', otherwise the Hon Henry Douglas. 'I fear,' Grey writes,

> he and I, who were chums in the keep, were sometimes rather noisy. The Reverend David Melville, a tutor, also lived near us, and was subject to fits of tertian ague. On one occasion he, knowing our habits, kindly sent for us and told us how he was suffering, and knowing we were the steadiest men in the keep, asked us to influence the rowdy men to keep quiet till he was well. We thought it was a most kindly way of reproving us.

These manifestations of high spirits, or rowdiness if you like, among the undergraduates, many of whom were destined to be ordained, in no way conflicted with that high seriousness in matters of religious belief and practice which was the subject of an earlier chapter.

In those early days, dinner was at four o'clock on weekdays, and to start with at two on Sundays, though this latter rather eighteenth century hour was soon changed to the more civilised time of 5.30.

There were Sunday lectures also, but these were dispensed with in 1842, though for the Easter term only.

In 1845 the Dean and Chapter decided that the undergraduates should be given the opportunity to attend the three state services held on 30 January, 29 May and 5 November, though attendance was not made compulsory. These three services were in the Book of Common Prayer until

1859, when they were removed, but the days became recognised holidays until 1872. The institution of their being holidays however continued after that in the form of Open Days; though these too were abolished in the early years of this century. The significance of these days may not be immediately apparent, but the first two marked the execution of King Charles the Martyr and the Restoration of the Monarchy with Charles 11, while the third, of course, marked the failure of the Gunpowder Plot.

The opening of Hatfield need not of course concern us; but the founding of Bishop Cosin's Hall in 1851 does. Before it moved to what became known as Cosin's Hall, the 'college' was disseminated among a few houses, on which the paltry sum of £850 was spent. The Rev John Pedder was made Principal at a salary of £100 a year. In 1856 these houses were let and the Hall removed to what was then known as Archdeacon's Inn.

Archdeacon's Inn had been in use as part of the University since the beginning, but the decline in numbers residing at the Castle had left it empty. As a hall of residence it had a lot to recommend it, being a Georgian building of exceptional elegance and grace. What may not be known is that it originally had very beautiful iron railings in front of it.

What should have been clear to any objective observer however is that the building, however gracious, could never be large enough for any hall accommodated in it to grow and become financially viable.

Pedder was Principal for only three years. He was followed by the Rev James John Hornby, who was Principal from 1854 to 1864.

Inevitably the Hall proved a failure, manifesting one could say in microcosm the faults that in macrocosm were only too observable in the University as a whole. It was taken over by University College in 1864.

By all accounts, though, Cosin's Hall was rather a jolly place at which to be an undergraduate. We know this from Scudamore Powell who, entering it in 1861 to read Medicine, was one of the last students there. During his time at Cosin's, there were only six other men in residence, and they took all their meals at University College. Powell has left us a few - all too few - reminiscences of his time up at Cosin's Hall.

Dr Hornby he describes as a fine-looking man who, though fond of athletics, was very shy. It seems the Principal had a private gymnasium, for the only time he ever spoke to Powell (one of his only six students, be it remembered!) was when he gave him permission to use this, which was situated in one of the lower rooms.

William Greenwell, who for some now unknown reason was known by the undergraduates as 'Neb', was as has been said, a fisherman. Powell writes of him once as hurrying back into the Hall from one of his fishing expeditions, with creel and rod, and in grey check trousers and long boots, rushing across Palace Green, and panting into the Galilee just in time for the service. His surplice did little to conceal his check trousers.

The Principal, the Rev J.J. Hornby, who was also in 1862 Vice-Master of University College, gave to the 1862 Commission of Enquiry an account of the arrangements at Cosin's Hall. Until 1858 it had been governed by a Principal who, as we have seen, received £100 a year; at the same time, University College was managed by the Vice-Master (i.e. himself) at the same salary. It was thought that great saving could be made by uniting the two offices and having a common kitchen for both College and Hall. In 1862 the men lunched and dined at Castle but had breakfast and tea in their own rooms. They paid 14 shillings a week for luncheon and dinner, inclusive of cheese and beer. At the Hall they paid a guinea a week for everything, including cheese and beer, coals and candles; and from five to seven guineas a term for furnished rooms. Despite the intimate connection between Cosin's and University College, which Mr Hornby thought should have attracted undergraduates to Cosin's, the numbers there had fallen dramatically - being down at the time he gave evidence to the aforesaid six.

It is extremely interesting to read what he has to say about costs. The highest battels he had ever known at Cosin's came to £73 10s. The average was about £68. At University College, as we have already seen, the men took over the furniture at a valuation. Hornby knew of one case where a man spent only £71 14s., including rooms and University payments, and the highest payment for a year he had ever known was only £138, which included everything. Cheapness was clearly still a prime consideration; for Hornby advised the closure of the Hall in order further to reduce costs. One of the financial problems of the Hall was the high rent that had to be paid to the University for the building; and when the undergraduates were down in numbers the rent was simply not paid. There were only twenty rooms in Cosin's Hall, though there were five more in an adjoining house; as compared to forty-seven in Castle and twenty more in adjoining buildings, and about forty-three in Hatfield.

It will come as a surprise to today's Castlemen that, at the time the

Castle was made over to the College, the upper part of the Great Hall, where the dais is now, and by the entrance to Bishop Cosin's staircase, was walled off and divided into two floors. The lower room thus formed was put to use as a Senior Common Room, and was known as the Black Parlour, while the upper room, which was formerly the Bishop's drawing-room, became a lecture room. In 1847, however, the same Mr Salvin who had been commissioned to rebuild the Keep in 1840 was called in. He removed the partition wall and floors, and thus restored the Hall to its former length northwards, though he retained Bishop Fox's partition to the south. The tracery of the north window was inserted, designed from the still existing remains of the original window, and Salvin's craftsmen may well have used some of these original remains.

Two of the windows on the east side of the Hall, and one on the west, were restored at the same time to their original length. Fowler, in an article in the *Durham University Journal* dated 8 July, 1882, writes that the substantial cost of all this was borne, not by the Fellows, as was commonly believed, but by the Warden; and from what we have already learned of Thorp's generosity, as well as his somewhat eclectic passion for building, it is easy to believe this.

Charles Grey Grey's little book provides us with invaluable information as to what life in the Castle was like in the Eighteen Forties; what it was like in the 'Sixties is told us in a letter to the *Durham University Journal* dated November 1914. Headed *Tempora Labuntur*, and signed only by the single letter 'P', it starts off with the claim, 'It is nearly half-a-century since I first went to the Castle . . .' This dating puts 'P's' residence at around 1864. While 'P' goes on to say that his recollection of student life is, because of the time lapse, necessarily scrappy, what he gives us is a delightful picture of College life at the time.

One particular reminiscence of his, however, aroused criticism at the time it appeared in print, and some doubt about its veracity thereafter:

> University College and Hatfield Hall were the only colleges in those days. There was little acquaintanceship between the students, and I can remember one Castle man saying that he did not even know where Hatfield was until many years after he left Durham.

Subsequent issues of the *DUJ* contained protests at this reminiscence, though a subsequent correspondent who signed himself *Senex* put it in context, in a letter dated February 1915, by sensibly pointing out that this superior tone was a pose adopted by the Castlemen of the day. Whiting however, in his history of the University of Durham, refers to it with absolute seriousness: 'The contempt of the Castle for Hatfield was probably not so bad as 'P' records.'[3] He even goes to the length of quoting Fowler as a contrary witness, Fowler having written, 'I was at Hatfield from 1858 to 1861, and four of my best friends were Castle men.'

Nobody of course can be expected to take seriously such a preposterous claim as that made by 'P's' informant. Durham in the Eighteen Sixties was an infinitely smaller and more homogeneous place than it is today, and it is inconceivable that a University man then would not know the whereabouts of a sister college not much more than a couple of hundred yards away. The remark was obviously never meant to be taken seriously, and indeed much of 'P's' article is written tongue in cheek.

'P' tells us of an interesting division between the students. They were 'either undergrads or probationers, the latter being those who had not been fortunate enough to pass the Matric, but of whom better things were expected.'

Nearly all the men at the University were intended for the Church, [but] there was at the Castle a physical science student. He used to disappear at regular intervals, but who gave him lectures and what they were about nobody ever knew, and he would never tell.

Terms in the sixties lasted ten weeks, but 'P' comments rather acidly on the fact that the divinity students went down about two weeks before the arts men: 'We never heard the reason, but we supposed that it was because a knowledge of divinity was more easily acquired than a knowledge of arts.'

Even as far back as this, a favourite amusement seems to have been climbing over the roofs of the Castle.

The more dangerous the roof, the more popular it was. Happily no one ever came to grief. One Sunday evening, while we were dining in Hall, and all was peace, a succession of heavy falls was heard on the roof just over the High Table. The Dons were very much alarmed, but we were not. A messenger despatched hastily brought back word that a certain undergrad. was practising jumping on the roof to reduce his somewhat rotund proportions.

As in every institution down the ages, food was a matter for constant complaint.

Plum pudding was a staple dish at the Castle dinner. What we did not eat used to be served up to us next day in slices fried and bore the name of 'Resurrection'. A student, on payment of threepence, was permitted to have sweets from the High Table, which were of a superior class to those we got. It was not, however, considered good form to flaunt his wealth too often.

The Master of those days, Dr Joseph Waite (he was 'Warden' of University College from 1862 to 1865, when there was no Master, was appointed Master in that latter year, and continued so until 1873) was 'very much liked. He was very kind hearted and was a capital tutor.' On the debit side, however, are the following.

He had his pet phrases. His favourite was, 'Gentlemen, will you just take a brief note?' but the note which followed was not always brief.

Worse is to come.

A student on one occasion, with a furtive eye on a brief note he had taken down earlier in the term, repeated the note verbatim, when the term's work was being revised. The Master was delighted, and said, 'Dear me, Mr Jones, that is good, that is very good. May I ask where you got it from?

The Castle was not without its hazards - leaving aside its tempting roofs. Fire was, as earlier, an ever-present danger. Candles of course still provided the lighting in the students' rooms, and on this account,

A man who had rooms in the Norman Gallery once nearly set fire to it. He had stuck a lighted candle into a brass candlestick, which was still hot owing to the previous candle having burnt to the socket. He left the room to visit a neighbour. On his return he was horrified to find that the candle had melted and fallen on to the table, which was in a lively blaze. Fortunately, he put it out without the Gallery suffering any injury.

'P' adds: 'he shudders now when he thinks of what might have happened.'

Two institutions mentioned by 'P' in this letter call for extended comment. One is 'Keeping Day'; the other is the Choral Society.

For the first, Keeping Day was the system by which a man was 'marked' on his attendance at chapel and lectures. As 'P' succinctly puts it, 'If a student missed . . . [either], he lost a day, and so many days lost meant a lost term.' Evasion was not unknown.

One man who was anxious not to lose a day made a practice, after passing the Verger on Sunday mornings and being marked, of walking up the chancel of the Cathedral and making his exit by another door.

Later, the Proctor 'marked' men as 'present'. It was a heartily disliked system. The *DUJ*, as late as 27 February 1897, takes it to task.

To keep a day under this system is a matter of some difficulty - unprofitable difficulty too: and even when the day is kept, who knows whether one is credited in the Proctor's book with having kept it? One must attend a service in Galilee and all lectures, and therefore that service and each individual lecture gives a man a separate possibility of missing a day, not perhaps by his own fault, but by the imperfection of the arrangements for 'marking in'. In this respect the Galilee service is comparatively unobjectionable, as a list of absentees is published daily, and mistakes can be rectified.

The same could not be said for 'marking in' at lectures.

What security has a man that his lecturer or the Proctor's man notices his presence, or, if so, marks him in? And there is no means of finding this out . . . A weekly list of days kept, if it gave the Proctor a little more trouble during the term, would take off a good deal of work at the end, and would be more satisfactory . . . Compulsory lectures are the crying and unnecessary evil of the present system of keeping days.

The unsatisfactory nature of the system was eloquently put in a letter in the same issue of the *DUJ* from one signing himself 'A.B. Raham'.

if a man is wrongly marked absent from a lecture, the mistake cannot be rectified. Thus I lost 2 days (once wrongly deemed absent from Galilee and twice on successive days from 2 lectures). Fortunately the Proctor's servant remembered that I had informed him, at that time, that I had kept the 'Chapel' in question and so I was allowed this day. I managed finally to keep my term by attending at the Castle Chapel on the last day of term. This, after I had, as a matter of fact, kept either 49 or 50 days . . . if a man does not keep at least 50 days, he runs considerable risk of losing his term.

Once again the plea is made: as regards Galilee, 'a list of absentees is posted daily and mistakes may therefore be rectified. Why cannot the same be done in the case of lectures?'

Complainants were vociferous down into the twentieth century. In a letter to the *DUJ* of 6 June 1903, 'A Hard-Up Korkscrew' wrote in that two dons he had questioned about the system admitted they did not understand it. He then put three posers:

1) In the event of a man missing Galilee does he lose 1 day for each lecture on that day, even if he attends the lectures, or does the lost Galilee also count as a day lost?

2) If a man keep 45 and then refrains from Galilee and lectures, are days deducted from his hard-earned 45?

3) If a man through some misfortune lose 1 lecture in a day, are the Galilee and other lectures he has previously kept deducted as so many days lost?

As a pecuniary benefit to the University (he concludes) the screw scheme is a brilliant one, but not to

'A H-U Korkscrew'

If 'P' knew of a man who went in at one door of the Cathedral and instantly out at another, another correspondent to the *DUJ* of 11 June 1907, a man who signed himself 'Reverence', took issue on the matter of coercion at religious ceremonies, a regrettable feature in the life of the University being

> the practice, which is so common, of spending the time devoted to keeping day in Cathedral on Sunday in reading of a more or less secular nature. We all recognize that attendance at Cathedral is an irksome necessity, from which we would gladly be relieved. Those who would rather not attend public worship, or in particular that of the Church of England, can obtain their remedy if they care to seek it, and can be excused from attendance.

There was also, according to this correspondent, although sadly he does not go into detail, 'open jocularity and horseplay.'

Presumably this hooliganism came to a head in the Easter term of 1908, for on November 26 of that year the *DUJ* cryptically commented:

> It must be carefully remembered that the proposal to abolish compulsory attendance at Galilee has no connection with the disturbances of last term or with the punishment which was then inflicted. It is perhaps unfortunate that the two things should have happened together, because to some it may appear that the hand of the official has been forced by a handful of rowdies.

The matter became not simpler but even more complicated. The *DUJ* again, on 5 April 1909, noted:

> There has been of late a great increase in the number of men who break the University rule regarding attendance at Cathedral. Some time ago there was some unpleasantness which excused men who did

not sit in the Transept. This, however, has fortunately now been removed, and therefore we would draw attention to the fact that men may legally only 'keep day' by sitting in the Chancel or North Transept.

Chad's and John's men were still 'marked' in 1910 for, commented the *DUJ* on 5 March, 'the new arrangements made for marking [their] presence in Galilee . . . at the south-west door of the Cathedral are highly satisfactory to the members of the halls concerned.'
As for the Castle Choral Society, 'P' records that

There were some good voices among us, and there was a choral society which had concerts in the shades on Saturday evenings. 'She wore a wreath of roses' and 'Her bright smile haunts me still' were favourite songs, and so were others of the Haynes-Bayley type.

For quite two terms the most popular song by far was one which set forth the virtues of John Wesley and his little dog Tobit. It was set to an easy air - that of a well-known hymn - and was sung by all, both musical and unmusical, and in all places appropriate and inappropriate.

It's sad that a society which flourished for as many years as the Castle Choral, and which gave deservedly popular public concerts, attended by many of the notabilities of the city, sank, in this present vulgar century, without trace.
On Saturday, 9 December 1876, for instance, the Society gave the

usual concert in the College Hall. The music [wrote a critic in the *DUJ*] was on the whole good and showed at least that great pains had been taken in its preparation. Of the choruses 'The Cloud-Capped Towers' was especially well rendered, and the Rev T. Rogers, Mr Edwards and Mr Whitehead were favoured with an encore. The audience was a brilliant gathering of the elite of Durham, and the decorations of the hall were simple, tasteful and elegant. The applause was hearty, and the proceedings were a complete success.

At that date the Choral Society was, it appears, peculiar to University

College, for in the same issue of the *DUJ* a correspondent who attended this concert, confessing that he belonged to 'that part of the University which rejoices in the name of 'Hatter', laments that his College 'did nothing of the sort.' It was an omission which was soon rectified.

Down the years the *DUJ* recorded the successes of the Choral Society. Happily, these reports give us not only some idea of the musical taste of the time, but also a picture of Castle Hall as it appeared on those social as well as musical occasions.

In 1878, for instance, we are told that 'Three concerts have been given, listened to by large and appreciative audiences.'

In 1879, we hear that

Despite the unfavourable weather the concert usually given . . . was attended by a large and brilliant audience. The platform was, as usual, decorated gracefully with tropical plants. The well-filled Hall showed that the concert is regarded quite as one of the events of the season. With the single exception, perhaps, that there was an unique preponderance of instrumental music, the whole programme was well arranged and excellently rendered. The appreciation of the guests assembled was shewn in repeated encores, the response to which caused the meeting to break up somewhat after the customary hour.

In the December *DUJ* of the same year we learn that the Choral Society did not restrict itself to one, or even three, annual concerts, for 'the usual fortnightly concerts have been given.' These included violin and piano solos, and glees.

March 1880 records that the Society now numbered 32 members. December of the same year adds again to our picture of the great occasion.

The fair sex was in every sense more than fairly represented.

The orchestra, raised to a judicious height above the floor, was decorated with shrubs and flowers, and by an admirable combination of screens and lamps the stiffness and bareness of the conventional platform was entirely avoided. But the old old draughts were in full force.

The concert was, continued the *DUJ*'s critic, the outcome of steady work, and the natural climax of a series of fortnightly concerts, at which music was submitted to the criticisms of a purely academic audience.

March 1881 shows us even more abundantly what a glittering occasion the Castle Choral Concert must have been. It also records a miraculous improvement in everybody's personal comforts, for

Cold air and chilling draughts, hitherto one of the chief characteristics of the Castle concert, are now no more; the Hall, on the evening of the 12th, was equably heated by the system of hot-water pipes which has been lately introduced. Upwards of 600 friends of members assembled in spite of heavy rain. Red curtains served as a reposeful background. Lamps on stands, and very judiciously placed footlights served to give light.

The front of the platform was banked, as usual, with evergreens and plants.

Early 1882 saw the introduction of instrumental quartets into the Society; while the report of the December concert adds again to our picture of the scene, for as to the platform,

the lighting was effected by means of two clusters of gas jets, one on each side of the Hall, which were concealed from those in front by means of large and handsome white banners charged with the St Cuthbert's Cross. The usual dark red curtains at the back and sides of the platform gave an air of repose.

Back now to Charles Thorp, after what I believe to have been a necessary digression: necessary because such institutions as the Choral Society and 'Keeping Day' were initiated, or agreed to, by him, and continued with vigour throughout - and beyond - his century.

Warden Thorp's resignation, dated 19 June 1862, was forced upon him. In his letter of resignation he makes no bones about this, writing of himself as 'a party consenting under external pressure.' He was now, it is true, both old, being nearly eighty, and infirm; but one cannot view these his last days without sadness. The great work of his life seemed to be ending in failure and ignominy; the Royal Commission, before which, as I said, he refused to appear, was a grievous blow to him.

He died, on October 10 of this same year, 1862, at his beloved Ryton Rectory.

Whiting's valediction to Warden Thorp is a fitting one:

> The University owes him a great debt, both for its foundation and for the lines on which it was founded, and it would be a very fitting thing that at every one of our academic functions the memory of our chief Founder should in some way be recalled.[4]

---

1) Senate Minutes, 12 February, 1838
2) *Letters and Memoirs of Walter Augustus Shirley*, 1849, p.292
3) Whiting, p.115
4) *Ibid.*, p.111

Chapter 7

Good Clean Fun - And Games

The Smallness of the College

The smallness of student numbers throughout most of the College's early history, while making for cosiness and the creation of long-lasting friendships, clearly made sporting and other communal social activities something of a problem. Peaks in numbers tended to be greeted with great elation, as when the *DUJ*, in December 1878, applauded the fact that in that year 'a larger number of students are resident than has been known in the history of the University save about the year 1850!'. There was in consequence 'great *esprit de corps*', and the Societies were flourishing.

Things had not often been so. The following table shows the extent of the problem, particularly in the 'Seventies, a problem which was to be repeated in subsequent decades.

Number of Students in Residence

Year	Total	UC
1873	69	22
1874	76	27
1875	78	23
1876	92	43
1877	110	47
1878	125	50
1879	157	51
1880	191	61
1881	195	64
1882	205	79

In this last year, 1882, when the number of students for the first time exceeded 200, 112 were reading Arts, 93 Theology.

In 1884 however we find the numbers dropping again, the number at Castle falling to 57. Sporting and cultural activities were the first to feel the pinch. In 1884 the Choral Society, necessarily one of those most exposed, began its lamentation: 'owing to our comparatively small numbers this term . . .'

Fortuitous increases in numbers, such as occurred in 1905, were no guarantee that the Societies would be in all that much better shape. In May 1905, for instance, the *DUJ* reported that

> There has been a gratifying increase in our numbers this term, notably at University College, which, we hear, is in danger of becoming overcrowded. We understand that the total number of men in residence now at Durham has never been exceeded. One result of the increase has been that certain lecture rooms have been quite inconveniently crowded, some people even having to occupy such places as window-sills and table-tops as seats, owing to a lack of chairs.

Yet six months later it was compelled to deplore the fact that

> last year, so few men were up who could play Rugby, or indeed football of any kind, that it was quite impossible to raise a College XV.

Fluctuations there were inevitably, and great national calamities played their part in reducing the numbers of men in residence. Thus while in 1906 there were 'considerable accessions this term' and in 1907, 'The Castle is full, Hatfield is not', and indeed in 1908 the DUJ could crow

> The 'Varsity is in the happy position of having more men up this term than for many years past

in November 1914 we have it lamenting: 'Owing to the small number of men at present in residence . . .'

As the Great War progressed, of course the situation got worse. In December 1915 the *DUJ* bewailed again 'Our present depleted numbers', and in March 1916 lamented

> Only 70 men were on the University Roll at the beginning of term.

That small number has since been decreased owing to the number of men being called up. The place is very quiet.

The March 1916 issue however recorded that

Though so few men are in residence, we are proud to record that there is some College life.

One wonders if this 'life' were a last frenetic gesture in face of the dire prospects ahead of what few men there were in residence.

In November 1922 again the *DUJ* reported that 'In the Durham Colleges the total of undergraduates in residence is larger than ever before.' And in December 1925, 'The number in the Durham Colleges this term represents an increase of nearly 50 over last term, and 20 over all previous records.'

It went on:

The last 21 years in the Durham Colleges have been years of steady progress. 21 years ago there were 3 professors and 13 lecturers on the staff of the Colleges. There are now 12 professors and 26 other lecturers, apart from the staffs of the various Colleges.

Yet the year previous to this the *DUJ* was again complaining about 'the smallness of the number of men in residence this year', while in March 1925, the peak year, the DUBC was feeling the pinch because of 'the small number of men in residence.'

The year 1928 saw a further fall, the number up at Castle being a mere 34, fewer than at any College save Neville's Cross; for Hatfield boasted 80, St Chad's 48, St John's 62, Bede 110, St Mary's 51, St Hild's 35. Neville's mustered but 30.

These were necessarily lean years. In 1931 Castle had 38 men up, and in 1932 just 42. The *DUJ*, when giving the annual statistics in this latter year, put its finger on the problem when it commented: 'Considering the economic situation it is pleasing to see the numbers keeping up so well.'

The Depression had much to answer for, to University College as well as to the country at large. The *DUJ* pointed out in December 1933 that

The increase of students is all the more notable as the teaching profession is overcrowded, and the Board of Education announces there will be a reduction in the number of places available in 1934 and 1935.

It may not be generally known that at this time promising young men were given grants by their local authority to go to university only on a written guarantee that they would not, on graduation, make an attempt on the grossly overcrowded teaching profession.

So much for the statistics. The fewness of the men up at Castle, and the other Colleges, must have made the playing of team games difficult. J. Henderson, writing in the *DUJ* in 1920 on 'The University College Beagles, 1859-1863', says apropos the football played:

> it was Rugby, of course, and that of the roughest. No soccer in those days. No limit to the numbers on each side, and very little scientific play.

We have already heard how, in 1854, the Choral Society was finding it difficult to find singers, and how, in 1904, so few men were up who could play Rugby, 'or indeed football of any kind', that it was quite impossible to raise a College XV. Clearly, the men who were up, as in Canon Chase's and Canon Corden's time (1934-8 and 1931-7 respectively), were expected to play everything, as well as back the Societies, take a full part in the spiritual life of the College, and read for a degree. One can only stand back in amazement at how far they succeeded.

Rowing seems to have remained a pretty constant activity, and we shall be looking at this in more detail in a moment; but all the sports, one can confidently assume, were waging a constant war on two fronts: one against opponents, the other against the difficulties inherent in there being too small a pool of talent from which to draw.

The war years of course proved catastrophic. 'Durham University Rugby Football Club has resumed its activities after a lapse of five years,' wrote the *DUJ* in March 1920. And in July 1919 it reported that 'after a lapse of four years the Cricket Club has been revived . . . although the numbers are still very limited . . .'

The composition of the football teams for Michaelmas term 1876 shows the public school background from which Durham men were coming: St Bees School, Durham School, Repton, Marlborough, Loretto, Ambleside, Christ's Hospital, Radley, Hurstpierpoint, and Harrow. This background undoubtedly made for the popularity of sports such as Steeplechasing and Beagling.

We are fortunate indeed to have a programme of the University Sports of 1857.

The University Sports of 1857

Durham University Steeple Chase

March 4th, 1857

AT CROOK HALL

Stewards

O.P. Cambridge
H.V. Austin   R.G. Benson

First Race. - Flat Race - One Hundred Yards

1st Prize. - Silver-Mounted Newmarket Whip

2nd Prize. - A Gold Pin

K. Woodward . . . . .   White - Pink Cap
T.F. Dodd . . . . .   Rose - Blue Cap
A. Master . . . . .   Pink - Purple Cap
J.L. Clarke . . . . .   White - Dark Blue Glengarry
H.L. Whatley . . . .   White - Blue and Red Cap
W. Langley . . . . .   White - Red Cap
C.H. Henzell . . . .   Pink - Black Cap
W. Jowitt . . . . .   Black and White-striped - Cap, ditto
C.H. Biddle . . . .   Black and Red
R.W. Teasdale . . . .   Light Blue - Red Cap
W.H. Wardell . . . .   Rose - Blue and White Cap
F. Fawkes . . . . .   Red and Green Tartan - Blue Cap
J. Raven . . . . .   Dark Red

Second Race. - Steeple Chase - One Mile

1st Prize. - Hunting Stock

2nd Prize. - Pair of Silver-Mounted Drinking Horns

3rd Prize. - Hunting Knife with a Set of Studs added by O. P. Cambridge

M.G. Hubback	White - Light Red Cap
K. Woodward	White - Pink Cap
A. Master	Pink - Purple Cap
T.F. Dodd	Rose - Blue Cap
A.C. Baillie	Crimson - White Cap
P.H. Douglas	Chocolate and Blue - Blue Cap
H.L. Whatley	White - Blue and Red Cap
C.H.W. Hoskins . . .	Black and White Plaid - Cap, ditto
A.D.C. Thompson . . .	White - Light Blue Cap
R.W. Teasdale	Light Blue - Red Cap
G.R. Bulman	Blue - White Belt - Black and White Cap
T.W. Huthwaite . . .	Pink - Lilac Cap
W.H. Wardell	Rose - Blue and White Cap
W. Jowitt	Black and White-striped - Cap, ditto
J. Raven	Dark Red

Third. - Throwing the Hammer

Prize. - Gold Pin

A.C. Baillie	Crimson - White Cap
J.L. Clarke	White - Dark Blue Glengarry
P.H. Douglas	Chocolate and Blue-striped - Blue Cap
M.G. Hubback	White - Light Red Cap
W. Jowitt	Black and White-striped - Cap, ditto

G.R. Bulman	Blue - White Belt - Black and White Cap
W.H. Wardell	Rose - Blue and White Cap
C.H. Henzell	Pink - Black Cap
C.H. Riddle	Black and Red

Fourth. - Height Jump

1st Prize. - Gold Pencil Case

2nd Prize. - Hunting Flask

T.F. Dodd	Rose - Blue Cap
H.L. Whatley	White - Blue and Red Cap
J. Farmer	Red - Red-striped Cap
J.L. Clarke	White - Dark Blue Glengarry
C.H.W. Hoskins . . .	Black and White Plaid - Cap, ditto
F. Fawkes	Red and Green Tartan - Blue Cap

Fifth. - Length Jump

1st Prize. - Beagle Hunting Whip

2nd Prize. - Silver-Mounted Walking Stick

F. Fawkes	Red and Green Tartan - Blue Cap
S. Woodward	White - Pink Cap
T.F. Dodd	Rose - Blue Cap
H.L. Whatley	White - Blue and Red Cap
J. Farmer	Red - Red-striped Cap
W.H. Wardell	Rose - Blue and White
C.H.W. Hoskins . . .	Black and White Plaid - Cap, ditto

Sixth. - Hurdle Race

1st Prize. - Pair Silver-Mounted Drinking Horns

2nd Prize. - Silver Pencil Case

S. Woodward	White - Pink Cap
J.L. Clarke	White - Dark Blue Glengarry
T.F. Dodd	Rose - Blue Cap
H.L. Whatley	White - Blue and Red Cap
J. Farmer	Red - Red-striped Cap
C.H.W. Hoskins . . .	Black and White Plaid - Cap, ditto

No second prize will, in any case, be given, unless three, at least, start.

All persons whose names are entered for the Mile Race, must be on the Ground punctually by *One* p.m. in order to walk over the Course. The racing will begin punctually at 1.30 p.m.

Three things in this old programme are interesting. First, of course, the quite small number of participants: twenty-one in all for what were, after all, University Sports. What is clear too from the note about Second Prizes is that the number entered was no guarantee that that number would actually be participating. Secondly, there is the very stylish attire, one reminiscent of jockeys in a race. Thirdly, the decidedly 'County' nature of the prizes, all but one - the pencil case - being among the essentials for those whose entertainment consisted in the main in killing everything in sight that had fur or feathers and moved spontaneously.

The University College Beagles

An invaluable article published in the *DUJ* in July 1920 adds to our picture of what I have called the 'County' character of the undergraduates of the time. Written by a J. Henderson, who went up only two years after the

Sports programmed above were held, it describes the state of the University College Beagles between 1859 and 1863. It will be noticed that some of the men mentioned as being Beaglers have appeared above as participants in the 1857 Sports. The A.C. Baillie-Hamilton is the same as the A.C. Baillie who took part in the Mile Steeplechase.

I entered University College as a Freshman on [sic] 1 October, 1859, having obtained a Foundation Scholarship in May, together with my school companion, J.A. Chalmers. We were both from the V1th Form in Durham School in the days of Dr Holden. My connection, however, with 'the Beagles' did not begin until I had taken my degree in 1862. The Master of the Beagles in 1859 was Sam Woodward, and the Whips were J. Farmer, H. Whatley and the Hon A.C. Baillie-Hamilton. The pack was afterwards hunted by my great friend Tom Philpott. When he left in 1862, the Mastership was held by two or three for a very brief time and it seemed likely that the Club would be broken up and the pack dispersed. The Rev J.J. Hornby, the Head of Cosin's Hall, and afterwards Headmaster and Provost of Eton, was particularly anxious to carry on the Club and asked me to become Master, to which I consented on condition that he would help me both in my reading (I was in my Divinity year) and in the hunting of the pack, about which I knew little or nothing. It was a heavy demand upon my time, because even when not hunting the dogs had to be exercised. But as Hornby put it, it was worth while because it afforded good healthy recreation during the Michaelmas and Epiphany terms to men who might otherwise be loafing about 'old Harry's' and other billiard-rooms in the town. Football, I may remark in passing, was not so popular as it now is. It was Rugby, of course, and that of the roughest. No soccer in those days. No limit to the numbers on each side, and very little scientific play. My first business as Master and Huntsman was to learn to distinguish each dog in the pack by name. I suppose it was necessary, and certainly each dog responded to his or her own name, and to that alone. Bachelor, Barmaid, Bellman, Beauty, Charity, Ringwood, Rattler, etc. This was not so very easy a task when you had a pack of about (I think) fifteen couples, all very much of the same shape, size and marking. But to me a much more difficult part of my business at first was to blow the horn. My first attempts were ludicrous - blowing till my eyes were nearly starting from my head and my cheeks near to bursting, yet for all the sound produced the horn might have been a peashooter, whilst at other times sounds issued forth at which scoffers said the very dogs looked up and grinned. 'Oh if you could only see him, blowing the horn without hearing the sounds he makes!' The tendency to laughter while attempting to blow was no doubt one contributory cause of my failure. But if I had to endure the banter of my friends I was able, as the sequel will show, to take my revenge out of the peaceful and innocent inhabitants of Durham who lived in Saddler Street and thereabouts. It was very wicked, no doubt, and if any of them should still be alive I would take this opportunity of apologising for my wickedness of fifty-eight years ago. It was on this wise. To learn to blow the horn properly I had to practise. This I did in the open window in my rooms, which were at the top of the Keep overlooking the town. The time chosen was after the evening's reading was done and lights out - about 11 or 12 p.m. I soon discovered the art, and the practice would have ceased, but that on one occasion a window at the back of one of the houses in Saddler Street was thrown open, a man's head in a white night-cap appeared, and then a volley of winged words was let loose. Oh, the pity of it! on the one side. Oh, the fun of it! on the other side. A new pastime had been invented quite accidentally, others were called in to enjoy the sport and to take part in it. For a time the horn was borrowed night after night 'to draw the town', and very seldom was it drawn blank. A score was kept in C -'s rooms where the serenade generally began - a request to 'shut up' counted as 1, a malediction as 2, and 3 for a night-cap.

Our kennels were at the point in the road between Neville's Cross and Four-mile, where a branch road leads down to Langley Bridge, and the kennel-keeper was a man called Peter, and a most extraordinary creature he was - a veritable wild man of the woods. He could neither read nor write, but I had to put myself under his tuition as to dogs and hares. When an old horse was killed to provide food for the hounds there were certain parts which he reserved for his own use.

The first hare of the season was always sent to the Warden - the Venerable Chas Thorpe [sic], in those days - and by him always suitably acknowledged. Visitors frequently came to our 'meets' and were always welcome, except when they came on horse-back. Our hounds were real beagles, not like the semi fox-hounds one sees so often nowadays, and being small were slow. We should have regarded it as unsportsmanlike to hunt a hare with the bigger and swifter hounds. This did not suit some of our equestrian friends who would occasionally try to 'lift the hounds' especially when the hare was running in a circle. A very welcome visitor was one who is now an Honorary Canon of Durham and a faithful Parish Priest, then a boy at Durham School, but as I have no permission to use his name he must be nameless. He was a keen sportsman and a splendid runner as his record at Cambridge afterwards proved him to be. All, however, who joined us were not such as he, and if sometimes a nuisance, were sometimes also a source of amusement. The one great object of most novices is not the hunting, but the killing of the hare, and of one such it is reported that when the hounds were drawing a field of turnips a hare sprang up almost in the very midst of the pack, and, bounding over one or two of the outside hounds, darted down one of the furrows. At, or near the end of this furrow, was our friend, who seeing the hare making straight for him, sat himself down 'on his hunkers', as the pitman would say, on his heels and with outstretched arms prepared to capture poor puss. She dashed into him, striking him full in the chest and sent him sprawling; I have occasionally seen hares run in this way when pursued, running as if they were looking behind and not in front of them.

I have vivid recollections of many splendid runs, not all by any means ending in a kill. Indeed, I was rather glad than sorry that our hare escaped if we had had a good run - on one occasion I had to submit to a good soaking in having to follow some of the hounds which had crossed the Browney at a part where it was of considerable depth, and where 'bridge there was none.' But I think my most trying, not to say humiliating, experience as Master of the famous pack of University College Beagles was in an attempt to take the pack over to Mr Parrington's - somewhere beyond Brancepeth - to be in readiness to hunt the next day, being half-term 'open-day', November, 1862. None of my whips turned up. Only Mr Hornby was with me, but as we could go all the way by road we ventured forth. All went well until we came within the boundaries of Brancepeth estate, it then became evident that numerous hares had crossed the road and that scent was strong. Many attempts on the part of the hounds to break away were stopped, but eventually the whole pack broke away, and in twos and threes went off each after their own particular objects. In our help-lessness and bewilderment a gamekeeper, and I think another man with him, came and helped us to collect the dogs and started us back to Durham, but not until we had been exposed to a violent storm of thunder and lightning as far as language was concerned.

Having mentioned the name of Mr Parrington I cannot conclude without saying how gratefully I recall all that he did in aid of our Beagles' Club. Long before I became Master I had heard him spoken of as a thorough sportsman, and a true friend to the Club at all times. He used to take many of our hounds and keep them, and helped us to find homes for others, during vacation times free of charge except Peter's wages - 10s. a week. I noticed a few remarks upon his life some time ago which spoke of him as a gentleman with all the instincts of a true English sportsman - a description with which I fully concur. So far as I know all the old beagling friends of my happy and, I trust, not unprofitable days at Durham, are gone with the exception of one with whom I communicated before writing these reminiscences, hoping that he, who was much more able to do so, would undertake the pleasant task. I regret, however, to learn that he is now unable to write.

My last farewell sight of our beagles was a year or two after my leaving the University and came about in this way. In 1863 I became junior Curate of St Nicholas, Newcastle, and as I was passing the Central Station on one occasion I saw a huntsman with a few couples of beagles and was told that they were hounds of the old University Beagles, which the then Earl of Tankerville had bought. I felt very much inclined to give a good 'view halloo' and lift his hounds for him, but it would not have done, so I mentally said farewell to those that I fancied I could recognise. There was 'Bachelor' - a bit too long in the leg and apt to overrun the scent. There was 'Bellman' - fat and slow, but sure - probably the keenest-scented hound we had - and there was 'Beauty' - the affectionate little dog who would always come to be pat-ted and to lick your hand.

The pack was broken up and the Hounds sold in 1874. The account book of the Club from its commencement to its close was kindly sent to me and I forwarded it to the Rev T.H. Philpott, who had a prior claim to it, having been Master before me. He died suddenly on May 22, 1917. A better, truer friend no man ever had than I had in him - a friendship which was affectionately renewed in the last years of his life. Mrs Philpott returned this book to me on hearing of my intention to write these few reminiscences, and from it I copy the list of Masters of University College Beagles' Club given below.

In conclusion, I should like to put upon record that I have to thank the beagles for cementing the life-long friendship between myself and the Rev J.J. Hornby - one of the many blessings which I owe under God's kind providence to my years at Durham University.

List of [Hunt] Masters

C.H. Ford	18-(illegible)	W. Kenyard	1862
A.C. Baillie	"	J. Henderson	1862
B. Schiffner	1851	F.T. Henzell	1863
Hon M.B. Portman	1853	J. Marshall	1865
H.S. Jackson	1853	H. Rhodes	1866
J.K. Watson	1853?	– Richardson	1866
W.J. Sergeantson	1855	C.N. Greenwood	1869
J.A. Bennett	1856	C. Gregson	1870
Sam Woodward	1857	J. Golightly	1872
T.H. Philpott	1861	A.H. Allen	1873
W.L.S. Orde	1862	W.K. Thomas	1874
F.R.H.H. Noyes	1862		

An editorial note to this article under the title 'The Beagles in 1857' runs:

Apparently the Committee of the Beagles' Club issued each year a card giving the list of hounds in their possession at the time. We give on the next page the list for the year 1857, two years before Archdeacon Henderson entered University College. It is possible that some of our older graduates may possess similar cards or other documents illustrating life and sport in the earlier days of the University, and which might be worth reproducing. The Editor will be glad to receive any such, and whether reproduced or not, they shall be taken care of and returned if the owner so desire.

No later edition of the *DUJ* refers to any such ephemera having been received, and one must therefore assume that none remained, or at any rate was sent.

Muscles and Muffins

Another kind of hare was also pursued. Paper chases are recorded. That of March 1887 starting from Prebends' Bridge, we may confidently assume that this was the starting point for all of them. Forty 'hounds' and two 'hares' were involved.

Swimming was popular. Whether a swimming club was ever in existence before 1879 is unknown, but races were held in that year over the course at Nab's End, the first cup being 'a handsome silver-mounted oak' affair, which was presented by H.R. Harrison, described in the *DUJ* as 'the energetic founder and secretary of the club.'

And there was, of course, fives, the court being reached from Fellows' Garden, though it was taken down in 1956 to make room for the Library extension.

A Lawn Tennis Club was struck in 1880. It met in that year on the Race Course, and numbered about a dozen men.

To the disgruntlement of some, however, more sybaritic pleasures beckoned. 'Muffins, crumpets, tea-cakes, bread and butter,' the *DUJ* bewailed in 1908, 'the students would rather forgo their games than their tea.'

Billiards

Billiards, despite its overtones of close rooms overhung with the smells of tobacco and porter, and played by pasty characters in shirt-sleeves and weskits, seems nevertheless to have been very popular. Readers will remember Archdeacon Henderson's claim that beagling at least took men away from 'loafing about "old Harry's" and other billiard-rooms in the town.' The College and Hatfield Hall had facilities for play, though where in Castle the table or tables were situated is unknown. The game was wide-ly popular in the nineteenth century, and in the first years of the twentieth century it still had a respectable - in both senses of the word - following. The Handicap Tournament in 1903 was won by a Castleman, one W.A. Jackson, with another Castleman, one clearly born to play billiards, W.E. Poole, coming a close second.

On the River

To turn now to what Lieutenant-Colonel Macfarlane-Grieve, in his *History of Durham Rowing*,[1] has called 'the oldest sport in the University of Durham.' It would be impertinent of me to attempt to summarise this book, well-known to devotees of rowing, and particularly of Northern rowing, and indeed such a summary would be out of place in this history, but the book has in places a somewhat wider appeal. There is, for instance, much to interest the general reader in the section of thirty-five pages on 'Durham Rowing from 1815 to 1876. With special reference to Durham University.'

Macfarlane-Grieve's claim seems to be amply justified since, as he put it, 'Undergraduates were first admitted in Michaelmas Term 1833, and in June 1834, we find the "Sylph", belonging to the Durham University Original Club, competing in the race for six-oared boats in the Durham Boat Regatta.'[2]

The racing coincided with the Waterloo celebrations, concomitants of which were the pealing of the Cathedral bells, the firing of cannon, the playing of rousing patriotic music by an aquatic brass band, and a Grand Ball in the Assembly Rooms; and Macfarlane-Grieve convincingly argues that 'it was largely owing to the University that the Waterloo celebrations of previous years developed into the annual Durham Regatta.'[3]

Readers will find it of interest that in 1834 all the races in the Regatta after the initial one were postponed until eight o'clock in the evening, 'As all the Gentlemen of the University were engaged on this day (the last day of the Easter Term) to dine with the Bishop of Durham.'[4]

Of interest too are the curiously anachronistic archery trials which pre-ceded the actual racing in these early years. There was, at Old Durham, a little way up the river, an Archery Ground where the competitors used to shoot between the races. In 1835, for instance,

On Wednesday [June 17] took place the Durham Regatta. The sports commenced with a trial of skill in archery. The candidates, selected from the several crews, one from each four-oar, and two from each six-oar, contended on the Flats below Old Durham garden, the prize a silver medal was won by Walter Scruton, Esq., Mr Hills of the University being second.[5]

Deplorable behaviour is always of interest, and the following is worth a mention.

During the night of Monday last [the year is 1842], some evil disposed person, or persons, did wilfully and maliciously bore four holes and otherwise injure a gig-boat named 'Tiger', belonging to Thomas Wills whilst lying near the Prebends' Bridge; the object evidently being to retard its progress whilst racing at the Regatta.[6]

One has to turn to Thomas Hughes' book, already mentioned, to fill in the human picture, rather scantily furnished by Macfarlane-Grieve. One can assume with confidence that rowing practices current at Oxford were also to be found at Durham.

The crew had had their early dinner of steak and chops, stale bread, and a glass and a half of old beer a piece at two o'clock, in the Captain's rooms. The current theory of training at that time was - as much meat as you could eat, the more underdone the better, and the smallest amount of drink upon which you could manage to live. Two pints in the twenty-four hours was all that most boats' crews that pretended to train at all were allowed, and for the last fortnight it had been the nominal allowance of the St Ambrose crew. The discomfort of such a diet in the hot summer months, when you were at the same time taking regular and violent exercise, was something very serious. Outraged human nature rebelled against it; and although they did not admit it in public, there were very few men who did not rush to their water-bottles for relief, more or less often, according to the development of their bumps of conscientiousness and obstinacy. To keep to the diet at all strictly, involved a very respectable amount of physical endurance. Our successors have found out the unwisdom of this, as of other old superstitions; and that in order to get a man into training for a boat-race now-a-days, it is not of the first importance to keep him in a constant state of consuming thirst, and the restlessness of body and sharpness of temper which thirst generally induces.[7]

Again, just before the start of the race, the St Ambrose Captain

took a sliced lemon out of his pocket, put a small piece in his own mouth, and then handed it to Blake, who followed his example, and passed it on.[8]

The *DUJ* in March 1910 reprinted the Regulations for Training for Boat Races of 1882-5. It can be seen that many of the earlier misconceptions about diet still remain.

1) Rise at 7, or not later than 7.30. Cold bath, and short walk or run before breakfast (about a mile).
2) Breakfast (8 o'clock). Chops, steaks, cold meat (beef or mutton), bread as stale as possible - better toast - the less butter the better; eggs, water-cress; tea (no coffee), not more than 2 ordinary breakfast cups.
3) Lunch. A little cold meat (not necessary), bread and butter, and half a pint of beer.
4) Dinner. Roast beef or mutton, fish or fowl in small quantities, vegetables (very little potato or green food), no pastry, jelly, beer - one pint.
5) Dessert. Oranges, wine - 2 glasses at most of port or claret, not sherry, no cheese. Tea - 2 small cups at most.

Bed 10, or not later than 10.30.

NO SMOKING

The *DUJ* of the time added:

Printed rules will NOT get you through Elvet Bridge unless you keep them, and we do not hold with those who think that so long as you eat half-raw beef it does not matter whether you go to late dances, or hot [sic] concerts, or make night hideous with skylarking in the Keep.

For a serious look at University College rowing, the reader is of course recommended to Lieutenant-Colonel Macfarlane-Grieve's book.

Some Esoteric Recreations

Fowler records that about 1842 a debating society, which appears to have been called a 'Union Society', was begun at University College; then of course the only college in the University. It is not known how long this debating society continued. There is in the earliest minute-book of the 'Union' a memo that Durham University Union Society (so-called) was revived in 1872, when Hatfield Hall and Unattached men were allowed to join it; and the society was then first called the 'Durham University Union', though the name Durham Union Society' was restored in 1873. At first the Reading-rooms of the Castle and Hatfield Hall became the meeting places of the separate branches of the Union.

At the College, the Read and Weed was a prestigious society. Details of its founding are hard to find, and the Minute Books have disappeared; but the society had, as its name suggests, a literary origin, its members combining the high-minded aim of cultural advancement with the dubious 'pleasure' of imbibing nicotine. Enough has already been said about the popularity among undergraduates of smoking. The Read and Weed had its own ritual initiation ceremony, about which more will be said later, and admission was dependent on there being no single blackballing of a candidate. It had at one time its own blazer, as the following letter from a caustic correspondent, 'Ridens', to the *DUJ* in May 1887 shows; but by 1947 only a Read and Weed tie distinguished members.

A reading society was started some time ago in the College to read Shakespeare and other noble works, in order to improve the minds of its members. They have at length produced a blazer. We have known for some time back that the mountains were in labour, but a 'blazer' was beyond our wildest expectations and - such a blazer! The members of the Read and Weed are humble-minded mortals,

144

for the said blazer suggests to our mind the vests of stud grooms, ornamented with the brass buttons daily to be seen on gyps, or still better the cloths on cab horses waiting at railway stations.

I hope the men who invented it will have the good taste to keep in their own rooms, as visitors might think they were the judges' attendants.

We have heard that one gentleman objected to the Castle blazer because it did not suit his complexion - does this one? If so, preserve us from such beauty. If, as was suggested at the time, the College give a Masquerade Ball they will be useful. Oh may their proud possessors reserve them for that time.

This letter has additional interest in that it gives us some indication as to what the College gyps were wearing.

'Varsity men seem to have been amazingly touchy about apparel, as will be seen in a moment.

For the time being, however, for all that has been said about the sparseness of men on the ground, there seems to have been no shortage of societies competing for their membership. An editorial in the *DUJ* of December 1909 fulminated rather pompously about the plethora of these.

There is a great deal too much going on in the Durham Colleges. There are too many societies which occupy men's time and thought. We do not need any more. It would be better to abolish some of them. The average Durham undergraduate, after he has passed the Freshman stage, has hardly one minute to himself. This is partly the inevitable outcome of our two years' Arts course, but we cannot attribute it to that alone.

The Battle Against the Beaux

To return to the matter of dress, and with it that of knowing one's place in the pecking order and keeping to it, the College, like all closed institutions, was rigidly hierarchical and men who, out of ignorance or - worse - 'side' transgressed the immensely complicated code were subjected to such abuse as today we find hard to understand. The *Durham University Journals* down the years are a mine of such detail.

In February 1885, for instance, it reported with the undisguised horror it kept for such solecisms that 'the latest novelty in costumes for the river is flannels, a blazer, and spats.' In March 1887, 'the latest form of academical dress lately observed in Durham is a blazer, a gown and a hood dangling about the ankles. It would look very well on the stage, probably, but really, in Cathedral service at 4 p.m. on Sunday it is too much of a good thing.' In the cold February of 1896, 'The following . . . was on view quite recently, and surely eclipses all previous attempts at originality so completely ... Shoes, socks (coloured), bare legs, white shorts, light coloured dust coat, surmounted, and trimmed off with Cap and Gown!'

Umbrellas unfailingly raised the cholesterol level of the editors of the *DUJ* and the small army of spies they appear to have deployed solely to report on such irregularities. In February 1898, 'Yesterday's rain fortunately brought to our notice the umbrella, cap and gown fresher, without notice of whom no first issue of the *Journal* would be complete.'

In this last instance, of course, the offence was compounded by the fact that the offender was a freshman, this perennially appearing breed being as doomed as grouse to be shot down in season. In the following month of the same year, the editors 'would call the attention of clerical freshers to the fact that a brown satchel with light coloured leather straps is admirable for very young girls to carry their books in, but scarcely suitable for a University student.'

In the same issue an outraged correspondent, one 'JTF', quoted a letter he had just received:

> a Cambridge man met me yesterday. He has been to Durham to look around, and, to his astonishment, he saw several undergraduates in *gowns and whites* and he cast one more stone at Durham.

Clearly, insularity was not peculiar to the new University of the North. Such deplorable fashions, or blatant disregard of the decencies that fashion dictated, died hard; say rather, such being the happy resilience of the human spirit, they never died. For in 1898 again, 'a certain undergraduate [was seen] parading the city in blazer and whites, with a cap and gown.'

Another glorious fashion, much in favour among sporty young gentlemen, was called into question in that July.

Knickerbockers [thundered the *DUJ*] do not harmonise with academic garb.

Matters refused to improve, and as the year wore on the *DUJ* was help-
lessly reduced to resorting to satire: 'A tie is evidently regarded as a superfluous article of apparel, whilst the umbrella is looked upon as quite the
thing.' Even old-established undergraduates prove themselves remiss. 'It
is not the custom in Durham to wear a frock coat and a top hat,' the *DUJ*
reminded them, adding caustically - 'unless you wish to show yourself a
fresher.'
Curly-brimmed bowlers, alas, seem to have been restricted to the
dandies of the City.
The homely satchel continued to be occasionally sported, and in the following year, 1899, offenders were again taken to task: 'All tradition is
against the use of a bag [for books] by a student in cap and gown.' Most
probably the satchel was an anathema because of its inseparable association with school, which of course almost every undergraduate had only
just left.
Moustaches too were forever open to criticism, and there are endless
derogatory references to these adornments.

What a wonderful thing a moustache is! So must have thought two
students the other morning in Galilee; for during the short time [fif-
teen minutes] spent in that edifice the above-mentioned gentlemen
were unceasing in their attention to that appendage . . . We should recommend the possessors of these articles of beauty to rise ten minutes
earlier, so as to give sufficient attention to them before going to keep
day.

Late risers were, as will be seen shortly, always prone to unseemly
behaviour and improper dress in chapel. Repeated strictures appear
against the pernicious custom of wearing slippers in Galilee.
Ostentation of any kind seems to have been viewed with the greatest
disquiet; the desirable objective of most undergraduates, but not presumably of many freshmen, being so totally to efface themselves as to be invisible. In the 1900's, for instance, red waistcoats were anathematised, they
having apparently sprung up overnight like gloriously colourful toad-
stools.

The complexities of 'Varsity protocol are reminiscent of those found in British India in the days of the Raj. 'It is not considered very good form,' the *DUJ* laid it down in December 1902, 'to wear a palatinate blazer, won for cricket, when the wearer is one of the spectators of a boat race.' In November 1905 it somewhat vindictively harried an offender with the disclosure of a previous offence.

We understand that the Castle man who wore his 'soccer' palatinate throughout the Cricket season is up again.

That he is now wearing the same blazer, but this time with a U.C. Inter-Collegiate cap!

In May of the same year a letter to the *Journal* from one 'ABC' protested against the bad taste shown by several men in wearing Inter-Coll and other Boating blazers while on the cricket and tennis field. 'Are some men,' the writer enquired, 'ashamed to wear their ordinary College blazers?'

Things went a stage further to the bad in 1906, in June of which year the following assault was launched:

The impression created on the uninitiated by the blazers of many colours worn by certain men seems to be far from that which the wearers of the said blazers imagine they are creating. One of them was accosted the other day by a semi-intoxicated pitman and asked where he came from. On being enlightened, the pitman replied, 'Oh beg pardon, I thought there was a circus in!'

It seems that prejudice ran even to fashion in academical dress. The *DUJ* in December 1902 pontificated, significantly in Biblical style:

We know a man by his friends, but we know him better by his gown. Let him, therefore, take heed that his gown be torn and his cap battered to the utmost limit of the most correct conventionality; that so may his name go down to posterity as one who lived all-honoured of his fellows, a very son of *Alma Mater* and the foremost of his times.

The Freshman - Open Season for a Despised Species

One suspects that the above convention served to distinguish men who had been 'up' some time from the ever-despised freshmen. These, as readers of *Verdant Green* will remember, were considered not only fair game but also inherently absurd. A John's fresher, for instance, was reported in 1900 as having declared: 'Well I'm blessed! I came across that quotation today, "Greater love hath no man than this, etc." I always thought it was Dickens before.'

Freshmen's inherent comicality could to some small degree be considered engaging; the solecisms they perpetrated could not. In December 1881, for instance, the *DUJ* reported that 'A senior left the usual card on a freshman one day, and was astonished to find his call returned at 8.40 the next morning with: 'Did you wish to see me very particularly?'

Freshmen were of course almost expected to contravene the conventions regarding what was considered proper dress. The *DUJ* again in the March of 1884, a year particularly conscious of aestheticism:

> We have not heard much of the freaks of freshmen this term, but a young man in cap and gown was observed one day walking across the Palace Green and swinging a very lovely walking stick. Evidently he thought the effect must be quite beautiful.

The wet November of the following year brought down on some hapless fresher the following rebuke: 'A new academical costume has been observed in the case of one of those who have newly joined us: straw hat, gown and umbrella. The effect,' it added caustically, 'was striking.'

Umbrellas have already been noticed as calling down upon those sporting them Zeus-like thunderbolts of lightning.

Freshmen, like children, were evidently to be seen (preferably very rarely) and not heard from.

> Though few in number, those [freshmen] of January 1896 seem to have reached the climax of bumptiousness. Quite the latest is to call on the Seniors; and one may often on returning to one's rooms find kind notes of invitation from 'unobtrusive freshmen'.

As the century wore to its close, things went from bad to worse. In November the following year the *DUJ* noted with horror that

> the bumptiousness of freshmen is invariably a cause of complaint, but this term's display really breaks the record. Even if they do join

the group of seniors after lunch, they will do well to confine their chaff to those of their own standing.

But this ill-behaviour was nothing compared with that howled about in May 1898:

The freshman of today is to be known by the loudness of his voice and his attire. He yells along the passages, bursts unasked into the rooms of senior men, and invites them to coffee with an air of easy condescension. At an 'at home', he forms the centre of admiring circles, whom he favours with gracefully delivered accounts of his own varied accomplishments. At College meetings he punctuates the remarks of the presiding official with humorous asides, and takes it upon himself to propose whom he thinks fit for the vacant posts. In the billiard room, his swagger and assumption may be seen at their climax; and, in short, it may now be said of our clubs, our athletics, our informal gatherings - 'the trail of the fresher is over them all.'

Even that last gratuitously offensive remark was outdone by what followed: 'boot leather is considered a good cure for taking the lead at College meetings in one's second term.'
Mind, not every rebuke was undeserved:

One [freshman], from Cumberland, observed, soon after his arrival, to one whom he did not know to be an officer of the University, that he thought it a good thing 'to grease in with the dons.'

Perhaps with the death of the old familiar century things could not but change for the worse. Certainly by November 1908 no improvement in this baneful species was to be observed, and the *Journal* felt moved to pontificate:

There seems to be an impression amongst the freshmen this term that they own the 'Varsity. It is not uncommon in the first week of term, but means have generally been found to disillusion them. But this term they seem to be quite untamed. A freshman should remember that he is without form and void - at least his attitude and opinion of himself should be based on that assumption.

Or was it simply that freshmen had always presented an obnoxious face to their seniors who, ultra-sensitive to what they themselves had been and had only just escaped from being, turned upon their hapless juniors to rend and destroy? Certainly, the fear of losing privilege seems to have been at the root of this paranoia, and in the February of the same year the *DUJ* came close to admitting it.

One of the more modest of the *Journal's* many functions is to see that 'Varsity rules are strictly kept by 'freshmen' and juniors, and perhaps these latter will be glad to know that it is their privilege on Sunday mornings in Cathedral to occupy the choir - *only* - and that to invade the North transept or the nave before the conclusion of the Litany is to violate the sanctity of the senior men's privilege, which the said seniors ought long ago to have noticed and rebuked in time-honoured manner.

Behaviour in general though seems to have been that of students down the centuries. Despite protestations to the contrary, Castlemen and, one must suppose, the members of the other Colleges occasionally drank to excess. In 1896, for instance, Canon Greenwell appeared to have made an attack on this lack of temperance. His allegations were not long in being rebutted. A letter from 'Decet' in the *Journal* of May 1896 expressed the offence caused:

Remarks by Canon Greenwell at the meeting of the Archaeological Society in the Lecture Rooms during the last vacation . . . insulting to Durham men, and especially to those in the Norman Gallery insinuate that not only do they drink but are sometimes to be seen in a state of intoxication . . . violent language. Those in authority will testify that never have the men of the University been of a quieter or more temperate character.

'Decet' of course quotes no evidence from the last sixty years in support of this last, towering claim, and one is left with the feeling that he protested too much. In the following month a disclaimer appeared from Canon Greenwell who, whatever he said to the bearded rows of sober archaeologists in front of him, shows himself to have been less concerned with temperance matters than with the preservation of the Castle fabric. The fire risk, he pointed out, was huge - particularly that in the Norman Gallery. On this account he had written to the Dean, who of course was also Warden, and the Dean brought the matter before Senate, who determined at the end of the current term to remove the students from the Gallery.

The Demon Drink

One assumes that 'Decet' was an intending parson. Alcohol abuse must have been of concern to prospective ordinands, who were sure to find it, in the parishes they would all too soon find themselves precipitated into, one of the great social problems of the time. Judged by the following, solutions urged by high-minded undergraduates seem to have been preposterously unrealistic. The *Journal* of February 1908 records of drunkenness in the Town that

> Temperance Sermons in the Cathedral are incongruous; temperance sermons in the Town are useless. Therefore are certain members of the 'Varsity giving a series of Popular Concerts, believing that the best way to make a man sober is to give him some recreation more profitable than alcohol and yet as delectable.

These Concerts, held on Saturdays of all days, of course elicited little, if any, response.

A strong temperance presence seems always to have made itself felt at University College. A letter to the *Journal* dated March 1884, from one 'Senrab' (Barnes?), complains that at Castle a slight breach of etiquette at the dinner table results in the offender's paying for a tankard of beer. 'We are sowing,' he gloomily forecast, 'the seeds which will germinate in the form of a drunken parson's life.' 'Senrab' rather miserably suggested, by way of alternative, a fine to the amount of a tankard of beer, the terminal total to be given to some local charity.

A letter to the *Journal*, written by one 'Vich Jan Vohr' in March 1897, and concerning itself entirely with the vagaries of freshmen, takes up this theme, only from the opposite standpoint:

> It is the fashion with some freshmen to support loyally 'total abstinence', and they emphatically disapprove of such things as 'Social

Evenings'. Nor is that all; some have gone so far as to libel them by informing non-attendants like themselves that those who are present have all to be carried home afterwards. Others have even let their prejudices obtain such a hold of them that at those all-important events known as 'Christenings', i.e. of cups, they have been known to pass the cup by with head erect and with an injured countenance and defiant air, without wishing their College better success in the future in the simple words of 'Floreat Collegium'.

Hooliganism in High Places

Mention has already been made of the rowdyism that traditionally attended Convocation, manifestations of high spirits it is hard to credit nowadays. This was a persistent cause of concern to the dons. As the century wore on this rowdyism grew more, instead of less, of a problem. In June 1885, for instance, the *Journal* felt obliged to make a public protest, one which gives us a nicely drawn picture of such functions of the time, this particular Convocation having been held in the Upper Lecture Room.

The 'chaff' on Convocation Day was a trifle more pointless and insipid than usual. We are familiar with the groaning and hooting at dons who have unpopular duties to perform during the term. Such manifestations, of course, come with us, as at Oxford and Cambridge, from the minority which sympathises with vice and lawlessness. But jeers directed against people's infirmities, or against ladies, are a new departure . . . It is only fair [the *Journal* felt obliged to add] that the attempts in this direction were immediately hushed up.

The *Journal* clearly felt that a more dignified venue than the Upper Lecture Room would have improved matters, for it added: 'If the use of the Chapter Library cannot be granted, the proper place for the ceremony is clearly the Castle Hall.'

Its point appears to have been taken by the authorities, for in December of that year it was reported that

The Great Convocation of this term was held in the Hall of University College. Those who remember the dreadful crush in

Lecture Room Number 5 will rejoice in the change. The size of the room, the convenience of the exits and entrances, and *the stone floor unfavourable to sound* [my italics], all helped to make the event less noisy and more orderly than usual.

But there was no real improvement, for traditions, bad as well as good, die hard. A letter in June 1891 from 'A Member of Convocation' questioned 'whether it be "good form" to create an incessant uproar during the whole of the proceedings of Convocation, and this when two Bishops are present to receive degrees, and publicly to hurl grossly abusive language at persons in high authority?'

Six years later a far more effective, because satiric, attack on disrupters was launched by 'One Who Was There'.

As making a row seems to be an essential part of Convocation, it would be as well if the students practised for a short time beforehand. A few singing lessons would be no bad thing, while copies of the funniest papers might be bought and extracts from them turned to local use.

And in May 1902 a correspondent to the *Journal* signing himself 'B.A.' resorted to the same weapon.

I attended Convocation this June after an interval of some years, and was surprized to find the same witticisms in vogue amongst the undergraduate spectators as in my day. Must not these have become a little time-worn by now? Cat-calls and requests to the proctors to speak louder, or even cock-crowing and bugle-blowing, have surely served their turn. May I make a modest suggestion, that some time before Convocation the SRC should hold a meeting and appoint a sub-committee to discover original jokes and quips to hurl at the dons on these occasions? This would surely add liveliness to the proceedings and prevent the local press from commenting on the lack of originality among Durham undergraduates.

Thanks to these letters we know a great deal about the form this persistent rowdyism took. In April of the following year, for instance, 'B.A.', pos-

sibly more incensed after a second attendance at Convocation, wrote again
to complain that there was 'nothing very clever in crowing like a cock,
mewing like a cat, or even in braying after the manner of the sapient ass.'

The musical accompaniment however seems to have got more sophisticated with the years. The 1904 Convocation was particularly distinguished
for this.

> The visitors were entertained for some time before the Warden
> entered the Castle Hall by a varied programme of popular airs played
> by certain undergraduates upon a weird array of musical instruments.
> The entrance of Senate etc. was heralded by a tremendous outburst of
> cheers and blasts from trumpets, etc. The Warden, however, soon put
> a stop to this by announcing that 'if any musical instrument is blown
> during Convocation the proceedings will be stopped.'

The Grand Convocation of 1906 seems to have reached a kind of perfec-
tion of hooliganism; for the Warden took the extreme measure of sending
men down for their part in it. This condign punishment was not let pass
without protest, as a letter from 'C' shows.

> I think the voice of the *Journal* for the new academical year should
> at least bear a word of sympathy to the deeply wronged victims of the
> Convocation episode. To be 'sent down' is surely the undesirable lot
> of anyone, whether he deserves it or not, but to be treated with the
> utmost rigour and severity of 'Varsity law for the mere maintenance
> of recognized customs is as ridiculous as it is splenetic. If the men in
> this place are wise, the next Convocation will possess an unparalleled
> record for that orderliness and silence which constitute absolute bore-
> dom, and can only spring from absent and disinterested heroes.

But the Warden's action seems to have had the desired effect. The Easter
Convocation of 1911, for instance, while noisy, was distinguished for unaccompanied voices.

> The students were in strong force, but their efforts were not nearly
> so provocative as on former occasions. When those introducing can-
> didates for degrees were heard to advantage, the students greeted the

achievement with lusty renditions of 'Bravo, bravo, bravo, bravissi-mo.' When mixed companies of successful students advanced to the Chancellor's dais, the hall rang with the plea, 'Put me among the girls.' The B.A.'s were greeted as 'jolly good fellows.'

Certainly the venue seems also to have had something to do with the decorum, or absence of it, during the proceedings, for in 1925 the *Journal* reported that

> Owing to the repairs to the Castle the June Week Convocation in Durham this year was held by kind permission of the Dean in the Chapter House of the Cathedral. The proceedings were therefore much more orderly, and certainly more dignified than is usually the case.

And Hooliganism in Low

But rowdyism was not confined to Convocations. Behaviour at lectures left a lot to be desired. Readers will remember how unmercifully the Rev Richard Harmony was ragged by Verdant and his fellows. The *Journal*, as usual, took up the cudgels on behalf of propriety in December 1897. Earlier in the year, in February, it had already made a plea for a more courteous reception to dons:

> It is rather a tax to have to cap a don whenever meeting in the street, but surely such a course is better than the familiar nod, with what we may call a coachman's salute.

Now:

> Making a disturbance during lectures . . . is a very contemptible proceeding. It is poor fun, and certainly ungentlemanly, even if it is systematically gone about [!]. We write this as having been present at many 'rows'.

The *Journal's* spies reported faithfully on behaviour as well as dress. March 1898 brought the acid comment: 'We sympathise with that undergraduate who is manifestly incapable of uttering the monosyllabic token of respect 'Sir' in the lecture-room . . . a defection of the vocal organs . . . an elementary lack of regard for a lecturer.'

The same issue exoceted an ordinand who failed to keep up to the mark.

> We are strongly of the opinion that Theology Scholars, as a rule, conduct themselves decorously on Sunday morning . . . one of these gentlemen would produce a greater effect if he strolled in a little later and kept both hands in his pockets instead of one.

In February 1910 the *DUJ* printed the entire sermon preached by the Bishop of Jarrow on the first Sunday in term. It added, 'We think our readers will agree that the sermon is one which every Durham man should keep. We heard on good authority that the Bishop saw one man reading a newspaper.'

The dons though were possessed, on occasion, of a ready wit. In June 1899 the *Journal* reported that 'A lecturer told a student that a cap and bells would suit him better than a cap and gown.'

However, things certainly did not always go their way. A letter from 'A Sufferer' in November 1904 protested 'against the childish and inconsiderate practice of vociferous applause, often quite uncalled for, which seems to be considered the correct thing in University lecture-rooms by a certain class of men.'

The 'correct' thing was not always done in examination rooms either. Cribbing was not unknown. To what an extent it was carried on it is impossible to say, but the fact that it went on at all with such a small number being examined says much about the inefficiency of both the system and the invigilators. Of intent, no time-table was posted up by the dons for the examinations, so that candidates, not knowing which paper to expect, could not come prepared with a crib. A not altogether coherent letter to the *DUJ* from a Hatfield man, Harold Greenwood, the President of the Union Society, speaks volumes:

> In your last issue a jotting with regard to timetables for Final Examinations in Arts and Theology has given me an opportunity, long wished for, of entering a protest against what I consider to be a disgrace to every Durham man. I have had the privilege of sitting for

three examinations during the last two years, and on two of these occasions I have seen men, or perhaps I should say a man, deliberately cribbing in paper after paper. While I quite recognise that those who 'vigilate' are in no way to blame, in that they cannot persistently watch every man . . . I have no doubt that 'the candidates are greatly inconvenienced' by no timetables being issued, but I question whether anything else should be the case where examiners cannot trust to the honour of the men they examine.

At any rate, personally, I am grateful to a system which disappoints a man who will crib, and who by his action disgraces his university and lessens the value of every degree taken at that university.

Behaviour at sporting fixtures was often not merely unseemly but quite reprehensible. A letter from 'Pax' in March 1908 protested against a

custom which is, most unfortunately, becoming common with some men. They stand on the touch-line at football matches and refer to the players in terms which are far from gentlemanly. In the match Castle v Hatfield, this afternoon, one spectator used such terms as 'beast' and 'dog' when alluding to the opponents of the team which he was supporting. Such conduct does not tend to foster good feeling between the Colleges.

But a letter from 'Sirius', dated 29 May 1916 best sums it all up. Interestingly, this was written only a month before the infamous assault on the uncut wire of the Somme.

It is with great regret that I find it necessary to 'rush into print' at a time like this, and on a subject which is not a particularly pleasant one, namely, the apparent ignorance which is constantly being exhibited of the traditions of our University. Surely, in spite of the war and all that it means to the 'Varsity and to us as individuals, we are still gentlemen; but I must say some of us seem to have forgotten that. There are, of course, very few men up, but that is all the more reason why each and every one should do his best to keep the old place going, so that when at last we have peace again, and the gallant fellows come back, they may find the habits and customs of 'Varsity men very little changed.

It is not my intention to particularise to any extent, as there are so many things going on which, to say the least of it, are not done: this last phrase, by the way, in the good old days, was very significant, but now that the Sphinx is no more, it is hard to strike home to individuals who do not conduct themselves as they ought. But one or two things which one sees every day are so glaringly, shall I say vulgar, that one cannot ignore them. For instance, what are the townspeople to think when they see a 'Varsity man going down to the playing-fields in flannels, blazer, (I do not care to say of what colour), and a *tweed cap*! Or another coxing a college tub *with a pipe in his mouth!!* Or another sculling on the river arrayed in *a black vest and shorts!!!* Such things as these stamp a man at once as a tout, and it really is surprising that we have not a more instinctive sense of what is bad form. Then again, we constantly see men going about the streets of Durham wearing a blazer with ordinary clothes, not flannels, as a rational being would do; it is more ridiculous, if possible, than playing tennis in dark grey trousers.

And, Mr Editor, what on earth is this 'Varsity coming to when a man leaves a game of tennis to go and talk to some tout girl on the tow-path! Why, such a man would have been boycotted in the pre-war days. I cannot imagine that anybody could so lose his self-respect, and not only that, which, after all, does not matter so very much, but respect for his University. It is a great mistake to make ourselves so cheap. Perhaps the misguided fellow knows no better, but I hope that if this letter meets his eye, he will learn that this sort of thing is *taboo*. We are not woman-haters or celibates, let us hope, but there are times and seasons for all things. Finally, I should like to draw attention to a matter which is not so much a question of bad form as of rank foolishness, that is, the craze for sliding seats in college tubs, exhibited by men who hardly know which end of an oar to hold. It is crass folly to imagine one can row on a sliding seat without having been coached by somebody who, at any rate, knows something about rowing, and there is naturally a shortage of such men now. It does neither the men themselves nor the boats any good, and is fatal to the great sport of rowing, which we hope will some day be in full swing again.

Sir, may I appeal, through you, to the men of Durham, to stir themselves, and remember that there *are* traditions attached to our Alma

Mater; let us be 'Varsity men in the true sense of the term, and conduct ourselves at all times and in all ways as such. It is distinctly lowering to the caste to indulge in punting clad in ordinary clothes, and making an ass of oneself generally; it also savours too much of the 'townee' to walk out after dinner with a hat and walking-stick. Such things were never done before, and we do not want the old order to change, giving place to new, for the old one grew from the habits and customs of hundreds of finer men than there are here now, and we cannot do better than imitate them.

Ragging Conceived as a Fine Art

Ragging of course was ineradicable. Indeed it must have been very much a part of College life in 1908, for a motion debated by the Literary and Debating Society was 'That the abolition of the system of "Ragging" is undesirable.' Significantly, the motion was lost.

From an entry in the *Journal* in March 1896, it is clear that the ingenuity that Cuthbert Bede writes of as having gone into the ragging of freshmen was as alive at the end of the century as it was at the beginning. Their boots were whitewashed. They were marched as a volunteer corps through the City to the derision of the townsfolk. They were made to sit fake exams, and to undertake fake medical examinations. They were induced to attend fake auditions for bogus musical and dramatic societies. They were penned in a lecture room from 9.30 to 10.15 on the first Sunday morning of term to learn the Collect for the day.

A rather pious letter from a Castleman who signed himself 'B.A. Univ.' deplored the whole practice of ragging and opined 'there will never be *esprit de corps* in the University under this system.' He had heard an Eton and Oxford man the other day - one who had spent some terms at Durham - saying he could number the gentlemen of Durham on his fingers.

Assuming this latter opinion to be true, it speaks volumes for the nature of the ragging to be found at Durham, for it is inconceivable that anyone who had experienced the savage Eton of the day would not have been thoroughly acquainted with the practice, one conducted there in a far more inhumane way than one would normally credit.

In 1903 ragging flourished as it had never done, and the best advice the *DUJ* felt it could give was 'passive resistance'.

The wrecking of students' rooms had always been a feature of College ragging, and was so even in 1916, half way through the War, when mention is made of rooms belonging to students who showed 'eccentricities' being reduced to chaos. The reminiscence by 'Vich Jan Vohr', already referred to, in the *Journal* of March 1897, both castigates the eccentricities of the freshmen of his day who were deserving of being taken down a peg and, most interestingly, applauds the loyalty of that race of College servants long unknown to us - the gyps. One such freshman, who had made no secret of his dissatisfaction with the 'humdrum life of Durham', had

> heard from his gyp that his rooms had been turned upside down; he unfortunately never saw them in a state of disorder, thanks to the exertions of his gyp, and when he arrived upon the scene tidiness and neatness prevailed throughout.

A man was fortunate if he had a good gyp. Not all were as obliging as he who restored the forward fresher's room to unaccustomed order and decency.

Lastly, a satiric sketch by one 'Onlooker', in the *Journal* of May 1904, deserves quotation since it alludes to many of the things which have been mentioned already. The style should be familiar; it is of course a copy of any studied dialogue of Oscar Wilde.

A Conversation on Palace Green

The Time: 8.30 a.m.

The Characters: A. (an undergraduate).
B. (a stranger).

A. Now we will wait here, and watch the life of Palace Green. We shall see how the men keep their day, and what they have to do for it.

B. But are the men forced to keep their days? Surely they need no pressure to drink at the well of knowledge and learning? Do not they do it of their own free will?

A. Oh! no! Don't you understand? The men are obliged to 'keep' forty-five days to count their term - it's only 'rotters' who keep more.

B. It seems very strange. And what is that bell ringing for?

A. That is Galilee bell, which rings for ten minutes and frightens the freshman who thinks he won't be in time unless he gets there before the bell stops, but it also serves to remind the 'old bird' that it is time to get out of bed. Now watch - here come the 'early birds'. They are chiefly 'freshers' and 'good' men, who are always down to breakfast in time and like to have as long as they can in Galilee. You see, they think the Dons will notice it. Now they are beginning to come in large numbers. These are the men who make a principle of having at least ten minutes for breakfast, and so have plenty of time for a quiet stroll to Galilee.

B. The bell has stopped now. There won't be any more coming, will there?

A. You wait a minute. The flower of the 'Varsity are still breakfasting and never leave more than half-a-minute to get to Galilee.

B. I'm sure they will miss their day.

A. No, here they come! The 'flowers' are bursting forth to the toil of the day.

B. How they run!

A. Oh! yes! They're sporting men and full of vigour and energy. Notice how deftly some balance well-worn slippers on their feet. Their cap is no longer a square: it is a mass of cardboard. Their robe is no longer a gown: it is a bundle of rags.

B. Why are their gowns so torn? Is it because they are poor?

A. My friend, you are quite mistaken. No! it is because they study style and good form. They are torn and dishevelled to distinguish them from those unnameable 'rotters' who keep sixty days or so, go to bed early, never break a rule, and spend two years at the 'Varsity with a gown like a lady's best dress. I can't tell you more about this, because here they come from Galilee, and I want to point out some of the men to you. Here, first, are the Dons, whom I will not dare to criticize. It's so very unoriginal to criticize the Dons. Those behind them are the 'birds', who go in last and come out first. Then you see a long stream of ordinaries. There is no need for me to point out the lady students. Please do not question me about them, for anyone heard uttering their names is 'sent down'. But I want you to notice some of the 'ordinaries'. Look! some of them carry large bundles of books. Those are the men who catch each precious word that falls from the lecturers' lips like precious jewels and store them up in ponderous note-books, as recommended by the lecturers themselves, only much larger. They are sure to 'get through', because they never do anything wrong. Notice how some of them push their way forward to catch the eye of a Don and wish him a polite 'good morning', oh! so nicely! Others, you see, would not deign to carry a book, except a paper-covered 'key' which slips easily into the pocket. You will notice how all have a saintly look, as if refreshed by the fifteen minutes in Galilee, and ready to endure the toil of the day. Now they are making their way to the Lecture Rooms. The 'good' ones go in first, because they like to sit in front and display their diligence to the trusting lecturer, and perhaps pick up his pencil. I am afraid you can't follow them in, as you are not *in statu pupillari*, but if you care to wait here you will see, between lectures, some of the 'birds' basking in the sunshine and planning a 'rag' to help them through the night.

B. It all seems very strange and funny to me. You don't seem to work for work's sake, and you -

A. Oh! no! We don't work, as a rule; only 'rotters' work, besides it's 'bad form'. Goodbye, I'm going to play 'pills'.

B. Well, I am surprized - and I always looked upon a university as a seat of learning!

June Week

There remain June Week and the June Ball.

First, however, a word is necessary to explain the attitude of the authorities to any form of social intercourse with women students. The *Journal* of 1909 groans:

> Cruel is the despotism of the chaperon! A young gallant of Castle fame desired to treat to afternoon tea two sister-students, on the day of the Sports. His aunt was with him - surely a sufficient safeguard against frivolous behaviour. Nevertheless, before the damsels dared to enter the Pavilion on such an Invitation, the Principal must be asked. She refused consent.

The first June Week took place in 1889, when for some reason, possibly to ape the practice at Oxford, it was known as Commemoration. The proceedings of that first great event extended over three days, during which the weather was perfect and the visitors numerous. It was given a solemn enough start! On the Sunday morning the sermon at the Cathedral was preached by Archdeacon Watkins, and in the afternoon Dr Ince, Regius Professor of Divinity at Oxford took the pulpit. A cricket match was played on the Monday, the University playing the Old Harrovians. During the afternoon, music was provided by Mr Amers' String Band, and the several hundred visitors present were served with refreshments. In the evening, a University Concert took place in the large Lecture Room.

Tuesday morning was given over to sight-seeing, and visits were paid to the Colleges and the grounds. Convocation, at 2 p.m., was well-attended by that other musical *ensemble* of which we have heard something already but nothing to the good, namely what the *DUJ* of the time euphemistically called the 'penny trumpets'. After these lively proceedings, the Archdeacon gave the sisters and the cousins and the aunts of the undergraduates a conducted tour of the Cathedral and Chapter Library. At 4, a Garden Party was held in Fellows' Garden, when Mr Amers' String Band played the guests a medley of old English songs. Meanwhile, the Library, with its 32,000 volumes, was thrown open to the studious, or maybe the merely curious, by the Librarian, the Rev J.T. Fowler.

In the evening came the Grand Finale - a Torchlight Procession of Boats, which started at 9.30. The Banks were thronged with sightseers, and the river was filled with craft of all kinds, all decorated and all competing for the Prize for the best decorated boat. The three Judges (in those pre-feminist days three ladies, two being the Archdeacon's wife and Mrs Plummer, wife of the Master of University College) were rowed up and down for the judging, their deliberations being aided by a constellation of lamps and glorious nebulae of Chinese Fire. The Procession rowed twice up and down, after which it massed by Prebends' Bridge to sing 'Auld Lang Syne' and the National Anthem.

Later June Weeks provided interesting variations on this first, by no means inglorious, celebration. In 1899, for instance, there was a debate on the Friday at Hatfield; on Saturday a Concert in Castle Hall; and on Monday a Garden Party in Fellows' Garden. At this last the Band of the 1st York and Lancaster Regiment played. In the evening the Castle Grounds were illuminated by tiny lights, about which more in Chapter 14, and Chinese lanterns. Sunday was of course given over to devotional matters; but Monday saw a Lawn Tennis Tournament, and Tuesday the Regatta.

We have what bears every sign of being an authentic description of the 1900 June Week, in the form of a fictitious letter written by one of the ladies supposedly present, 'Gertie', to her correspondent, her 'dear Cissie'. This is a wholly delightful as well as invaluable piece of ephemera. After describing the Concert in Castle Hall on the Saturday, when the chairs seem to have been arranged in 'clumps', presumably to facilitate the serving of coffee and tea during the interval, 'Gertie' proceeds to Monday's Garden Party.

It ought to have been in the Dons' Garden at the Castle, but it was wet, so they held it in the Castle Hall. The Band were in the Gallery. We were received on the steps by some of the Committee. In the evening it was fine enough to have the Promenade Concert out of doors. We first went into the Hall. The Committee, or some of them, received us at the door; it was awfully swell being bowed to by a lot of young men in evening dress and gowns. They looked so solemn, but one of them, I'm sure, winked at me. When it got dark we went into the garden. It was very pretty, all lit up with hundreds and hundreds of lights, and 'Floreat Universitas' in coloured lights on the grass slope.

Some of the men turned up in blazers! When we went, there were some of the Committee at the gate to say good night.

On Tuesday and Wednesday we went to the Regatta, and the

Fireworks in Pelaw Woods.

And now we come to the Ball. There were about seventy or eighty people there, and the Hall looked very nice. Three or four of the undergraduates had been hard at work all day decorating it. The floor was a little sticky and treacherous at first (Dick really did let me down in the Lancers) but got all right later on. There were some lovely sitting-out rooms, where nobody could see anybody else, and the refreshments were upstairs. And such refreshments! Tom says I ate six ices. Dick walzes [sic] like an angel. The band was awfully good. There were four stewards; two of them danced quite nicely, and the other two walked about and made everybody comfortable. There were not so many 'Varsity men there as I had hoped for, and a good many of them didn't dance. The stewards wore such pretty rosettes, palatinate centres and white edges and ends.

The ices 'Gertie' so gormandised were, no doubt, Mrs Johnson's, whose confections were singled out for high praise again in 1902, when they were provided for the Garden Party and Promenade Concert in 'University College Gardens'.

Glorious sunshine in the afternoon and brilliant starlight in the evening made outdoor conditions perfect, and the grand old Castle Hall was not to be matched as a retreat for the enjoyment of light refreshments, and, above all, Mrs Johnson's Ices. The band was a good one, and played bright music all the time. In the evening, the guests, as they were received, were ushered into the Hall where the band played in the musicians' gallery, while refreshments were served. Afterwards a move was made to the gardens, and under the influence of the lovely night and the music, great progress was made in those June Week acquaintances which are dear to the hearts of Durham men. Eleven o'clock came all too early, save for the musicians and the energetic officials and members of the committee.

Unfortunately, the 1904 June Week was, 'owing to various reasons', celebrated on a quieter, indeed more modest, scale. As the *DUJ* nostalgically pointed out,

The absence of the usual garden parties was a great disappointment to many people, and rightly so, seeing that the surroundings of the Castle grounds are almost unique. What enchanting descriptions one has heard of the appearance of the Dons' gardens when lighted up by many-coloured globes, and peopled with a gay throng of prome-naders. Is this now to remain a dream of the past? We hope that next June will see its reappearance.

That June certainly did not, for it was to be two years before the next June Week was held. Part reasons seem to have been the inertia of the dons, and the apathy, or even the downright opposition, of some of the under-graduates.

June Week returned in 1906, though again in truncated form. There was a 'splendid' Concert in Castle Hall, and in the Garden, traditionally 'illu-minated for the occasion'. And there was a debate. The Cricket Match with Manchester University was, in order to make the Visitors feel at home, rained off; but the Inter-'Varsity Boat Race with Edinburgh did take place.

1907 saw a more musical emphasis. On the Thursday an Organ Recital was given in Hatfield Chapel by the Precentor of the Cathedral; on Saturday, the 'Varsity Boat Race took place against Edinburgh; while the Union Debate, an Inter-'Varsity affair, was held in the evening in Hatfield Hall. Sunday evening saw (or rather heard) Haydn's *Creation* in the Cathedral. On Monday and Tuesday the 'Varsity played a cricket match against Manchester, while on Wednesday and Thursday it played against Edinburgh. There was a Concert in Castle Hall, where apparently the *pièce de résistance* was a Dr Sweeting's *Burial March of Dundee*! The report of this latter event says tellingly that the string band which accompanied the choir, and which had been 'raised with difficulty', was a 'vast improve-ment on the exiguous strains of a piano alone, to which we are accus-tomed, and which are all too mean either for a 'Varsity Concert or the Castle Hall.'

The Regatta was held on the Tuesday.

The report has another passage of interest. Writing that the 'illuminated Fête in the Fellows' Garden was most enjoyable', and that the 'secluded nooks were as well haunted as of yore', it goes on: 'The perennial ducks still seem to cause as much joy as ever in their pond.' This pond was still to be seen, though sadly overgrown, in the Fellows' Garden as late as 1991, when it gave way to the new Office; its occupants had however disappeared - let us hope they had taken wing - many years before.

It seems to have been the custom for notable recipients of Honorary Degrees to be greeted at the railway station by a rag. In this same year of 1907 it was the great Kipling's turn to be thus fêted, he being given a Doctorate of Letters. The November 1907 *Journal* reported that 'the Kipling rag was very well organised and equally well carried out. The procession was one of the best we have ever seen, even better than that which met Baron Takaki. Some of the costumes were very fetching.'

The 1908 June Week was, like the others of the new century, haunted by the ghosts of past glories.

At one time visions of ancient and laudable customs revived, such as a 'Varsity Ball, and Tea on the Terrace, were dangled before our eyes.

But -

These are followed by an ominous rumour that, unless there is a greater display of enthusiasm on the part of all concerned, the famous June Week activities will be dropped.

Post-War generations attempted to revive the Week's pristine glories, but it was a long haul. June 1919, spirits buoyed no doubt by relief that the long wicked misery was over, did its best.

The end of last term saw a revival, in a small way, of June Week. On Saturday evening, June 28th, there was the Union Debate, and on Monday . . . an excellent concert was given, in the Castle Hall, the conductors being Madame Blanche Newcombe and Mr E.V. Stocks. It had been arranged that a band should play in the Hall from 9.30 - 10.45, and advantage was taken of this to get up an impromptu but very successful dance.

Madame Blanche Newcombe was the wife of Dr Pace; she had long been prominent in the Choral Society.

'Varsity Rags

The 'rag' element seems from now on to have taken precedence over everything else, perhaps because, unlike balls and garden parties, rags were logistically less demanding and required little or nothing from the authorities save permission for them to take place. In 1920, for instance,

the custom of a June Week 'Rag' was revived. It took the form of what was advertised as a Jazz 'Sircus'. A procession of weird-looking animals and fantastically garbed human beings started from the Hospital and marched through the Town to Palace Green, where a mock auction was held. The auction was as quaint as the procession. A box of chocolates went for a sovereign, while a 'chimpanzee' went for two shillings. The proceeds, together with the money collected in the streets, came to more than £70, which sum was handed over to the Durham County Hospital. The *Birmingham Daily Post* of June 29 said:

'Durham University students have set a new standard in "rags", for their programme yesterday was of a constructive rather than destructive type, and as the procession marched through the city a collection was taken for the Hospital. This is a good example to the student world, and calculated to do much more to commend culture to the people than those meaningless orgies which have taken place elsewhere in the past, to the destruction of property and the detriment of law and order.'

1921 saw a similar format, but with a distinct attempt to revive the distant glories. The *Journal* reported:

The June Week festivities were very successful this year. A new feature was the University Dance in Hatfield College. On the last Saturday of term the Union Society held an Inter-University debate, at which the principal speakers included representatives from Oxford, Glasgow, St Andrew's and Leeds. The motion 'That the Trades Unionism of today is a menace to Industry' was carried by a considerable majority. The debate lasted nearly three hours, but this did not matter, as the oratory maintained a high level throughout.

On the Monday afternoon the usual 'Rag' took place. It was described as 'potted pantomime', each College being responsible for its own special 'pantomime'. There were represented in the procession, 'Beauty and the Beast' (University College), 'Ali Baba' (Hatfield), 'Cinderella' (St Chad's), 'Dick Whittington' (St John's), and 'Aladdin' (Bede). In addition there were a Jazz Band and a nigger troupe. The sum of £80 was collected for the Durham Hospital.

The June Week proceedings also included the usual University College Concert, which was a great success.

By now the Rag seems to have attracted most of the energies and the talent of those undergraduates who wished to make June Week a success. Their initiative, organising ability and ingenuity can be seen from the description of the 1922 Rag.

The 'Rag' last summer term was quite the best since the War. The subject was 'The Marriage of Caesar and Boadicea'. A procession of Ancient Britons, Druids, Roman warriors and prehistoric animals marched down the North Road to the Market Place, where a 'human sacrifice' was offered. Outside the County Hotel there was a combat with a savage 'bull' which was ultimately brought down by six gladiators. The Romans then embarked on some 'triremes', and took a majestic departure up the river, where they were shortly afterwards attacked by a yelling mob of Britons in 'coracles'. When every canoe and 'trireme' had been upset and all the combatants were in the water, Father Neptune arose from the waves and made peace by ordering the immediate marriage of Caesar and Boadicea. This took place the same afternoon at 'Stonehenge' which apparently had been recently moved to Palace Green . . .

1923 did see the return of the Garden Party - but at Hatfield! This was the period when the College was in great danger of slipping down the hill, and indeed the celebrations of two years later were 'shorn of many of [their] ancient glories owing to the repairs going on at the castle.' The Thursday Concert, for instance, was actually given in the Miners' Hall, as was the Debate; and as accommodation there was limited, a smaller number of invitations than usual was issued for the Concert. Durham seems by now to have been gaining acceptance, since there were representatives at the Debate from no fewer than six other universities. The external features, of course, did not suffer. On the Friday afternoon 'the usual Tennis

Tournament' was held; and the Rag on the Saturday seems to have been the usual success, though it was a particularly cold day. It took the form, in this year, of a

Norman invasion gallantly opposed by a number of Anglo-Saxons. A sacrifice [another!] was offered in the Market Place, while outside the County Hotel the Witan met and conferred the degree of D.D. on two strangers from the 'University of Stonehenge'. The final scene was on Palace Green, and represented the storming of a Norman castle by the 'Anglo-Saxons.'

Inevitably there was some repetition of the more successful tableaux. The Graeco-Roman historical themes, the set-piece battles, and the sacrifices crop up time and again. The Rag of 1926, the last year we shall look at,

intentionally violated all historical probabilities and showed a vivid imagination on the part of the originators. Cleopatra, complete with baby and nurse, came down the river and was received at Hatfield boat-landing by Antony and a mixed crowd of Roman soldiers and Egyptians. They celebrated their reunion by a banquet in the Market Place. The Ku Klux Klan by a prodigious effort projected themselves back through nearly two thousand years of history and carried off the lady, the nurse following with the infant, propelled in a soap-box on wheels. On Palace Green Cleopatra was about to be offered as a burnt sacrifice when she was rescued by the Romans, and the reunited enemies next marched to the Old Elvet where, outside the County Hotel, the Sacred Bull and a few dancing girls were sold by auction.

All good clean fun!

---

1) A.A. Macfarlane-Grieve, *A History of Durham Rowing*, Andrew Reid, Newcastle-upon-Tyne, 1922
2) *Ibid.*, p.13
3) *Ibid.*, p.15
4) *Ibid.*, p.14
5) *Ibid.*, p.16
6) *Ibid.*, pp.21-2
7) Thomas Hughes, *Tom Brown at Oxford*, p.139
8) *Ibid*, p.144

CHAPTER 8

Alfred Plummer and Walter Kercheval Hilton

On the death of Charles Thorp, The Wardenship of the University becoming one with the Deanery, Dean Waddington became the second Warden. For three years there was no Master of University College, until Dr Joseph ('Joe') Waite was appointed Master in 1865. As Dean Waddington occupies only a peripheral position in the College's history, we will pass on to his successor Lake.

It is appropriate here to add what Bishop Hensley Henson has to say about the two other Deans, Waddington's successors, who were Wardens of the University, men clearly not of the calibre of the scholar, traveller, and founder member of the Athenaeum, Waddington.

> Lake (1869-1894) seems to have left no considerable memory.
> Kitchin (1894-1912) to the outer world was mainly a rather obstinate 'little Englander'. . . . of none of them [including Waddington] does one hear anything religious. Kitchin, baffled by the Chapter in some effort of nepotism, sulked in such wise that he would no more attend the daily services in the cathedral. Annoyed by the ill-behaviour of some students, he shut them out of the cathedral as a body!

Lake was set in as limited and parochial a mould as was possible to find, and the justification for mentioning him here is that his misconception of his role as Warden did nothing but contribute to Durham's, and therefore University College's, decline in the latter half of the nineteenth century.

That Durham's plight was of concern to people well outside it was shown by the *Times'* address to the Prime Minister in 1869, when the deanery fell vacant, for it urged him to appoint some vigorous educational expert who would restore life once again into the moribund university. Gladstone however appointed the Rev William Charles Lake, rector of Huntspill in Somerset, and prebendary of Wells Cathedral. Lake had been a tutor at Balliol, and had served on several royal commissions on education. Sadly, his views on Durham ran directly counter to those of Van Mildert and Thorp: Durham's function, he believed, was simply to train clergy. In 1874, the then Archbishop of Canterbury Tait, who had been a tutor at Balliol when Lake was an undergraduate, visiting Durham addressed the University in the Galilee Chapel and made it plain that his idea was the same.

During the 'Seventies Owens College, Manchester, began to agitate for university status, and it was inevitable that reference would be made to Durham, as an example of a 'new' university, when the matter came up for serious consideration. It is instructive to read the views of those who expressed an opinion.

As early as 1874, the Liberal Robert Lowe, who it will be remembered had served on the 1862 Commission, and was now Chancellor of the Exchequer in Gladstone's cabinet, in a public speech declared that the only thing which would reconcile him to the foundation of such a place as Owens College as a university would be that it would certainly swallow up the 'effete' University of Durham. This charitable remark can only be excelled by his other description of Durham as an 'abortion'.

In 1877 a number of distinguished men were asked their opinion on Owens College's pretensions. That civilised apostle of culture Matthew Arnold thought it would counterbalance in the north-west Durham in the north-east. A Dr Carpenter, however, thought it would be better for Durham itself if it surrendered its privileges and merged itself with the proposed new university of Manchester, an essay in logistics which could only be entertained by an academic. A Professor Jack thought that 'the pathetic position of Durham' served to warn the government against 'the rash creation of new universities',whose creation he considered 'viewy and theoretical.' On the other hand, Dr Lyon Playfair diagnosed part at least of Durham's trouble when he said that it had lately, through Newcastle, 'been trying to get back to the original intention of universities, but she is too ecclesiastical to succeed.'

In 1871 Senate decreed that in future there should be one uniform academic year, of three terms, extending over twenty-six weeks, for both Arts and Theology. Thus one bone of contention that had divided the two Faculties was decently buried. Reforms such as this did little, however, to raise either the standard or the popularity of Durham in the outside world.

Numbers remained pitifully low. In the eighteen seventies the total number of students was under a hundred; the total number of tutors about ten. As late as 1871 there was still an eighth class - said to be popular! Most of the undergraduates were still intending parsons. Curiously, as well as the usual young men from the public schools, there was a number of middle-aged business men, attracted to Durham by the shortness and cheapness of the course.

It must have been abundantly clear to Durham men that the future of their University lay in their own and not in the authorities' hands; and it was for this reason that the Durham University Association was founded in 1866. The distinguished part played by the Association in furthering the cause of the University has no special place in this history. However, on a more social than academic note, what Whiting has to say about the protracted battle waged by the Association over the projected colours of Durham hoods is of interest; for at their meeting in July 1883, Canon Whitley, who had been Reader in Natural Philosophy from 1833 to 1855, said that when the colour of the M.A. hood was discussed by Senate, his proposal that it should be black and amber was outvoted on the ground that people would call it 'Durham mustard', there being a mustard factory in the City at that time. Mr Telfair, the University tailor, afterwards produced a piece of a purple coat which had been worn by Van Mildert, and it was this colour which was adopted for the M.A. hood. This particular piece of Van Mildert's coat was, in time, bequeathed to Mr Sewell, Mr Telfair's successor; whether it exists today is very doubtful.

In 1880 the number of professors was at last increased to four, when the Venerable Henry William Watkins was appointed to the Chair of Hebrew. Watkins was unusual, academically, in that he was a graduate of King's College, London; though on graduation he did proceed to the almost statutory Balliol as a scholar. He was made Professor of Logic and Moral Philosophy in the University of London in 1877. A canonry went with the Chair of Hebrew at Durham; and it is clear that things in the Church of England had not changed overmuch since the days of the University's foundation, for with this canonry Watkins successively held the Archdeaconries of Northumberland, Auckland, and Durham. He retired in 1920, and died two years later. One of the stalwarts of Durham's eccentrics, Watkins never took breakfast; objected so strongly to smoking that not even a bishop dared light up in his house; and was a lifelong total abstainer. At the outbreak of the Great War he wrote to the military authorities: 'I am seventy years of age, I am called the Venerable, but I can walk twenty miles in a day and I can shoot. If you can make any use of me do so.' Nobody ever called him 'Professor': he was always 'the Archdeacon'.

For those who read English at Durham, the following will be of particular interest. It was proposed as early as 1846 to found in the University a Readership in Anglo-Saxon and Old English Literature - an indication of the suspicion with which 'modern' literature was viewed in academic circles. Nothing was done about English Studies however until 1882, when the Rev Herbert John Randall Marston, M.A., Fellow of the University, was appointed Reader in English Literature and given the arduous task of delivering two open lectures (that is, to include the general public) in each of the two winter terms. Experimental at first, the Readership was continued until 1889. Marston must have been an exceptional scholar and lecturer, for he was appointed though he was blind. In 1889, when Marston retired, a Classics lecturer, Henry Ellershaw, was appointed, who became the first holder of the Chair of English Language and Literature. In 1919 Ellershaw became Master of University College; holding the office until 1932.

In the 'Eighties the by now expanded University was feeling pinched for space, and it is interesting to note that one of the reasons given for founding a new college was that it might do something to mitigate the antagonism between University College and Hatfield.

1882, of course, was the year of the University's jubilee. University College commemorated this by putting in the great window behind High Table in Hall; and this window now demands a mention. As has already been noted, the upper part of the great Hall was originally walled off and divided into two or three floors, the lowest, the Black Parlour, being a dons' Common Room, the room above being a lecture room.

In about 1845 the partition wall and the floors were taken away, the Hall was restored to its ancient length northwards, and the tracery of the north window was inserted. It was this tracery that was filled in, in 1882, by C.E. Kempe and C. Hodgson Fowler. The *DUJ*, commenting in July 1882 on the insertion of the tracery of nearly forty years before, gave it as their opinion that the tracery was 'certainly very heavy', but forbore to criticise further since 'It is a monument of their regard for their University on the part of the Fellows of that day, for it was they who bore the cost of it.'

There had clearly been some criticism of the glass's being 'too pale'; but the *DUJ* will have none of this: 'we cannot think that any deeper colouring of background would in the least enhance either the dignity or the harmony of the window.' Perceptively, the writer compliments Kempe's work on having managed to avoid 'that common fault of heraldic windows - patchiness.'

An explanation of the design should be of interest to all Castlemen.

On a mead of blue flowers - asphodel - stand four ecclesiastical figures, the outermost on either side being the bishops who played the chief part in building the Hall itself: the warrior Bishop Thomas de Hatfield, a liberal benefactor of that Durham College at Oxford with which we started this history, and Bishop Richard Fox, the friend of Henry V11. Between these two stand two saints, George and Cuthbert, patrons respectively of England and the diocese. Each of these four carries a heraldic banner. Between the two saints there grows a luxuriant tree, that of either Knowledge or Life, whose trunk is partly concealed by the centre mullion, but whose branches, with their tender white foliage and bunches of red and green berries, fill up all the rest of the window and support the armorial shields which record the history of the University and University College. Entwined with these shields are ribbons bearing the motto of the University. The topmost branches, in the cinquefoil at the head of the window, curl round the Insignia of the University, granted in 1843 under patent of His Grace the Earl Marshall and the three Kings of Arms. Below this, in the two quatrefoils, are the bearings of the Bishopric of Durham (the Cross being patoncé) and the Archbishopric of York. Between them, in a triangular opening, is a tiny shield bearing the designer's (Mr Kempe's) own coat of arms. The charges on this suggest that he numbered the great Cardinal Kempe among his kin.

Every one of the four main lights contains four shields, making sixteen in all, of which ten are Episcopal and surmounted by mitres and coronets. They represent the arms of the six successive Visitors of the University: Bishops Van Mildert, Maltby, Longley, Villiers, and Baring, and of course the Visitor of the day, Bishop Lightfoot; and also those of four of the chief bishops who had to do with the building of the Castle: Bishops Tunstall (or Tonstall), Cosin, Nathaniel Lord Crewe, and Butler. Lord Crewe's shield can easily be picked out by its having a baronial helm and coronet in addition to the Durham mitre.

Of the remaining shields, those furthest to the left contain the bearings of the three Wardens, Archdeacon Thorp, and Deans Waddington and Lake; while those in the opposite compartment are those of two of the three Masters to date of University College, the Rev Herbert Edward Booth, and the reigning Master, Dr Alfred Plummer. Charles Thorp was, of course, already accounted for. The shield without arms contains the simple initials of that Master already mentioned in this history, poor Dr Joseph ('Joe') Waite, who alone among this assembly had not inherited any such glories from his ancestors. The Rev Herbert Booth, a man totally unknown to Castlemen, was Master for only a year, in 1874.

At the foot of the tree are to be seen four figures. Among these, Bishops Hatfield and Fox are dressed alike, but are seen standing in different attitudes while the colours and the folding of their robes differ. They wear mitres, are clothed in dalmatics and copes, and bear in one hand their pastoral staff, with vexillum, and in the other a banner with their arms. The cope of Bishop Hatfield and the dalmatic of Bishop Fox are especially interesting for 'those with an eye to such things,' for the ruby and purple glass of which they are composed is etched so that the patterns show either white or pale crimson. The jewel work on the copes too is particularly rich and luminous. Bishop Fox's face was no doubt intended for a likeness; for the face is drawn and the eyes are closed, indicating that Fox himself was blind - though to be strictly accurate blindness did not come upon him until after he had been translated to the see of Winchester. Bishop Hatfield's cannot really be said to be anything of a portrait, if one takes into consideration the massive features on his effigy in the Cathedral. St George, standing between Hatfield and the tree, is represented as a young man, crowned with laurel, and in silver armour damascened with gold. The dragon is, as is usual with dragons, under his feet. St George's right hand holds a martyr's palm; his left the standard of England. Beyond the tree stands St Cuthbert, in the eucharistic vesture of a bishop. His mitre, of a curious and antique shape, is like all the other mitres in the window white; his chasuble is purple; his dalmatic sage-green. His left hand carries his characteristic if macabre emblem, the head of St Oswald the King. The interesting thing about this particular feature is that St Oswald's head is supported on a reliquary and not on Cuthbert's open hand, the reliquary being drawn after an old representation of the actual casket which contained the relic. Cuthbert's right hand holds a white banner, embroidered in crimson and showing his familiar cross - the badge of the University.

Beneath the whole is the Latin inscription:

Universitatis hujusce jam L annos fundatae memorem hanc
fenestram alumni posuerunt, MDCCCLXXX11

University College boasted its first royal member in 1884, when at a spe-
cial Convocation held in the Chapter Library the degree of Doctor of Civil
Law was conferred on Leopold Duke of Albany, youngest son of Queen
Victoria, in recognition of his interest in, and work for, education. The
Duke of course expressed a polite wish to be enrolled as a member of
University College. Of interest is the fact that the parchment of the degree
was presented to him in a casket made of old oak from the Castle, decorated with a carved design representing some of the sculptures and carv-
ings to be found there. Unhappily, our first royal member died very soon
afterwards.

After the short Mastership of Booth came the long one of the Rev Alfred
Plummer: from 1875 to 1902. Plummer was a Fellow of Trinity College,
Oxford, the original, it will be remembered, of the old Durham College;
was one of the foremost New Testament scholars of his day; and produced
about a dozen commentaries on various books, together with volumes on
Church history, and translations into English of various works of the
German historian Döllinger. On his death in 1926, the *DUJ* painted a telling
little picture of him. At that time there were few members of the University
still resident in Durham who remembered him; but

hundreds of old men of the Castle and Hatfield and St Cuthbert's .
. . will never forget the pale-faced bearded figure, and the deep voice
which said, 'My dear fellow,' or the lectures on St Luke which covered
about two chapters a year. To the man who wished to get through an
examination and nothing else they were a subject for grumbling; but
the men who were really keen learned from him something of his
scholarly methods of slow and meticulous examination of every word
of Holy Writ.

A tremendous worker himself, Plummer had little sympathy with the
idle. A story about him tells how, when one of his colleagues had been set-

ting on foot some new organisation, one of whose aims was 'to get the men together', Plummer started one of his lectures with a weary: 'I see Dr - is getting up a scheme "to get the men together." Now I exist here to keep the men apart and make them work.' Another tells how he scorched another lecture-room with the following:

There are a good many men who come up here from time to time with considerable industry but very little brains, and we are all very sorry, of course, but they are ploughed. There are also a large number who come up with very fair ability, but they won't work. Unfortunately there is a third class of men who for some reason or other make Durham their Alma Mater, those who have no brains and won't work either.'

Plummer was a scholar of the first rank and, in the words of the *DUJ* on his retirement after twenty-eight years, 'contributed to directing the attention of the learned world of Europe and America to Durham as a centre of scholarly and theological studies.' Come of a noted Durham family, closely associated with the professional, industrial and political life of Durham and Northumberland, Plummer was educated at Lancing, where he gained an Exhibition at Exeter College, Oxford. He was elected in 1864 to a Fellowship at Trinity. He made himself a Döllinger specialist, early on in his scholarly career translating some of Döllinger's historical researches. In 1871 the University of Oxford commissioned him to take to Munich the Diploma of the Degree of D.D. which they had just conferred on the Catholic historian. Plummer spent many Oxford vacations visiting Döllinger at Munich, remained a close friend of his until Döllinger's death in 1893, and published fragments of their conversations which are on a par with the volume of Döllinger's table-talk produced by Frau Von Kobell.

When Plummer was appointed Master of Castle in 1874, the University, though it was showing some signs of recovery from the deep depression of ten years before, was still a long way from being flourishing. A man of his international stature in scholarship was needed if University College, and indeed the University with it, was going to be put on its feet. It was important therefore that Plummer continue to produce scholarly works despite his commitment to the University, the College, and the welfare of his undergraduates. His speciality was New Testament exegesis. He produced noteworthy Commentaries on the Gospel and Epistles of St John, for the Cambridge Greek Testament for Schools and Colleges Series, and, as may be inferred from what was said of him above, a monumental commentary on St Luke.

Plummer was, by all accounts, and despite the grumblings of students who had to listen to his meticulous piecemeal analysis of Luke, a first-rate lecturer, dedicated to making difficult things easy. His lectures on Logic were apparently models of pellucid style and arrangement.

On his retirement in 1902, the Board of Faculties meeting at Durham presented him with a handsome silver cup carrying the following inscription:

> Aluredo Plummer S.T.P. de Universitate Dunelmense per XXV111 annos egregie merito eruditionis et amicitiae memores faustum non sine libris otium discessuro precantur collegae. V1 Kal Jun MCM11

This was offered to Plummer by the Warden, Dean Kitchin, who had been a tutor with him at Oxford.

A month later, after Hall, Castlemen made their own presentation to their retiring Master. This enviable gift consisted of a solid silver soup tureen, sauce tureens, and a pair of entrée dishes, all engraved with his crest and motto, and carrying the inscription:

> To the Rev. A. Plummer, MA,DD, Master of University College Durham, from the members of the College, as a mark of esteem and gratitude.
>
> June 21st. 1902.

In reply, Plummer referred to the nickname by which he was known to generations of Durham men, saying he had long been aware of its existence and had always felt proud of it. He assured all the contributors that their present would be handed down to many generations of Polycarps after him.

He retired to Bideford, where he took an active part in educational concerns. He died suddenly on April 17 1926, while playing - a nice touch - a favourite tune of his wife's on the piano.

The latter part of the century seems to have produced, apart from Dr Plummer, some notable servants of the College. One such, who came as Bursar in 1877 was Walter Kercheval Hilton.

Hilton was not an *alumnus* of Durham, having graduated from Corpus Christi, Oxford, but he gave the University, and the College in particular, his total devotion. Plummer contributed a telling recollection of him to the *DUJ* on his death in 1913, at the age of sixty-eight, after he had given the College and the University thirty-six years' service.

Walter Kercheval Hilton was born in 1845, the youngest son of John Hilton, of Bentcliffe Old Hall, Eccles. He and his two brothers were educated at Lancing; Francis and Louis being Plummer's schoolfellows. Though Hilton entered Lancing only in 1859, a year after Plummer had left, Plummer got to know him well there, for he often stayed at his old school when an undergraduate at Exeter College and later when Fellow of Trinity. He also saw a great deal more of him when Walter Kercheval followed his two brothers to Oxford.

Hilton took his B.A. in 1869 and his M.A. in 1872. When the first Education Act was passed in 1870, he was appointed an Inspector of Returns, a post he held from 1871 to 1873, at which time the office expired. He also held one or two other educational posts, both before and after this two-year period.

Plummer recollected how, when in the Long Vacation of 1874 he left Oxford to become Master of Castle, he found at the College three officials in residence: the Rev F. Copeman, University Tutor and College Censor; the Rev T. Thornton, University Registrar and College Censor and Bursar; and the Rev J. Atkinson, University Lecturer and College Chaplain - all three in Orders, be it noted. When Thornton was presented to the Rectory of Shadforth, it occurred to Plummer that Walter Kercheval Hilton would be an excellent man to take his place. He accordingly persuaded the Governors of the University to appoint Hilton Registrar, while he himself appointed him Bursar. Hilton later became Censor, as well as Bursar, on the death of the Rev Copeman and the retirement of the Rev Atkinson.

Hilton went into residence at Castle in the Easter Term of 1877 and, as Plummer rather touchingly remembered, 'dined in Hall for the first time, Sunday, 22nd April.' His arrival was timely, for in 1877 the Castle presented an unpretty picture of squalor and decay, and the improvements he brought about were therefore both many and substantial.

First, the Chapel. Before Hilton's arrival, the undergraduates had been petitioning the Master to improve the condition of the College Chapel, which was in an extremely dilapidated state. On the evening of March 15

1877 a meeting was held in the Choral Room of University College, under the Chairmanship of the Master, to discuss the plans and the various estimates for the restoration. Hodgson Fowler exhibited his plans, and these were, not surprisingly, unanimously acclaimed. The estimates topped £1000. The Dean and Chapter promised their support in the raising of this large sum. Subscriptions had been invited as early as July 1876, the recipient being appropriately enough the Rev E. Castle.

It is at this moment that Hilton appears on the scene. Hilton had good taste, something not always found in 1877; and he was devoutly, one might almost say over-devoutly, religious. Although a layman, he was more regular in his attendance at Galilee and Chapel than any other member of the staff. His considerable energies were given first to this matter of the restoration, and certainly by March 1878 the restoration had progressed so far that it was hoped to re-open the Chapel at the start of the following term. It was indeed opened on the Tuesday of Whitsun-week, after having been closed for nearly three terms. The roof had been cleaned, the stonework renewed where necessary, the windows reglazed, and the whole building reseated, the handsome old oak stalls having been cleaned and new oak seats made to match them. In order to increase the accommodation, the screen was pushed back several feet nearer to the western wall, and consequently the Chapel now seated 62. The Restoration Service on that memorable day consisted of the whole of evensong, instead of the customary shortened version; the Master taking the first part, and the new Censor, though a layman, the second.

The restoration work to the Chapel, as well as other general improvements, continued. In 1883, for instance, the Members of the College proposed putting in a stained-glass window in memory of W.E. Gabbett, who two years after having been appointed classical tutor in the University had fallen three to four thousand feet on the *Dente Blanche*, near Zermatt. A Gabbett Challenge Cup, as we all know, still exists. In the event though, the thick iron bars which were set in the windows of the Chapel put stained glass out of the question, and the money collected was instead devoted to rehabilitating the East end of the Chapel, which the earlier restoration had left almost untouched. The East end at the time was, in the words of the *DUJ*, 'in anything but an artistic condition.' It was proposed to restore it 'in the Italian style', and this work too was put in the hands of Hodgson Fowler.

It may not be generally known that the floor, before the 1883-4 work was put in, was of wood, with slate steps. These were replaced by the present tessellated pavement with marble steps. A foot-pace, also of marble, was added; and the oak panels, taken originally from the Cathedral pulpit, were reset and freed from the heavy and inharmonious moulding which then disfigured them.

The East wall had been plagued by damp, which had begun seriously to damage these panels; and this was now lined with waterproof concrete. At the same time, the central heating was continued along Tunstall's Gallery into the Chapel.

The *Journal* however was still not satisfied. 'What is chiefly wanted now,' it complained, 'is a handsome reredos to take the place of the beautiful but inadequate Arundel copy of Perugino's Crucifixion.'

All this beautification however seems not to have improved the quality of the services. Indeed the Chapel, like the Courtyard Clock, and the behaviour of 'cads' in Galilee, was a source of perpetual complaint. In 1886, for instance, 'A Second Year Man' wrote to the *Journal* :

> It has rarely been my misfortune to attend a duller or more dreary service than the daily Evensong in our Chapel . . . The singing is very feeble; and there is woefully little of it. Surplices on Saints' Days were discontinued under the impression that their use was thinning attendance . . . not the case . . . they should be resumed again; anything to render the service less slovenly.
>
> Is it generally known that the flowers in the altar vases are artificial, or at any rate 'everlasting'?
>
> Finally, why are the large candles at the entrance of the Sanctuary never lighted? Are the reasons for all this neglect of decency and order in the externals of our service 'Protestant', or economical?

Either way, of course, they were equally to be deplored!

The Chapel Organ also came in for restoration. In 1879 the Dean and Chapter, at the request of the College, gave the Choir organ portion of the old Cathedral organ to the Chapel. Again the details of cost make our inflationary eyes blink, for the enormous sum demanded for putting it up was around £155. This work was completed, and the organ was ready to be played, by the start of the Easter Term, 1880. This instrument, by all reports a handsome one, remained in use until 1926.

This new organ, incidentally, which was the work of Messrs Harrison of Durham, was placed in the Chapel of University College as a memorial to the twenty-five members of the College who fell in the Great War. Even this instrument, it is comforting to note, contained portions of the old one which it replaced.

Some of Hilton's improvements to the Hall have already been mentioned in connection with the meetings of the University College Choral Society, he having got rid of the unsightly gas brackets, and substituted for them elaborate wrought-iron chandeliers. He also got erected the screen at the south end, and put panelling all round. His also, of course, was the heating system. What Dr Plummer calls 'the warming apparatus' had its *fons et origo* under the dais in the Hall. Under this dais was a room which, during Plummer's first couple of years, was a lecture-room. Here, unbelievably, the Choral Society held its fortnightly concerts, to which a few Uitlanders used to be admitted. This room turned out to be the only suitable place for the furnace of the 'warming apparatus', so from this time on the room ceased to be used as a lecture-room, and the concerts, to everybody's benefit, and certainly the College's, were promoted to the Hall itself from these poky quarters.

Hilton's religious zeal was famous. Plummer, in his Recollections of him, said that it was 'impossible for anyone to tell what he did in promoting a healthy moral and religious tone in all the circles in which he moved, and especially in the College in which he was for so many years Censor and Bursar.' He mentions one of Hilton's more surprising innovations in this context.

At the beginning of Epiphany Term, 1882, he told me that the work in College on Sunday made it difficult for the servants to go to any service in Cathedral, which was not very suitable for them, and which probably was not often attended by them. Their opportunities of religious worship during term-time were not great. Could we not give them a short service in the College Chapel at 7 p.m., when they could nearly all attend? I said that it could easily be done, but I should like to have some evidence that such a thing would be appreciated by the servants. It would be better not to begin, than to have to cease because hardly anyone cared to attend. I consulted Freeman the butler. His reply was, 'It is the best piece of news, Sir, that I have heard for a long time.' He was confident that it would succeed. We began on the 4th Sunday after Epiphany, 29th January, 1882; and during the remaining twenty years of my residence these services never ceased, and were almost always well attended by servants, some undergraduates, and often some outsiders.

Plummer also recollects that, after the Cathedral had given the College 'as much of the beautiful old Cathedral organ as was suitable for the Chapel,' Hilton was often, and latterly always, the organist.

Another obituarist, W. Hooper, sheds an interesting light on Hilton's religious zeal and his expression of that zeal in his ministry to the more unfortunate of the undergraduates. For the first,

it shewed itself most prominently in an intense revolt against all that savoured in the least of conventional unreality . . . [This] doubtless diminished his popularity among men, for he never hesitated to denounce in even too unsparing words anything that might seem to him in the least to be untrue.

For the second:

To no call of need or distress could he ever turn a deaf ear. Many and many a weary month was spent in vacations helping in various ways some unfortunate undergraduate, and to more than one he ministered even to the point of death.

The then Master, Dr Gee, in his Eulogy of Hilton, given in College Chapel after Hilton's death, made no bones about the dire physical state of the College before the new Bursar came along:

I can speak from personal experience of the skill and taste with which he brought the furnishings and general arrangements of the fabric and surroundings of the Castle out of the squalor and confusion in which he found them in 1876. I have still a vivid recollection of the very general decay and decrepitude of all things about the Castle in those days.

As well as being one of the most substantial and efficient members of the

Choral Society, Hilton was active in the management of both the College and the University Clubs and Societies.

The Boat House, which dates from 1884, was his work. Hilton fought a lively battle against the Chapter over the issue of its appearance, the canons favouring black painted brickwork, he the plain red brick. A quite clever and amusing little poem, 'Durham Banks', which appeared in the *Journal* in this year, and celebrated the struggle, implies that Hilton lost this part of the battle, the red brick piles having been 'blacked' at the insistence of the Chapter.

What also deserves recording is Hilton's devoted service to another well-loved 'Varsity institution. In W. Hooper's somewhat curious words:

he contributed very largely to the initiation and perfecting of the annual gathering known as 'June Week'.

To Hilton also the whole University owes the 'beautiful cricket-field which is the envy of the other Northern Universities.' He it was who 'secured it for us, he financed it, he added to it, he managed it, he was still trying to improve it.'

Hilton, like all those who love Durham, and the Castle in particular, was a repository of stories about the place. And he had the true lover of Durham's nostalgic yearning after a past which, in a place like a University, and especially a collegiate University, all too quickly slips away. Though a man dedicated to change, he was no slave to change for change's sake; for appealing customs such as the following endeared themselves to him. In his early days it had been the custom, when one of the dons was going away by train, to notify one of the university police-men. That worthy man, in a top hat with a gold band, brought along a cab, rode on the box to the station, and proceeded to the ticket office in front of his charge, where he bought him a first-class ticket. Hilton, bearded, ami-able, his finger-tips together, would add, when recounting this story: 'Ah, those were the days!'

Certainly every Castleman should remember Walter Kercheval Hilton whenever he sees the College's crest, for it was he who chose the College motto *Non nobis solum* . For him the words were no empty formula, pulled at random out of the Classical air: they expressed his entire philosophy for, as Dr Gee expressed it in his own Eulogy of the man:

he was constantly teaching us that the Castle was never meant to be for ourselves alone. We were never put here to lead a selfish life or to use upon ourselves merely the good things which we have here . . .

On account of bad health, Lake resigned the Deanery, and with it the Wardenship of the University, in 1894. He is only peripheral in a history of the College, but his minor achievements, as well as his eccentricities, merit him some small place in it.

Lake seems to have been a capable administrator who put the University's finances on a stable footing. His appointments to the teaching staff were, by all accounts, good; and he broadened the regulations of the University - none of which somewhat boring accomplishments make him in the least memorable. Certainly, under him the numbers in the Colleges crept up to and slightly topped the two hundred. But Lake's place in Durham history is achieved by his simply being an impossible man to get on with. Something of this knack of his for alienating everybody about him has been referred to already. Three short anecdotes deserve a valedictory place here.

A writer in the *Globe* on 13 June 1905, referring to Durham said:

I am reminded of an instance in which I was worsted in an informal contest in logic with another professor in that seat of learning. It was back in the eighties, and having spent three years in Edinburgh, I wrote to the Dean [Lake] asking, 'Will you be good enough to inform me if it is possible for a man who has kept three years at Edinburgh to receive credit for one year at Durham?' No reply was forthcoming, so I ventured to write again, and then received this laconic answer: 'You asked if it were possible. It is not possible, so by your own showing your letter required no reply.'

Again, Thomas Rogers once dining at a New College 'Gaudy', the guest next to him said, 'I suppose you are the only person in Durham that the Dean has not quarrelled with.' Rogers was able to reassure his companion that he had had a mighty row with Lake immediately before coming away.

Finally, at a Lambeth Palace dinner, Miss Tait, the Archbishop's sister, once asked a guest from Durham how 'they' were getting on there. 'Oh, very quietly,' the Durham man replied. Archbishop Tait, overhearing this, said: 'What, is my old friend Lake dead?'

CHAPTER 9

Fin de Siècle

The fractious Lake was followed by the much more amiable Kitchin who, like Waddington, was a scholar.

The new Dean seems to have been a progressive: at Durham he was particularly active in bringing about the admission of women students; and, himself a Liberal of the Lloyd George persuasion, he gave sermons at the time of the Boer War which inevitably, at that time of jingoistic hysteria, caused great offence.

Kitchin was a gentleman. Always impatient of bad manners, he was heard to expostulate at one uproar at Convocation: 'Gentlemen! gentlemen! If you are gentlemen.'

On 20 May 1895, a year after Kitchin became Dean and Warden, a supplementary Charter was awarded the University by the Crown. Its main provision was to permit degrees to be given to women. This heralded some measure of progress, but things were still very much awry with the University as a whole. In the main, it was the B.A degree which was at fault, since disastrously it could still be taken in two years. More, Convocation had become simply a rubber-stamp affair, University patronage being, as in the old days of Thorp, in the hands of the Warden: indeed it was commonly said that many appointments to the teaching staff were made in the Dean's drawing-room.

For a time however the focus of attention was less on the insular City of Durham and its University than on the brown Veldt seven thousand miles away. In the Cathedral City, as elsewhere, the Second South African War roused frenzied passions. The Senior Men of the Colleges patriotically echoed the sentiments of the men in their charge, of whom about seventy are supposed to have expressed their readiness to join a volunteer company, if permission were given to raise one. The news of the relief of Ladysmith, on March 1 1900, was celebrated by a great procession of students through the streets of Durham, a firework display on Palace Green, and the burning of an effigy of the Boer president Kruger on the Green, after it had been contemptuously carried through the town.

Thus it came about that an honorary DCL was conferred at the end of the summer term on the brother of the Earl of Durham, Captain the Hon Hedworth Lambton, who had brought up the naval guns to the relief of Ladysmith; and after Convocation, the horses were taken out of the carriage in which the two brothers were to ride, and the carriage itself was dragged by rejoicing students round the town. In the evening there was a torchlight fancy-dress procession organised by the Students' Representative Council. When the whole vulgar and sleazy war was over, another torchlight procession was cranked up in June 1902, to celebrate the peace; and in the summer term of 1903 a DCL was conferred on 'Bobs' - Lord Roberts.

With regard to this latter visit, the *DUJ* percipiently pointed out that 'the work of other recipients of honorary degrees has perhaps more direct claim upon the attention of a University', but there was of course no doubt that popular enthusiasm would be centred on Lord Roberts. It added that the reception accorded him would be worthy of Durham, and somewhat optimistically hoped that no opportunity would be afforded of greeting him in a fashion which, though hearty, might be injudicious. This was a reference to Lord Lambton's remark, after his being fêted at Durham, that he had never been so near death as when an admiring crowd of undergraduates insisted on dragging his carriage down the hill from Palace Green. 'It would be a pity', the *DUJ* wrote, 'if the soldier who has survived so many campaigns should find Queen Street more perilous than the Khyber Pass.'

After Plummer's retirement in 1902 the new Master of University College became Henry Gee, who came up to Durham with the reputation of being a good scholar, a good teacher, and a popular Vice-Principal of St John's College, Highbury, of which he had been the head for many years. Under Gee the College, whose numbers had fallen, filled up again, and in 1905 the number in residence reached a record. This increase in numbers though seems to have been general to the University as a whole; for Hatfield was full, the Unattached men formed a considerable body, and before long two new Colleges were to be founded: St Chad's in 1904 and St John's in 1909.

While what is to be briefly recounted concerns more the University as a whole than the College, clearly the effect of these events was of the greatest importance to University College.

One of the two main features of the early years of the new century was the timely shift of government from the Dean and Chapter to the Senate. The former had, for seventy years now, been technically the governing body of the University, though they rarely interfered with Senate; but the situation was, and was seen increasingly to be, an anomaly. Indeed, the Commissioners of 1862 had stressed the importance of vesting the whole government of the University in the Senate. The weakness of the present system was there for all to see: those responsible for governing the University were a small number only of men who represented a small interest, one moreover which was coming under increased pressure in an increasingly secular society. After considerable and very acrimonious discussion, agreement was reached between Durham and Newcastle on the general principles of a Bill which it was intended should be presented to Parliament as soon as possible. It was so presented, in January 1908.

It is worth noting that, in the prolonged discussion leading up to the Bill's presentation, the Durham graduates were for the very first time determined to flex their muscles. Oxford men ran Oxford, it was said; Cambridge men ran Cambridge; and Oxford and Cambridge men ran Durham, all too often without any great commitment to, or any great belief in, the University's future.

For many of these men - there were of course notable exceptions - Durham was a staging post; they saw little future in it, had less interest, and showed accordingly not a lot of will towards its improvement. In circulation were the acid comments of those who had come for a while, then gone away thankfully to their spiritual homes in the South. A Professor of Divinity had bewailed in Oxford his 'sojourn in Boeotia.' One Warden even had spoken slightingly of the place it was his task to govern. Another had spoken contemptuously of the 'rough lads' it was the unfortunate job of the Professor of Greek to teach. One who clearly had read Johnson said that the best thing about Durham was the railway line that led straight down to London.

It is these domestic aspects of the governing of the University by non-Durham men that Durham men found particularly galling. A Newcastle graduate, Sampson Harris, M.B., B.S., put the case neatly in a letter to the *Journal* in May, 1907:

A short time ago a writer to the *Journal* asked why was the

Palatinate purple never seen in the stalls of the Cathedral, but always Cambridge white or Oxford red. In the North-East of England, with its large population and wealth, Durham should hold its own with any university in the world - but we must submit to be managed by a Dean and Chapter - always either Oxford or Cambridge men - whose sympathies are entirely opposed to our University.

The *Journal*, in the Editorial of the same issue, summed up the graduates' grievances - and, quite fairly, the fears of the Chapter:

The Durham-Newcastle problem is still with us. Since the government of the 'Varsity is vested in a close and self-elected oligarchy, it may be reasonable to say nothing about it, but . . . The most prominent feature of the Senate is the infinitesimal number of Durham men upon it. Out of 17 members there seem to be only three who are Durham graduates by residence and exam.

Again, the aspect of Convocation is hardly less cheerful.

The question persists in rising: Is Durham now what it should be? Is she taking the place she ought to occupy as the University of the North? Is her influence what the influence of the third 'Varsity in England should be? We have heard strange things of her management in the past. We have heard of a time when scholarships were awarded on the nomination of members of the Chapter, and we have heard of a time when the funds of the University were kept in a chest and drawn on as required . . . When we see the sweeping changes which the present Bill forecasts, we might wail for the benefit of the Chapter: 'Your house is left unto you desolate' - but the Bill is not yet passed. We tried to state the claims of the Chapter justly. It is hard to be hoisted from one's position by children one has brought up; but this seems to be the custom all the world over.

The Bill's intricacies need not concern us here; but the chief changes were these.

There was to be a Chancellor, who was to be appointed not by Senate but Convocation on the nomination of Senate. There were to be eight Durham graduates on Senate, which as a result would be increased from thirty-seven members to thirty-nine. Three Durham graduates were to be appointed to the Council of the Durham Colleges. The seat of the University was to be at Durham - no mean victory this, since the danger had existed that it be moved to Newcastle, leaving only a dismal Theological stump at Durham.

The totally unjustifiable system of *ad eundem* degrees would be abolished. Under this iniquitous provision, any Oxford, Cambridge, or Dublin man could take his Durham degree simply by paying over a small fee. The Cambridge or Dublin LLD could even take the DCL at Durham in this fashion, and thereafter peacock it before an unsuspecting public as being possessed of two doctorates. No Durham man, of course, was permitted to take an *ad eundem* degree anywhere else.

Further provisions of the Bill were that the Dean and Chapter were given six places on Senate, and that the Head of any College or Hall of Residence with twenty-five or more students would have a place on the Council of the Durham Colleges.

Dean Kitchin now became the first Chancellor of a University which was to consist of two 'Divisions', one at Durham and the other at Newcastle. Durham was left free to develop along its own distinct and distinctive lines.

Dr Gee perhaps best expressed the changes at the sixth annual dinner of the Sheffield Association of Durham Graduates, in April 1910, when he said that 'the anachronism that in the twentieth century we should have been like a glorified choir school' had been done away with.

That first Chancellor, Dean Kitchin, who had presided at Convocation for the first time at the age of eighty-two, died three years later aged eighty-five.

CHAPTER 10

A 'Nineties Diarist: C.F. Turnbull

C.F. Turnbull, who wrote his memories of the College he loved over sixty years after he had left it, went up to University College from Rainton on 7 October, 1896. He went with a Foundation Scholarship in Classics. It is a prosaic account of his life there that he gives, dry, factual, not without some moralising; its distinguishing characteristic - understatement. And yet . . . 'I hardly realised at the time in what a good ground my lot had fallen, and I did not then know, as I later did, how beautiful and historically interesting my new home was.' And the word 'beautiful', together with the fact that sixty nine years later he saw fit to write it all down, just as it was, even to his failure, through illness, to get the expected First, show that the three years he spent in Castle represented some sort of transfiguration. Certainly the beauty of the place made its mark on him, for two Octobers after he arrived, when the realisation of how transitory was his stay there added an additional poignancy, he wrote how glorious the Castle looked ranged round the moon-flooded Quad. 'I expressed a wish,' he remembered all those years later, 'to be a poet, to express my feelings in immortal verse.'

Writing about the Keep (his first home was No.45) Turnbull recalls what we have already noticed of other times: the very hierarchical structure of the College. As a freshman, he was not supposed to sport his oak, and he could indeed be fined for doing so, by any second or third year man who caught him offending. The procedure was simply to send in the culprit's name to the Bursar, who thereupon entered the sconce on his weekly battels.

Social life among the undergraduates was much the same in 1896 as it always was and would be for years to come, with minor differences. Condensed milk then was 'in great demand', biscuits and cakes ('Windermere's at half a crown were favourites') were on hand for friends 'who would drop in in ones and twos or in hordes in the late afternoon after rowing or games . . . before changing for dinner.'

And there were then, as there always are, those merry men for whom social life took precedence over the academic. Such a man in Turnbull's time was Blackett, who held the record for sitting finals, since a Pass degree man could take the examination an indefinite number of times. Blackett was Captain of Boats one year, and at the same time 'President and King Pin of the College Musical Society.' He must have spent a fortune, Turnbull mused, on private coaches. Such jovial souls, like the Poor always with us, are always popular; and great was the rejoicing in College, in Turnbull's last year, when Blackett passed.

Blackett, for all that he diverted his energies into other than academic channels, must nevertheless have 'kept terms'. To remind the reader, Keeping Terms involved, as well as attending lectures, being present at morning chapel, held in the Galilee from a quarter to nine to nine every week-day, and dining in Hall at half past six. Any day on which one missed any of these three requirements was counted as 'lost'. However, as one was allowed to lose one day in four, the rule, certainly in the 'Nineties, cannot be said to have been stringent.

Turnbull was called early in the morning by Fred, who was gyp to perhaps half a dozen men altogether, and was 'very smart in his gyp's uniform with large buttons and tails.' He would bring from the Buttery two large jugs or tins of water, one hot and the other cold, and set out his young gentlemen's hip baths. He would clean their boots; and he would fetch from the Buttery the breakfasts they had ordered on being called. Turnbull saw a lot of Fred.

Not so though with the bedders who, despite their being 'by ancient statute *mulieres senili ac deformi vultua*', seem to have been, again perhaps also by ancient statute, rarely seen. However, they curtsied charmingly on entering or leaving a room, if a Castleman was studying there.

Turnbull had to be in College at ten of nights. The wicket-gate in his time was locked at nine, so that later entrants had to ring the bell, when 'Old William Robinson', or his daughter, would open up. Between ten and eleven there was a fine of sixpence, between eleven and midnight half a crown; and thereafter a guinea. William Robinson, who died in 1902 at the age of 88, was born in the year before Waterloo. Turnbull's *Memories* contain Old William's obituary, as it appeared in the *Durham Advertiser* of 20 June 1902, as well as the following (perhaps apocryphal) story about him:

A man who had been told he would be sent down the next time he came in after midnight slipped a sovereign under the gate before Old William admitted him. Next morning though he was rusticated for the rest of the term. Furious he asked Old William why he had reported him.

'Because you were late.'
'But didn't I give you a sovereign?'
'Yes, sir.'
'And you took it?'
'Yes, sir.'
'Then why did you report me?'
'I was bound to do my duty, sir.'

The coin appears as a guinea in the story as Turnbull was told it, but, as the writer remarks, 'guineas went out with George 1V' - hence the apocryphal accusation.

The formality of undergraduate life was often engaging. For instance, during one's first term senior men, as we have already seen, invited freshmen to their rooms by leaving their cards on them. Indeed formality seems to have been a characteristic of Castle life in Turnbull's day, not a surprising circumstance when one remembers the class background of most of the undergraduates, as well as the preponderance of ordinands among them.

The dons too were in the main in Orders. Turnbull gives short biographies of those who taught him. Dr Plummer, who was Master of Castle for close on thirty years, and whose edition of St John's Gospel achieved a worldwide reputation, was reported to be so thorough a scholar that he had counted the number of times the conjunction *KAI* (and) occurs in the original Greek. Turnbull recommends his readers, if they look for a specimen of Plummer's thoroughness, to read his notes on the first verse of the first chapter of this Gospel, in the Cambridge Greek Testament for Schools series. There are, he tells us, sixty pages of Greek text in this Gospel, fifty two pages of Introduction, and three hundred and twenty pages of closely printed notes! The Master lectured to Turnbull, throughout his three years, in Greek history and, in his first year, in Ethics. Turnbull tells us, thankfully, why Plummer was called Polycarp: it was because he had studied the Fathers so much.

Professor Kynaston, another notable scholar, taught Turnbull Greek and Latin Literature, and Composition. Camden and Browne Medallist and Porson Scholar at Cambridge, Kynaston published his *Theocritus* in the Clarendon Press Series. This had 'reached a fifth edition in 1924'. He was not however an inspiring teacher. Kynaston was a rowing man, who had rowed stroke for Cambridge. There is a photograph of him, when aged sixty-six, in Macfarlane-Grieve's *History of Durham Rowing*. This, Plate V111, facing Page 184, shows the white-bearded canon resplendent in a top hat (one of only three among a float of boaters) and flourishing across a copious middle a wealth of gold watch-chain. The Bursar, W. K. Hilton, was, Turnbull notes with detectable surprise, 'a Southerner'. He merits mention in Turnbull's *Memories* for two things. For having once remarked that 'a Yorkshireman was a man who from the top of the tower of York Minster could see more counties than there were.' And for being nick-named Agag: 'because he walked delicately.'

The formality of much of Castle life seems to have been counterbalanced by the ubiquitous ragging, which has already received mention in these pages. Few rags that Turnbull tells us of deserve immortality by being printed here, save perhaps a sophisticated one on a man called Gilmour, who had taken a violent (but alas unreciprocated) fancy to a member of a female orchestra which came to perform in the Town Hall.

Gilmour managed to get a letter to the lady, confessing his consuming passion for her, and asking her to meet him on Prebend's Bridge. Arriving at the trysting place, he found not just Her but - the entire orchestra. With conductress! One suspects that unsophisticated Gilmours were given this treatment in every town on the orchestra's tour.

Turnbull was cox for the College, and he also rowed. He was asked to cox the University crew for the Regatta of 1897, but refused: being 'a reading man' as well as a rowing one, he did not think he could spare the time. There is a lot in the *Memories* about the sporting life of '96-'99; but games played and races run or rowed are as ephemeral as yesterday's news - and indeed yesterday's rags.

Of more general interest is Turnbull's account of the club life of his years at Castle. Once again that characteristic formality makes itself felt. Some of this, one suspects, must have been due to the greater seriousness of the age; but one must remember too, as I said, that many of Turnbull's contemporaries were destined for the Church. Most of his friends indeed. He gives later, at the end of these *Memories*, a list of those who 'became digni-taries of the Church.' There were:

Adams an Archbishop (of the Yukon), Bennet [sic] a Dean, Phillips a Canon, Palmer a Prebendary, Bagshaw [sic] Domestic Chaplain to the Earl of Londesborough, Gillingham a Chaplain to King Edward V11, [and] Gillingham, Knight, and Froggatt [became] Hon Canons of Southwark, York and Durham respectively.

Few Castlemen who have had experience of it would recognise the once prestigious Read and Weed in the even more prestigious *Patres Placidi* of Turnbull's day. Turnbull, who was 'elected on Wed. 10th Nov., 1897', gives a very full account of the *Patres Placidi*, who 'on special occasions' called themselves 'the Mystic Nine.'

Men did not apply to join, so blackballing (an odious thing really) was avoided. A man's name was proposed at one of their meetings, and, if agreed to unanimously, he was invited to join . . . The club met on Tuesday evenings at 8.30. On the table was an alabaster death's head, life-size, lit up by a wax candle inside. We wore a special club blazer, with a skull and crossed churchwarden pipes on the pocket, and the motto *While I smoke I read* in Latin underneath, *Dum fumo lego*. Hence the alternative name, since while we read aloud a play of Shakespeare, we solemnly smoked (or, in some cases, pretended to smoke) long-stemmed white clay pipes . . . Everything was done in due form, the Secretary advising each member, by letter, on special Club notepaper, bearing, in addition, the College arms, what play would be read at the next meeting, and usually assigning parts, though (but this was rare) parts were sometimes not assigned and we read in turn. This notification beforehand gave members, if they wished, an opportunity of reading their parts beforehand, and made for a more finished and enjoyable performance . . .

On winning the University Classical Scholarship I had solemnly conferred on me the title of Avus, and so was no longer Pater, but Grandpater . . .

It was all very enjoyable, reading for an hour, and ending up with tea (or coffee) and cakes, and animated talk for another hour or so.

Two further accounts of the proceedings of the *Patres* add a good deal more colour to this rather prosaic general description. On 16 November 1897 Turnbull wrote up his diary after his own initiation. The Masonic intimations make interesting reading:

Ordained a member of the Mystic Nine tonight in Trietschel's [a fellow undergraduate's] rooms - incense - death's head - Ego Pater te Patrem saluto - oath - solemnity - eyes blindfolded - suddenly on floor on rug - raised: presented with emblem and declared Pater. 8.30 Romeo and Juliet in Adams' room. Coffee - disbanded at 10.

And on 1 November 1898:

At ¼ to 8 Howard (*Pater Supremus*), Turnbull (*Avus and Pontifex Maximus*), and Adams (*Sponsor*) initiated Cummins and Evans in due style to the *Society of the Mystic Nine* . Great sport, especially our dresses. Met in Howard's rooms. The initiation in Adams'.

Turnbull, together with his friends Koch and van der Heyden, came together at the start of Turnbull's second year in another gathering which, while not a club, was a successful literary fraternity. This Literary Trio were

to meet turn and turn about in one another's rooms on Sunday evenings at 8 o'clock, to read aloud an essay by a well-known writer, each member reading quarter of an hour till the essay is finished, and to discuss it, when read, till 11 o'clock, when the meeting should break up - the host of the evening to write . . . a summary of the discussion, the said summary to be read out at the beginning of each session, like the minutes of a meeting.

These evenings tended, of course, to go on longer than 11 o'clock. The list of essays read is impressive, and says a lot for that seriousness of Turnbull and his friends which has been referred to above. At the first meeting, Arnold's 'Spinoza and the Bible' struck the required note. Macaulay on Machiavelli; Grant Allen's 'recent book about God' (probably *The Evolution of the Idea of God: an Inquiry into the Origins of Religions*, Grant Richards, 1897); the autobiography of Mrs Besant; Carlyle's 'Inaugural Address at Edinburgh, 2 April 1866, on being Rector of the University'; Arnold's 'The Study of Poetry'; Froude's 'Essay on Spinoza' and 'The Science of History'; Döllinger's 'The Policy of Louis X1V'; Macaulay on Pitt; Carlyle again on 'Boswell's Life of Johnson'; Arnold again on Milton and Keats; Carlyle on 'The Opera'; Romanes on 'The mental difference between man and woman'; unidentified essays by Döllinger, Schlegel, Sainte Beuve and Dowden, as well as others by the Trio's favourites, Arnold, Carlyle, Macaulay - these form an impressive list.

Interestingly, Turnbull disclaims any thought at the time of deriving practical advantage from these readings and discussions: 'we engaged in them purely for pleasure and intellectual enjoyment.'

Also interestingly, and rather strangely, that Movement which has come to be inextricably associated with the 'Nineties, the Aesthetic Movement, seems to have completely passed the Trio - though perhaps not others in the College - by.

Not all College life was conducted at this superior level. In marked contrast to the *Patres* and the *Literary Trio*, a group in Turnbull's third year, of whom he so thoroughly disapproved that he disclaims knowledge of their names even, set themselves up to 'make as much noise as possible in one another's rooms.' The life of the 'Brass Button Brigade' was necessarily of short duration; the very energy they expended must surely have burned them out quickly, even had the disapproval of 'the men generally' not been visited on them. Turnbull recalls hearing them, on the occasion of someone's twenty-first birthday, 'roaring out songs accompanied by a horn, till they were tired.'

Turnbull's account of his Third Year makes sad reading. A Foundation Scholar and a First Year Exhibitioner, he was now also a University Classical Scholar, and thus might, according to custom, 'look confidently to a First Class in his final.' His friends Adams and van der Heyden, who together had won the University Mathematical Scholarship, looked equally confidently towards their Firsts; and they were not disappointed. The wording of Turnbull's Scholarship Award also gave him confidence. While the other two Awards pinned up read merely, 'The Hebrew Scholarship is awarded to . . .' and 'The Long Reading Prize is awarded to . . .', that announcing the Classical Scholarship read: 'The examiners are unanimous in awarding this scholarship to C.F. Turnbull, University College.' It was signed by Kynaston, Plummer, and one H.A. White (a triple Oxford First).

While he seems to have been a good examinee, Turnbull only rarely did not think he had done miserably. Once was in the Theological portion of his finals, which took place in December 1897. He was questioned on Paley's *Evidences*, Greek New Testament, St John, and the Acts. While on this occasion 'all our men passed but one', the 'plough lists' in this partic- ular examination had in the past been somewhat heavy - 70%. In Classics, however, Turnbull need not have worried; he had sat, when seventeen, for a Senior Classical Scholarship at Cambridge and been placed third in a year when the second man was so good that the examiners awarded two scholarships instead of the usual one.

But - in his seventh term Turnbull's health broke down. He took the whole term off.

The Master, Plummer, took the unusual course of excusing him from keeping the full nine terms, and he returned to College for Epiphany term, to take his finals in June. He moved into 6 Hall Stairs.

Turnbull's Finals, in that year 1899, began on Saturday 10 June. The Pass-list came out at four o'clock on the 16th. He had got a Second.

What is engaging about this dead and gone Castleman is his modesty: indeed his humility. Though 'a brilliant First' had been confidently expect- ed, and one of the examiners had been overheard saying that 'Turnbull had done a brilliant paper in Ethics', he can write the following:

> I was not woe-begone because I did not gain a First. No, I was too thankful at having gained a Second. Firsts are quite rare, at any University, and all my family and friends were delighted. To break down early in November, to be forbidden to study, to miss a term, so near the date of the Finals, to be given the all-clear as it were on the 7th March, and to have to sit a gruelling examination lasting five days only three months afterwards: who was I to dare to expect even a Second?

Turnbull died in 1967. His death was recorded in *Castellum* in the fol- lowing year.

Charles Frederick Turnbull: schoolmaster at Scarborough, educationist, Italian lexicographer, Latinist in life as well as in letters, lover of your College; Castlemen such as you need no eulogy. You are, when all is said and done, part of the weave of the College: like the pocked yellow walls of Master's Garden, the Spring wallflowers along the cobbled path to the wicket, June Balls now dust and for some the dullest of ashes, and yester- day's laughter come flinging out of evening windows in the Keep. As you yourself would have put it: the *genius loci* - the everlasting spirit of the place.

CHAPTER 11

War and Inter-War

It might have been thought that, following the passing of the Durham University Act in 1908, and the death of Dean Kitchin in 1912, the University, and the College with it, would have prospered. The tragedy of the Great War put paid to any hope in that direction.

If Jingoism was to be seen, and particularly heard, in the country at large, it is not to be wondered at that it was to be found in the Universities, stocked as they were with that ideal cannon fodder: young men of intelligence and ideals.

The *Durham University Journal* in the immediate pre-War years makes sad reading, containing as it does continual references to that War Spirit which, as much as anything, contributed to the impending catastrophe. National Defence, patriotism - both are to be found nasally braying in issue after issue. Worse, the *Journal* of June 1915, after the Battle of Second Ypres and the first rolling discharge of gas over the British lines, asked the preposterous rhetorical question: 'how can a man die better and more nobly than on the battlefield?'

As early as 1904 some Hatfield men had formed a University section of the 4th Volunteer Battalion of the Durham Light Infantry. This was superseded in 1909 by a contingent of the Officers' Training Corps. The *Journal* of course took a keen interest in this latter organisation, which R.B. (later Lord) Haldane had established as part of his Army Reforms of 1906 - 1912. The *DUJ* of March 1909 reported that the Durham OTC, in proportion to the number of students, was the strongest of all the contingents so formed; and Haldane spoke to its members as follows: The university was . . . a place which should train for every phase of public duty. It should train for every one of the higher phases, and national defence was not the least of those phases. It was part of the law of the land that every man could be called upon to defend his country in time of emergency, and if that was their duty, it was a duty for which they ought to prepare.

Three of the officers of the OTC of those days were A. A.

Macfarlane-Grieve, 'Willie' Prowse and W.D. Lowe. The contingent had a good deal of pulling power, and indeed it is hard to believe that its members did not have a thoroughly enjoyable time. They drilled on Palace Green, doubtless impressing the impressionable young women who flocked to see them; and they went off to various jolly destinations for training and manoeuvres.

In March 1914, for instance, the *DUJ* reported that

'A' Company of the DUOTC put in its annual week of training in barracks at the end of the Epiphany term, the majority entraining in the Saturday night, March 14th. Richmond, Yorkshire, was again selected as our destination. The first - and largest - party travelled in the early evening under the command of Second-Lieutenant A.A. Macfarlane-Grieve, to be followed later in the day by another party, just released from the torture of the exam halls, commanded by Corporal Sladden . . . total 67. Captain Lowe and Lieutenant Longdon joined us during the week.

Sergeant-Major Prowse . . . [said] 'We do not forget how much [of the keenness and alacrity] we owe to the untiring energy and infectious enthusiasm of Captain Lowe, which is now clearly reaping its reward.

Both Macfarlane-Grieve and Lowe continued their connection with the OTC after the War. In 1914 Macfarlane-Grieve joined the 4th Highland Light Infantry as a Second Lieutenant; he left it in 1918 a Captain, having won the Military Cross and the Italian *Croce di Valore*. On his return to Durham, from which he had graduated in Honours Mathematics, he was appointed Adjutant of the OTC in July 1919. In 1927 he was appointed Commanding Officer, with the rank of Major, resigning this post, after eight years, in January 1935.

Incidentally, a brother, G.M. Macfarlane-Grieve, who like Angus Alexander was a pillar of the College Boat Club as well as of the College Rugby Football Club, went as a Second Lieutenant into the 3rd Battalion, the Black Watch, at the start of the War.

Lowe, who was Bursar and Censor, left the Durham Light Infantry as Lieutenant-Colonel, having won the DSO and MC. His *War History of the 18th (S) Battalion of the DLI* was published by Oxford University Press in 1920.

While young men like Macfarlane-Grieve and Lowe, together with the younger dons, went off to the Front, the University, and the College with it, seized up. Hatfield and St John's were commandeered. The cases in the Museum were piled on one side to make a temporary lecture-room. There were but a handful of students: a few women, fewer men and those physically C3, and some *mutilées de guerre* . College life was drastically affected, the Rugby, Cricket and Boat Clubs being of course quite unable to survive. Other College Societies also felt the pinch; they met just when they could - and that was infrequently.

When at last the endless war came to an end, things struggled slowly, painfully, back towards some shadow of the normality that had existed before the cataclysm. Students came crowding back. These were not, however, the callow youths of before the War, but for the most part mature men who had fought, killed, and suffered.

Much the same situation of course occurred after the Second World War, when the Government of the day, repeating what had been done in 1918, provided grants to ex-service men to return to University to take a degree, had they been up at the commencement of what was euphemistically called 'hostilities', or to take up residence for the first time if their university career had been postponed.

Certain important changes had recently been made in the University regulations governing the Arts course which were certainly for the better. For instance a B.A. degree other than that *in litteris antiquis* was instituted in 1910. The courses for this were exactly the same as those for the old B. Litt., which was accordingly dropped in 1912. The drawback to the B. Litt. was that while in theory it was to take three years, the first year examination could be taken before one came up to University; thus a year was saved - but at the expense of Durham's reputation, for its name as a place to get a cheap and easy degree was firmly established. The new B.A. degree required a second-year examination and a final in the third. And in 1918 the dreadful two-year pass course *in litteris antiquis* was abolished, necessitating every undergraduate from that time on to stay up for the full three years. Between 1913 and 1917 too, several new schools were added to the somewhat restricted choice open to selection, namely Classics, Mathematics and Theology. Honours schools in Science began in 1913.

The War had been over only a year when Dr Gee gave up the Mastership of Castle. He had, it will be remembered, succeeded Dr Plummer in 1902.

Gee, now become Dean of Gloucester, was succeeded by Henry Ellershaw, miraculously a Durham man, who had been a Foundation Scholar in 1883, and subsequently Newby Scholar (1885) and Van Mildert Scholar (1886).

Ellershaw was a Hatfield man. He was a keen oarsman, who rowed in the senior crew. After taking only a Second in Classics and Theology, he was, somewhat surprisingly, made Fellow of the University. After being ordained he became Chaplain of University College, and later, Lecturer in Classics. Although he was a graduate in Classics and Theology, his great passion since boyhood had been English Literature, and indeed in 1910, while still Master of Castle, he became the first occupant of the newly constituted Chair of English.

Ellershaw was clearly able to combine both jobs successfully, as a lengthy article of his on Byron shows, which was spread over two issues of the *Durham University Journal* in 1925-6. He was Vice-Chancellor during the last two years of his life. He died in 1932.

Ellershaw was a good-looking man - for a change, one not heavily bearded - and genial, if at times sardonic. The *DUJ* of 6 June 1932 painted a touching picture of his last days:

> The last months of his life were very sorrowful; the loss of his youngest daughter, followed so quickly by that of his brother, sadly depressed his usually cheerful spirit, and a good many of us noted with some anxiety that the Master's step was not so brisk as it was.

Rosalind Ellershaw had died on 13 December, on the boat on which she was returning from a holiday in Sweden.

Ellershaw was no great scholar but he was apparently an eloquent and inspiring teacher. Whiting, in his *History of the University*, writes rather curiously that he 'hated that showy and pretentious kind of writing in which the style seems everything and the matter nothing.'[1] An assessment which perhaps reflects Ellershaw's less than flamboyant scholarly attainments, and one which is borne out by a Newcastle colleague, H.L. Renwick, who in the June 1932 *DUJ* wrote of him:

> I do not suppose anyone would claim for Henry Ellershaw penetrating or exhaustive scholarship in any one branch of his subject . . . But he had the qualities most necessary, and most effective, in a

teacher of English Literature - wide reading in more than one field, a deep love of the best, and keen enjoyment. Accordingly he was shy of symptoms of budding scholarship in honours students . . .

Macfarlane-Grieve, in an obituary in the *DUJ* of June 1932, pointed out that Ellershaw's period as Master of University College came at a time of extraordinary difficulty. For one thing, he succeeded Gee after an interregnum of more than a year, which year moreover covered the last few months of the War, when 'the College had very nearly ceased to exist.' His first term as Master was Michaelmas 1919, and this, as has been said, marked the beginning of the return to normal conditions. Further, almost as soon as he became Master the fabric of the Castle began to cause serious anxiety, and in the years following, Ellershaw gave all his energies to the work of educating and organising local opinion to the danger threatening the building, until the first appeal for funds to preserve the Castle was made. As the appeal for funds widened he never missed an opportunity of arousing interest in the work, and it was a great relief to him when the Pilgrim Trust came forward with the generous contribution that it did.

Another casualty of these immediate post-war years was William Douglas Lowe.

Lowe was born in 1879 at Kearsley Moor, 'a cockfighting colliery village' near Bolton, Lancashire. He went to a Mr Tudor Owen's Preparatory School at Llandudno, from where he won an Entrance Scholarship to Shrewsbury, where he was from 1893 to 1898. Lowe was primarily a rowing man, though he did run, and played football for his house for three years. He began his rowing career in his house second boat, bottom of the river, and ended top of the river in the first boat four years later. He rowed in the School eight against Bedford, won the school sculling, and the School pairs. With all this, he still found time to play three times in the winning House football team, to win the mile and two-miles in the School sports, and to become School 'huntsman', or 'captain of the runs.' Eventually he became head of his House, and for two years was a praeposter.

Shrewsbury in Lowe's time was under the notable Head Master Moss, who laid down in the young Lowe the foundations of his classical scholarship. Armed with this he gained an open scholarship at Pembroke College, Cambridge, which he entered in 1898. He took to rowing seriously at

Cambridge, and rowed in the winning boat in the Senior College Trials; but was then forbidden to row on medical grounds. Despite doctor's orders, he did row in the ensuing Lents, making four bumps; but concentrated thereafter on coaching. Lowe still ran, representing Pembroke two or three times against Christ Church, Oxford, and obtaining second place in the handicap mile at the Cambridge University sports. As if this were not enough (one must not forget he got 'his First' in the Classical Tripos) Lowe also served two years in the Volunteers - that precursor, as we have seen, of the OTC.

After a year in Germany, Lowe became a master at Radley; but within the year he was invited by Henry Gee to come to Durham as Junior Censor and Classical Tutor at University College. Here he remained, taking a Durham M.A. in 1905, and lecturing in the University on Education and Classics. In 1913 he succeeded his friend W. K. Hilton as Bursar and Censor of the College.

Inevitably Lowe became a rowing coach, coaching two 'Varsity boats who beat Edinburgh, four who won the Wharton, and six Senate boats.

In 1909 he was made a Doctor of Letters at Dublin University, in recognition of his work on the *Cena Trimalchionis*. Lowe, being one of the earliest members of the Officers' Training Corps in Durham, was called up a few days after the declaration of war, went to Newcastle to lecture to cadets, and then helped to train the 'Pals' battalion of the Durham Light Infantry, first at Newton and then at Cocken Hall. It was with the 'Pals' battalion that he went to Egypt and France, won the Military Cross and the Distinguished Service Order, and was mentioned three times in despatches. Eventually, after being transferred to the Yorkshire Light Infantry, and briefly to the 11th East Lancs, he commanded the 18th DLI till the end of the war. At the Armistice he became Acting Brigade Commander, and then Commander of the St Omer district.

After this highly adventurous, and astonishingly undonnish, military career he returned to Durham as Classics tutor, and here he stayed till his untimely death in May 1921.

Lowe was clearly a man of inexhaustible energy, which was not, as it so often is with academics, channelled into a single source. As if all the above were not enough, he found time to become a Freemason (in 1907), and thereafter a Royal Arch and a Mark Master Mason. He found time to edit the *Cena Trimalchionis*, and Longus' *Daphnis and Chloe*, and cooperated with

E.D. Stone in a memoir of Herbert Kynaston. He also edited thirteen text-books for the Clarendon Press. He translated under the title *A Prussian Cadet* Szczepanski's *Spartanerjünglinge* and Von Wildenbruch's *Das Edle Blut*. His *War History of the 18th Battalion of the Durham Light Infantry* has already been referred to.

It is a tribute to his connection with the College that Lowe's coffin, before its removal to the churchyard at Hinton St George, Somerset, was allowed to rest at the head of the Black Staircase.

After certain bequests, Lowe left all his books to the College to form the nucleus of a College Library, as well as a sum of money to provide book-cases. What the *Journal* called University College's 'annual reunion din-ner', on 15 January 1925, ended with an adjournment to the Lowe Memorial Library for a preview. Formed in 'a large room overlooking the Fellows' garden, the grey colouring of [its] walls and bookcases is very attractive, and the library will look equally well by night or day.' The Library was officially opened in the following month, its opening coincid-ing with the dedication of the new organ in the College Chapel - a memo-rial to those Castlemen who died in the war. In the afternoon of 19 February 1926, Lowe's sister, Miss Lowe, Head Mistress of the High School at Leeds, formally opened the Library. The room chosen for it was a room used by Lowe: his friends had decorated it; and Professor John How (later Master of the College) presented the portrait of him which is placed in the mantel above the fireplace.

The Lowe Cup, awarded annually at the Regatta, is another reminder of his name.

Lowe turned his hand to poetry, not only in Greek and Latin, as would be expected, but also in English. There is a 'Coronation Song', which writ-ten in 1911 bears the hallmark of the more awful qualities of the pompous and materialistic (though really rather jolly) age in which it was written ('music by A.D. Clarke, L.Th. U.C.'), and there is also a 'Durham University Song' ('music by John H. Batten, Mus.B., Hatfield'), which was 'entered at Stationers' Hall.'

This latter song was written in about 1905, the year in which Lowe took his Durham M.A. Clearly, the place had already begun to exert its magic on him. The words are to be sung 'With Vigour'.

You will find the song in the Appendix.

A little earlier than Lowe's death, in 1921, occurred that of one of the great characters of Durham's non-academic servants: Joseph Plato Freeman, the Senior Verger of the Cathedral. As he had at one time been head butler of University College, he deserves a mention here.

What Freeman did not know of the Cathedral, said his obituarist in the *Journal*, one could be certain that no one else knew. It was a tribute to his antiquarian knowledge that he was at one time President of the Durham Archaeological Society. The *Yorkshire Post* contained a lengthy obituary of this Prince of Vergers by one Arthur R. Dolphin, which deserves picking over.

Dolphin wrote that one evening during the war, in the largest hotel in Glasgow, he found himself one of a circle of a dozen people seated round the smoking-room fire. The guests came from America, Honolulu, New Zealand, France, Australia, and Japan. The talk turning to Durham, all were agreed that, while the cathedral was indeed remarkable, what impressed them even more was the verger who had shown them round - Plato Freeman.

His knowledge of the City, the cathedral, and the undergraduates was encyclopaedic, and he had that socratic method of imparting knowledge about all of them that befitted his name.

Freeman would take his parties round from morn till eve, returning home when his long day closed 'worn clean out, absolutely done, hoarse and footsore.'

Only once was this Prince of Vergers known to have been angry with one of his 'guests'.

A lady was amongst a party he was conducting round the library; and as he called their attention to the frescoes on the walls beneath the great hammer-beam roof, she displayed her acquaintance with similar ones somewhere in Italy. 'Yes, I have seen them,' said Freeman. And of Cathedrals in France. 'I have seen those also,' said Freeman. 'But how is it that a man in your position has been able to travel so much in Italy and France?' demanded the lady. 'Madam,' replied Freeman, 'we vergers are able to do a great deal, we are even able to overlook such a question as that.'

Arthur Dolphin ends:

[Plato Freeman] was one of Nature's gentlemen. He could have filled with credit any position - he travelled abroad with a Professor of Divinity; he went for a long day's fishing with the inventor of Greenwell's Glory; he dined with a director of Armstrongs; he cut up pigs by the score to feed starving British prisoners; and year after year he fed the inmates of the Durham Workhouse with their Christmas dinner. I never found the subject of which he did not know something, or the patch of life in which he showed no interest.

---

1)   Whiting, pp.240-1

CHAPTER 12

The Castle in Danger

While death laid its hand on so many of the great ones of Durham in the years just after the war, the secret ministry of Mutabilitie was scratching at the great stones of the Castle which might have been thought to outlast eternity. For built not on solid rock but on a bed of made ground, of sandy clay, broken freestone and underlying shale, the foundations were already insufficient without the heavy buildings which successive bishops had overburdened them. In June 1921 ominous cracks, which appeared to be of some years' standing, were first noticed in Castle Hall. Careful watch was kept on these, and then in May 1922 evidence of fresh movement showed that these were extending. At once the matter was reported to the Estates Committee, and at the same time a request for permission to open out and examine the foundations was made. Although the Architect considered the failure was entirely local, in view of the great amount of Colliery damage in and about the City, permission to consult a mining expert was sought.

On the instructions of the Committee, steps were taken to verify the movement; the cracks in the Hall and in the buildings on the west of it were labelled; and steel wedges were inserted. Permission was also given for the foundations of the west wall of the West Courtyard to be opened out.

In November 1922 an interim report gave out 'that many of the labels were cracked, several of the wedges had fallen out, and that there was undoubted evidence that a movement was taking place, that the West Courtyard was built upon a thin layer of broken freestone, and that the wall had sunk eleven inches towards the north end, and that unless precautions were taken there was every probability of a collapse into the river.' It was recommended that the Courtyard wall and buttresses should be grouted and underpinned.

In July 1923 Mr Henry Armstrong, who had been asked whether the damage might have arisen from colliery workings, gave it as his opinion

210

that the failure was a local one and not due to these at all; whereupon the Committee called for a joint report from both Mr Armstrong and Mr W.T. Jones, FRIBA, on the state of the walls and foundations and the steps that ought to be taken to render them secure.

This joint report again recommended the immediate grouting and underpinning of the Courtyard walls and buttresses to arrest the movement that was undoubtedly taking place.

A shaft was accordingly sunk outside the Courtyard wall on the slope down to the river to find out the level of stable rock.

The Committee asked the opinion of yet another expert, Sir Francis Fox, before entering on the enormous and costly work already advised. Fox reiterated what the others had said: that the walls ought to be grouted by power to consolidate them before underpinning. This final recommendation was accepted by the Committee, who placed the work in the hands of John Thompson and Son of Peterborough, specialists in the use of the special process required.

The cause of the movement makes interesting reading. A shaft sunk upon the western face revealed that the broken freestone on which the west Courtyard was built overlies a bed of soft marly shale with layers of unformed coal seams, to a depth of at least twenty-eight feet. At this level a fairly hard stratum of rock is found.

The foundations of the west wall and buttresses of the Great Hall are placed on a bed of sand overlying the broken freestone and shale, at a height of forty-five feet above the rock.

The wall and its buttresses, erected on the brow of the steep slope down to the river, appear to have pressed down, and to have pushed outwards the intervening mass of soft shale towards the river. This mass of shale in turn carried forward the west Courtyard wall and buttresses, splitting and disintegrating both, making the wall sink down no fewer than eleven inches at its north end.

The effect of the pull of the Hall wall and buttresses was visible on their east side, half way across the width of the Hall, in the splitting and damaging of the ancient arches there. Traces of damage were also found in the east wall of the Hall.

Both the work that had to be done and the cost of doing it were enormous. The work involved:

a) The drilling and grouting by power of the damaged walls, the bonding of the horizontal fissures, and the cross stitching of the buttresses to the walls where necessary with delta metal.
The grouting process involved drilling holes into the walls and forcing in liquid cement under pressure. The ties were of delta bronze, which admits no corrosion.

b) The anchoring of the bases of the two buttresses of the west wall of the Hall by steel ties bedded in concrete to the base of the east wall.

c) The underpinning of the west wall of the west Courtyard down to the level of the stable rock with massive concrete buttresses. These, while carrying the wall above, would form a containing wall to the material behind, and thus counteract the thrust of the buttresses and walls of the Great Hall behind.

d) The underpinning of the massive buttress adjoining the west wall of the Brewery and Buttery above, the rebuilding of the north wall of the Scullery, and the strengthening and repair of Bishop Fox's Tower.

e) The cutting out of defective facing stones and refacing with new ones, the renewal of defective buttress slopes and their rebuilding in places; and the pointing and rendering weathertight of the walls of the west portion.

All this was to cost at least £30,000. To obtain a realistic valuation of this, by today's standards beggarly, sum we must multiply the figure by twenty-five; the cost of repairs would therefore be in the region of £750,000.[1]

There still remained the rest of the Castle. In 1904 the Norman Gallery had been tied across with three rows of steel ties, in order to hold up the south wall which was overhanging two feet three inches. What else needed to be done at that time but wasn't, for want of money, was the grouting of the foundations. Now that a grouting machine was in place it was thought sensible to use it, thoroughly to grout the walls, which were merely two skins of ashlar filled with rubble, and to try to consolidate the old earthworks, largely composed of sand, on which the whole building was erected.

The south wall of the courtyard adjoining the moat garden largely required rebuilding. At the time of inspection this was propped up with old telegraph poles! The whole face of the early Norman building adjoining the garden also needed a lot of attention, the ivy needed removing, and the south-east angle rebuilding. On the other side of the Gatehouse, the wall ascending the mound required grouting and almost completely refacing; the parapet needed rebuilding; and the wall rendered weatherproof.

The walls facing the Courtyard, especially that of the Great Hall and its buttresses, 'cried out for attention.' Bishop Cosin's porch needed renewal, the walls of the Great Stair and Tunstal's Gallery wanted attention - and all needed pointing to keep the weather out. All the hood or drip moulds to the doors and windows were defective and needed cutting out and renewing.

The north wall ascending the mound needed a good deal of refacing and pointing, as did the walls and buttresses of Moat Side Lane and the old flanking Tower in Brewster's Yard. The parapets of the kitchen needed rebuilding, as did several of the chimneys.

Finally - if with a building like the Castle there ever could be a 'finally' - the lead roofs of the Chapel, which had been tarred to keep out the damp, the Chapel Entrance Tower, and the Great Hall required recasting and renewing; much of the underboarding needed replacing; and the gutters needed levelling and relining.

Those of a technical turn of mind will be interested to know that the drilling, grouting and stone dressing was done with a 9-inch by 8-inch Ingersol Rand Air Compressor, driven by an electric motor of 30 h.p. The average pressure obtained was 75. The machine worked continuously two drills and three pneumatic stone dressing tools, and in addition frequently two grouting machines.

Such a sum as £32,000, the final estimate, was not readily come by in 1926 - the time of the Depression. The Council of the Durham Colleges had authorised the expenditure of £21,000; beyond that it could not go, and even so £6,000 intended for educational purposes had to go on the repairs. On 6 May 1925 an appeal was launched in the Great Hall for the £30,000 which, it was believed, was all that would be required for the Castle's preservation. The committee appointed to raise the money formed various sub-committees, including a women's committee and one to arrange public lectures.

By July 1926 only £15,000 had come in for the Castle Restoration Fund, although certain influential bodies were aware of what was at stake. The Royal Institute of British Architects gave £100; that it was not usual for the members of the Institute to make grants for such purposes says much for their realisation of the importance and urgency of the work. The *North Mail* and the *Newcastle Chronicle* were both active in promoting the cause, and their efforts brought in money, sometimes from unexpected quarters. A Colonial visitor to England sent in an anonymous donation of £2,500 to the *North Mail* and *Newcastle Chronicle* Fund, as an expression of gratitude for

his Majesty King George's noble work in war and peace . . What fitter memorial than to complete the restoration of Durham Castle, standing as it does between North and South, a thing of beauty on one of the seven hills?

Just as, on the foundation of the University, its founders had looked in vain to Industry in the North for funds, now their successors looked in vain to the same quarter for contributions. This time, however, the shortfall could not be said to be due to niggardliness. As Lord Joicey wrote to the Bishop of Durham on 28 August 1928:

I can quite understand it [the feebleness of the response to the appeal] to a certain extent owing to the unsatisfactory condition of most of the large industries in the North, and the very heavy taxation which has swept up most of voluntary gifts.[2]

By December 1928 the Appeal had raised only £24,000. A national appeal issued from the Mansion House in July of 1928 had met with a very poor response. The Bishop of Durham, Hensley Henson, asked in the Lords in the same month if the Government could help, but was told that nothing could be hoped for in that direction. Curiously, this was no manifestation of niggardliness on the part of the Government of the day; they were simply not empowered to provide anything. The quaint situation was that while the Castle stood, the Government was powerless. If however a large bit of the Castle fell into the river, then the Government was empowered to take over what was left in an upright condition and preserve it as a historic ruin.

Another meeting was held at Mansion House in September 1928, with the Lord Mayor in the chair. By now it had become clear that £150,000 was needed, £3,750,000 in today's money, and indeed £50,000 of this would have to be raised before the work of preservation could continue.

In 1929 the Prince of Wales, journeying to Newcastle to open the North-East Coast Exhibition, stopped at Durham on the way to inspect the work going on at the Castle. Accompanied by Dr J.S.G. Pemberton, Mr W.T. Jones, the Architect, and Mr Hopkins, the manager of the Peterborough firm in charge of the restoration, he went through the whole building, passing along the tunnel to the western walls, the seat of the trouble giving most concern. He saw the grouting process in operation, and was told in detail of the way in which the Castle, through the medium of steel rods, was being anchored to the hill, while concrete foundations were inserted to a depth of thirty feet below. Shown the cracks and fissures in the walls, the Prince said: 'This is a shocking state of affairs.' This sentiment did not of course, take either him or the Castle Restoration Fund very far; however, it was rather a jolly gesture.

1931 saw the big break-through, when the Pilgrim Trust of America gave £25,000 towards the preservation of the Castle. The Trustees were, it was said, moved both by the need for protecting a great historical monument and by the adverse economic circumstances of the County of Durham at the time. The Trust administered a fund of £2,000,000, which was designed 'for the benefit of Great Britain.' The gift came at a crucial time for, as the Bishop of Durham said in a lecture to the Northumberland and Durham Association in London:

> We have got to the most difficult and dangerous part of the work. After binding together the walls, we have to undertake the task of underpinning the foundations.
> The Harkness (i.e. the Pilgrim Trust) grant could not have been made at a better time. Much more money will be needed, preferably another £100,000, but I do not think it too much to say that this gift will carry us over the danger period.[3]

1934 saw the work still going on. The whole of the western wall had now been securely underpinned by a concrete base to a depth of forty-five feet down to the rock. In the excavation of the enormous chambers necessary, the workmen had passed through two seams of coal, both of good quality, one over two feet in thickness and the other, further down, about nine inches.

By now though the money raised was nearly exhausted, and a new appeal was necessary. The Pilgrim Trust came to the rescue again in 1935, with a further grant of £18,900, payable in instalments spread over the period ending March 1, 1937.

By this year, 1935, the underpinning of the wall of the Norman Gallery was approaching completion. That of the Great Hall remained, as well as general repairs to the floor and stonework in every direction.

Somehow the money was found and the restoration completed. One crisis for the College was over. In a year or two another, the Second World War, was nearly to destroy it - although, like the phoenix in its ashes, this held in embryo the resurrection of the College and its rising to an eminence undreamed of by those founding fathers in the Chapter in 1832.

1) Richard Roberts, Schroeder Merchants and Bankers, Macmillan
2) *Durham University Journal*, 28 December, 1928
3) *Ibid.*, March 1931

CHAPTER 13

Hesterna - Goddess of Unchanging Beauty

Ellershaw was succeeded in 1930 by the Reverend J.H. How, Professor of Latin. An elegant address, delivered by How to the Classical Association three years after he became Master, illuminates not only an eminently civilised Classic, but also the somewhat limited orbits of the College and of the University of his day.

He called his address 'Hesterna'. 'Someone,' he said,

> has already asked me who she is. I regret that Hesterna is not a lady, not even a local goddess. But the title sounds classical and is convenient.

He was being a little disingenuous. Hesterna was indeed no 'living' being; rather Yesterday, the Past elevated to deity.

How's are 'a few·random recollections of yesterday'; and he has interpolated them with what he calls 'a few rhymes', witty and elegant comments on the Durham of his day. They are, by any standard, infinitely superior to those of Lowe.

A modest man, How suggests these rhymes may perhaps 'lend a sort of low novelty to an otherwise humdrum address.'

He begins:

> It was only yesterday - a generation ago - that I received one fine summer morning two invitations, both from men personally unknown to me, one to a famous Public School, the other, from Dean Kitchin, to Durham.

Choice was difficult but, as one would expect from such a man, 'at length sentiment rather than calculation' took him to Durham.

> Its ancient buildings, its historical associations, its northern situa-

tion, its old-world atmosphere, its academic tradition, its supposed quiet and aloofness from the busy hum - these things attracted a solitary . . .

I came to look at the place, riding a pedal bicycle from Hertfordshire. Why not in a car? Because I hadn't one. It was before the motoring age. Young men were not then careering over the country in motor-cars and on motor-cycles, much less young women - though, I think, bloomers on bicycles were not unknown - *horresco referens!*

A sensitive, How saw for the first time 'with an almost physical shock', the massive pillars of the Cathedral nave.

In October 1898 he went to Hatfield Hall, and after a term found himself 'in charge of its discipline.' No unlikelier task for such a man invades the imagination for, it seems, the discipline needed tightening up.

In the end, official foes became often private friends, and continued to be so. How mourned that the Great War took its toll of them all. But, 'They made good in life and they died well', he says in true Roman style, 'and we may not grieve for them.' And he gives as convincing a justification for his astonishing opinion as one can find:

> O iuvenes semper, non vobis tarda senectus
> Debilitat vires . . .

> Oh you young for ever; not for you slow age
> sapping manhood . . .

Scanning the serried ghosts of his past, he summons first Walter Kercheval Hilton.

> Of the Dons I learnt most from W. K. Hilton. He . . . was a pluralist, Censor and Bursar of University College and Registrar of the University. We can enjoy the amenities of this College today; but before Hilton's arrival it had few amenities; it was ill-furnished and uncomfortable . . The Castle students of those days came from wealthier homes than most of them today, and they were often inclined to be unruly. But Hilton knew all that could be known about undergraduates.. His ironical aphorisms were famous. 'The undergraduate is

always wrong.' 'The undergraduate cannot tell the truth.' But the undergraduate seldom resented his Censor's flagellations. If he did, he probably deserved them. Hilton's cool judgment, lively wit and sometimes scathing tongue made him at once a dread and a delight. His efforts for the adornment of the Castle, his devotion to the Chapel, his furtherance of facilities for games cannot be too gratefully remembered. Utterly self-effacing, he lived on a mere pittance, stinting himself in his continuous generosity to others. A classical scholar, too, though he did not lecture. I still possess his Lancing Greek Verse prize, and I possess, also, Pandora's Box, as it was called, in which Dr Fowler treasured some of the clever topical skits that came from Hilton's quill. Like Dean Kitchin, he was devoted to Jane Austen's novels: he seemed to know large portions almost by heart. Shakespeare attracted and finally repelled him. It was on this wise. Dr Walpole, later Bishop of Edinburgh, asked me to join a Shakespeare reading society, a very select society indeed. Now I dislike reading societies, especially very select ones. So did Hilton. But I contrived to substitute him for myself. Before each meeting the parts were allotted by post-card. So far as I could tell from Hilton's acid comments, the allotment was often injudicious. At length he informed me with humorous acerbity that he was about to resign. He had just received a post-card on which was inscribed: 'Hilton - Old Man, Fool.'

Hilton did more for Durham and for Durham men than is generally realized. He had his foes, no doubt, and they feared him; but he had his friends, and they loved him. His death deprived me of my closest Durham friend. His portrait hangs in the Senior Common Room.

There follows a not inconsiderable poem, a threnody to How's closest Durham friend. After which he goes on:

There is a window to his memory in the Chapel he loved so well, with the following inscription:

Non hic, longinquo requiescis, amice, sepulcro:
Sed genio gaudent haec loca sancta tuo.

You rest not here, my friend, in this distant sepulchre but all
these sacred places rejoice in your spirit.

Another Latin inscription, on the Groundsman's house, which was built mainly out of money provided by Hilton, records his care for and improvement of the Playing Fields.

With his refined taste and good breeding Hilton was an ornament of Durham society; and the Durham society of yesterday was very agreeable, if perhaps a little more fastidious than today.

Pursuing his theme of the hierarchic structure of the Durham of yesterday, How is both amusing and instructive.

Social gradations were then [in the 1880's], I think, more marked than they are now. Hilton often made play with what he called the First, Second and Third Circles.[1] It was said the Durham tradesmen had a regular scale of prices varying directly with the distance from the exalted precincts of the cathedral and its neighbour Colleges. Perhaps a tradition from an earlier period of Golden Canons. The Golden Canons were gone, but their tradition remained . . .

There was then, as now, a great deal of friendly and gracious hospitality, so that it was often hard to find time, save in the small hours of the morning, to do one's more serious tasks, or, in a phrase once current, to do the work for which one was paid. Then, as now, Durham supported many causes - other people's amusement societies Dr Fowler called them. He counted ninety-six - it seems an incredible number - to which he contributed or was expected to contribute. But, though there were so many societies, academic meetings were far fewer, as was only natural in a smaller circle with a much more restricted range of studies. Today things are different. Academic meetings are multitudinous and never-ending. I was once the reluctant chairman of a syllabus committee which took three years, more or less, to make its report . . .

Yesterday the range of studies was, as I have said, much narrower than today. The Dons had all been trained in the old Classical tradition. The Mathematical Lecturer was also a competent Classic . . . The Modern Language Lecturer, now retired from the Board of Education, read Plato's Republic in Greek every year . . .

The curriculum consisted chiefly of Classics and Theology with a classical tincture. We pronounced Latin in the old-fashioned way. The 'reformed' pronunciation came in soon after my arrival, and presently I found in the same lecture three sets of students, represented by 'vicissim', 'veechissim', and 'we kiss 'im.' The last method was preferred to the others.

There were a few women students. I did not know what to say to them if they came late to lecture; but they seldom did . . .

How far we have progressed or, if you like, retrograded, may be felt at once if you weigh the Calendar of 1898 against that of 1933.

How continues with a Gilbertian comic poem entitled 'A Shorter Syllabus.' It begins:

> We've Classics at Durham
> For those who prefer 'em,
> And lines in Theology, too
> Hebraic Linguistic
> And late Hellenistic,
> High German and low Parley-voo . . .

and ends its nine stanzas with the oracular:

> Meanwhile we're extending
> Our business by vending
> Pure Science to any who'll try
> Our Chemistry, Botany,
> Physics, but not any
> Mining until by-and-by.
>
> So every sensorium
> Will find our Emporium
> Attractive, and quite up to date
> In practical polity
> Quantity, quality,
> Enter, for fear you be late.

As might be expected, How develops his theme into first a pious (but alas unfulfilled) hope that the Classics, which he could cheerfully write of in 1933 as far from dead, would 'long retain their vitality in a University where they have long been cherished'; and then into a number of vignettes of Greek and Latin scholars who taught at the University.

Foremost among these is Canon Evans, who was appointed by Bishop Baring in 1862 and was Professor of Greek for twenty-eight years. Though not a Castleman pure and simple, Evans deserves a place in this chronicle by virtue first of the fact that he taught generations of Castlemen, and secondly by his right to a pre-eminent place in the long procession of notable Durham eccentrics. His portrait hangs in Castle Hall: 'a grave face and a kindly, full of character.'

Evans began his education under a stern uncle, who disliked the east wind and put off lessons when it blew. The boy secured some holiday and an eventual thrashing by fastening the weather- cock in an eastward direction.

Dr Greenwell told How a like story of a Canon of Durham who, coming from the south and disliking the colder winds of the north, sent a workman to fix the weather-cock due south, and said he felt much easier in consequence.

Evans went on to Shrewsbury, then under Butler . . . He won the Hexameter Prize when quite low down in the Sixth. At Cambridge he won the Porson, but was debarred from Classical Honours by failure in Mathematics. [Evans had his revenge by writing his *Mathematagonia*, which twisted the theorems which had defeated him into Greek which defeated the mathematicians.] He taught first at Shrewsbury under Kennedy [Benjamin Hall Kennedy, of Latin Primer fame], and then at Rugby, where Benson, the future Archbishop, was a colleague and a comrade. His chief interests were in Language, Architecture and Religion. Beautiful words were a feast to him . . . Benson quotes an example of his copious vocabulary - an outburst against an awkward gate: 'Thou gate! Thou a gate! My wooden enemy! My ligneous barricade! My timber antagonist!'

Durham was the very place for the study of Evans' three abiding interests. But in only a year after his appointment to Durham, he was prostrated by the death of his wife. In the days of his depression 'he found solace in his habit of Greek and Latin verse composition.'

How describes Evans as

a remarkable man, a great scholar, truly pious, and possessed, with-al, of a sense of humour and of the gift of expressing it. He has been called an eccentric of genius. His only eccentricity was his absent-mindedness, that is, his complete absorption in his favourite studies. Sometimes, no doubt, it made things a little awkward, as, e.g., when he forgot that he had invited students to breakfast and was wholly unprepared for them when they arrived, or when his examination papers were not forthcoming at the appointed hour and had to be served later on wet from the press, or when he placed his boots on the book-ledge of his Cathedral stall, or walked home past the pulpit instead of mounting it to preach.

Evans' predilection for swimming in the open-air bath at Durham School produced one such moment of forgetfulness, which How described in a poem called 'Vestments'.

> A Master, weary grown of school,
> Set forth to seek the bathing-pool.
> But, ere he reached it, stood aghast
> To spy a figure fleeting fast
> Across a playing field, unclad,
> Or nearly so; for naught it had,
> Altho' 'twas midmost afternoon,
> Save swimming suit, tall hat, and shoon,
> Withal a green umbrella Fox
> Had framed to shade from Phoebus' shocks.
> In doubt the wondering Master ran
> To learn if this were ghost or man.
> A man it proved, of men a prince,
> More learned none before or since,
> A Canon, famed of absent mind,
> In scholarship profound, refined.
> 'Where, Canon, go you, thus arrayed?'
> Began the Master, half afraid.
> To whom the Canon: 'Why? What's wrong?
> I'm on my way to Evensong.'

Another story he does not altogether vouch for makes very amusing reading, all the more amusing for its being written by How in verse:

An Inadvertence

A Cleric, tired of widowed state,
Thought well to wed, albeit late,
And, conning o'er the fairer sex,
He set his choice on Mistress X.
On Monday straight he went his way
To ask her hand. She answered 'Nay.'
They met as usual; Monday came;
Again the Cleric pressed his claim.
The Lady (can we wonder?) grew
Indignant: 'Sir, 'tis strange that you
Should persecute me thus, and seek
The hand that I denied last week.'
The Cleric stared with puzzled frown.
At length: 'Dear me! I put it down
For Monday - "Mem: Ask Mistress X."
Of course I mixed the dates. 'Twould vex
St Cuthbert's self. I came too soon
And then forgot. Good afternoon.'

Almost as good reading as this last of his stories of Canon Evans.

Dr Greenwell told me that at one time Canon Evans became deeply interested in problems of thought-transference and the like. Dr Greenwell himself happened at the moment to be interested in the more pressing problem of how to find material for a sermon he was due to preach in the Cathedral within a week. Now, Evans took enormous pains with his sermons and was in the habit of retiring alone to the Chapter Library to declaim his sentences over and over again, as he stood or paced up and down. On the occasion to which I refer Greenwell also was in the Library, unobserved by Evans. The Canon's rehearsal began, and Greenwell, quick to seize a golden opportunity, took down the sermon as it was repeated, and on the following Sunday preached it in the Cathedral to the unbounded astonishment of its author. 'My dear Greenwell, I have long suspected, but now I am sure that there is some strange affinity between us. How else could you have preached almost word for word the discourse I was about to deliver?' Greenwell opined that it was indeed remarkable.

How ends this short monograph with an engaging story that tells us more than almost anything else about the man whom Evans was.

He died in 1889, and with almost his last breath he described in a final verse the dark-coloured medicine he had to take:-

Atrae iuvencae lac Acheruntium.

The milk of a black lamb, victim to the dark gods.

---

1) He was perhaps thinking of Honoré de Balzac's *La Fille aux Yeux d'or*; or more probably Dante's *Inferno* itself.

CHAPTER 14

A 'Thirties Miniaturist

Just as, in his old age, Turnbull recorded his time up at University College in the 'Nineties, so Canon Geoffrey Williams, long after he had gone down on his last Long Vacation, wrote his memories of 'Life in Durham Castle for a Student there: 1935 -1939.'

It is priceless documents such as these, which tell of events and things both substantial and insubstantial, ephemera even like the '12-paged brochure' on the Castle and the College which he was sent when he first enquired about a Theological Scholarship, which are the very stuff of history, and which throw open doors on ancient sunlight which might otherwise remain forever closed. Geoffrey Williams' memories of his Durham years are however written in such minute detail as to be almost a photographic imprint of those vanished years; they stand in a class of their own.

The young Geoffrey's request for information about the Foundation Scholarship in Theology which was to be held at University College brought him in the post a letter from the Master and the twelve-page booklet mentioned above. The letter was what one might have expected from John How, that urbane and most civilised, if rather ineffectual, Classic. It was written in How's own hand, and read:

> Dear Mr. Williams [the first time the recipient had been so addressed!],
>
> Thank you for your letter. I wish you every success in the Scholarship examination. I should be glad to see you when you come up for it . . .

The information about the College was contained in a twelve-page brochure 8″ by 6″ printed on blue paper which Geoffrey Williams assumed (much later) was intended to suggest palatinate purple. On the front cover was a picture of the Great Hall (exterior) and inside a series of articles, the

226

first naturally entitled 'In the Castle - information about University College, Durham.' The literary style adopted was rather elderly and a little painful. That first article alone would, adds Canon Williams, 'be guaranteed to repel from application any would-be scholar today.'

Apart from records, it is possible to read a great deal of the Castle's history from its very stones. Who can mistake the old Chapel or Pudsey's doorway? Who cannot read what the stones of the Gateway proclaim? When we look at the outline of the Southern windows of the Great Hall, or see its double portal, do not the very stones tell their tale? Is not Cosin's staircase a very portent among all the circular stone staircases which are to be found, either still in use or broken . . ?

The article, the Canon maintains, continued to intimidate potential boarders with the following:

every year adds to the tale of good men and true who leave its portals to do their best in the world and for the world, not unmindful of the inspiring words which form the motto of this place - Non nobis solum.

But perhaps Canon Williams is looking back at the 'Thirties through the black-comedy spectacles of the unfortunate young of today. Pick up any book of the period and you will find the same not-to-be-despised unworldliness, and unquestioning belief in moral values, in individual responsibility and a sense of mission.

But to continue. The text at this point was interrupted by 'a dark and very badly printed half-page photograph of the Great Hall (interior).' It continued with the vital statistical information that 'Entrance Scholarships of various values from £60 downwards' were offered for competition annually in March, and the fees were £115 per annum for the Arts course of three years, and £121 for the Science one. These amounts included the fees for tuition and three terms' residence each year of sixty days each, which included breakfast, luncheon and dinner each day in Hall. Students were expected to provide their own tea. Each student was allotted a set of rooms consisting of a furnished sitting-room and bedroom. He was expected to provide his own crockery, sheets and towels. There was also the 'encouraging information' that the College has recently been brought up to date by the addition of baths. Electric light has been installed in nearly all the rooms, and the kitchens have been provided with the most modern equipment.

The stripling Geoffrey Williams was further told that 'ample facilities for healthy recreation' were provided, and mention was also made of the possession by the College of a boat-house and a Fives Court. Those repelled by the physical were not forgotten, since

for the less energetic there is the College Library, the University Library and the Union Society where men of all the Colleges meet and Debates are held from time to time.

The assumption seems to be that the sportsmen were rarely or never to be seen in either of the Libraries or the Union Society!
Let Geoffrey Williams now tell his own tale.

If this language [that of the first article] seemed somewhat quaint, what followed made it pale into the basic English of pedestrian prose. Headed by a small photograph of Tunstal's Chapel (looking east) we move to . . . 'A Remembered Yesterday' by Sidney Walton . . .
'How I envy the man who is going to begin his College days in Durham, those golden cloistered days in that city of cities. Perhaps he has left behind that grey mass of industrialism, a modern town. He casts a look around the room allotted to him at the Castle, and stumbles upon the window. At once he is under the spell of it; the whole city at his feet, a silver ribbon of river running among the streets, the seven hills standing silently by and the sacred shadow of the Cathedral over the whole scene.'
That quotation is indeed a ruby, but surely this is more precious than rubies:-
'Turn, you fortunate "fresher" and look down upon the "Quad" below. There merry hints abound of a vigorous University life, full from morning to night of most varied interests. The "Quad" - what a pang the name is to those who have "gone down", and gossip there no more, but yearn for it as the delightfulest bit of greenery in the whole earth! - is chequered it may be with groups of men in rowing

"togs". But our talk was not all of sport and sunburnt mirth. Gay and merry enough we were, after the undying wont of undergrads, but still it came to pass, as I can see so plainly now, that the Castle held over us a sway of which we were unconscious at the time, and its silent and stately stones fashioned us unaware.'

We shall hear a little more of Sidney Walton in a later chapter. Remember though, reader, before you dismiss him as a hopeless Romantic, he came to Durham late, and from a barbaric background in the North, and he must have been eternally grateful for what he found in Durham, and in University College in particular, and filled with a sense of incredulity that such wonders as were there should have been opened to him.

Sidney Walton's rather fanciful whimsy was followed by a much more sober article on the History of the Castle by the then Bishop of Durham, Dr Hensley Henson. Hensley Henson had of course never been an undergraduate at Castle, and so was able to see the place quite untinctured by the rose-coloured spectacles of someone like Sidney Walton, who had.

Geoffrey Williams has no sure information about how long the brochure which How sent him had been used, but Hensley Henson was not appointed to the See of Durham until 1920, and indeed he later discovered that the Bishop's article was a transcript of an address given for broadcasting at Newcastle on 8 October 1925.

Young Geoffrey had neither visited Durham before nor even seen a photograph of the place; he therefore never forgot the shock he received when the train taking him there from Manchester 'emerged from the cutting and began the slowing process over the viaduct towards the station.'

Arrived at Durham, he booked in at the *Dunelm Hotel*, where a room had been reserved for him. The *Dunelm* was along Old Elvet and was owned by a one-time Mayor of Durham by name of Patterson [Pattinson?]. It is now no more, having been absorbed into the *Royal County Hotel*. The University seems to have had a long-standing agreement with the *Dunelm*, for intending undergraduates were also booked in there eleven years later, in 1946. The reason is not hard to find. As Geoffrey Williams points out, 'Although all the candidates would be fully or very nearly eighteen years of age, the *Dunelm* was the only one considered possible because it was the only temperance hotel in the city.' There he was told that 'those young gentlemen who had applied for admission into University College were

229

required to present themselves in the dining room at a quarter after nine o'clock . . . as the Master would be coming down to the hotel to see' them. Let Canon Williams take up the tale again:

Accordingly, after dinner about two dozen prospective Castlemen presented themselves and we stood in a circle, the tables having been cleared and put to one side. Eventually Canon How appeared, tall, bearded and wearing a winter's overcoat on the top of which was his academic gown. I do not think he removed his square throughout the interview.

With hands clasped behind his back he approached each youth in turn and began the interview with a grunt. The questions asked were identical and the comments predictable. 'What is your name?' 'Which school do you attend?' - if the school was known to the questioner a comment might be forthcoming. The third and last question was, 'Why do you want to come to the Castle?', to which the only possible response was 'because it is the best', even though the expected sentiment might be expressed with differing phraseology. 'Quite right' and a grunt with monotonous regularity and then the aged clergyman moved on to the next victim. The circle having been completed, the Master stood in the midst and said, 'I hope you all pass the examination,' raised his square and bade us goodnight. That was the only encounter we had with anyone from the University or the College.

How, incidentally, Geoffrey would soon have found out, was irreverently known as 'the Gazeeka', no doubt because of his singular appearance; for he was very tall and possessed of an abnormally long neck. Of him was written a ballad which began:

If I were the Gazeeka, I would, I would,
I'd sit on the Castle wall so hard
And show myself at a penny a yard,
I would, I would, if I were the Gazeeka.

The examination for a Scholarship in Theology consisted of two three-hour papers on the Bible, and one paper each on Latin and Greek, in which translations of English into Latin, and Greek and Latin prose and poetry unseens, dominated the questions. Young Geoffrey had set off for Durham on the Monday; his last paper was taken on Wednesday afternoon; and on the following Monday morning he received a typewritten duplicated sheet, clearly a copy of the one which had been affixed to the notice-board on Palace Green, telling him he had been awarded a scholarship.

How's grasp of the reins of government were, by all accounts, lax; doubtless he was more at home with the Latin and Greek authors he so loved and who were his evening's entertainment for, as he writes in 'Hesterna',

> The fragrance of a choice cigar
> Has crowned dessert and wine,
> And Muses, Greek and Latin, are
> Expecting me at Nine.

So he seems to have left his prospective Castlemen more or less to fend for themselves. Young Geoffrey received no further correspondence from him beyond that initial welcoming letter; and the Canon Geoffrey was to become writes that if he had not known a man who was at the Castle, who had been two years ahead of him at school, he would have been 'completely at a loss to know what would be required either for articles of clothing or books to have read or acquired.'

On the second Tuesday in October 1935, Geoffrey made his second journey to Durham, this time to stay for sixty days.

I had previously bought from Wippell's shop in Manchester a scholar's gown - full length with no split in the sleeve - not unlike what is called a Geneva gown. Commoners had a similar garment but the sleeve had a rent through which the arm could be placed . . . My former schoolfellow was on the same train and was kindly disposed . . . He accompanied me to the Lodge where I was introduced to the inimitable George Embleton, who had been the Castle porter from time immemorial. He had a redoubtable wife whom we all called Spondee, because she had two big feet. I was told that I had rooms in Bailey House and shown my pigeon-hole in the letter-rack. The day's first delivery of mail was set out in alphabetical order on a table by the door into the Hall so that we could pick it up on our way into breakfast. All other correspondence was deposited in the appropriate section in the rack in the lodge.

231

Unpacking, Geoffrey put his required two sheets on the bed so that his bedder could make it up when she arrived in the early evening. This was a far cry from the bedders' custom in 1947 when, having made the beds, they were not to be seen until eight o'clock the following morning.

Geoffrey's mentor now told him to go to the House of Andrews, there to buy a timetable of lectures which would cost him threepence. This necessary purchase was a large sheet of paper for pinning onto the wall; it carried a complete timetable of lectures for every year in every course, and the appropriate room in which the lecture would be delivered. Another necessary errand was to Gray's shop in Sadler Street - forced now alas by market forces to migrate to a shadow of its former self in a lane by the North Road 'bus station. Here Geoffrey bought himself a blazer. There were other garments which might - or might not - be bought, such as scarves, flannel trousers, cricket shirts, and sporting outfits of all kinds; but the blazer, Geoffrey found out, was a 'must'. He also found out that it was a peculiarity of Castlemen always to wear their blazers with the collar turned up at the back of the neck. The blazer too, he discovered, was to be worn on informal occasions only - never with an academic gown. There were two exceptions to this rule: the one, those occasions when the student went out to the local villages during the week before the annual rag, which was held on the penultimate Saturday of the summer term; the other, the 'Castle Wine', when the blazer was to be worn instead of a dinner jacket, though dress trousers and a stiff-fronted shirt were *de rigeur*.

Woolworths in the Market Place was the next port of call for Geoffrey - for crockery. It was of course possible to buy what one needed from a student who had gone down the previous term, or get what one wanted from one's gyp, who acted as a middle-man between his new master and his 'previous gentleman'. A kettle was indispensable; a reading-lamp desirable. Woolworths was still, in 1935, the 'threepenny and sixpenny' stores it had long been, but only clever manipulation enabled it to claim to be so. Since Geoffrey's table-lamp consisted of a number of exploded parts, the whole ensemble cost him half a crown: wooden base (6d - for which read sixpence), stem with bulb-fitting (6d), shade-holder (3d), shade (6d), bulb (3d), flex at 3d a yard.

Geoffrey was allotted an imposing suite of rooms. If, at the end of the year, he wished to change, he was told he might write to the Master, expressing his preference for a different suite; the Master almost invariably obliged. The sitting-room furniture consisted of an arm-chair, sometimes two, and a couch or a chaise-longue; with two, or even three, chairs, a book-case and a cupboard. The floor was usually carpeted. Apart from the bed, the bedroom contained a wash-hand stand and toilet-set: ewer and wash-bowl, soap-dish, tooth-brush holder, and slop-pail. There was of course a chest-of-drawers and a looking-glass. Whatever the slight differences between one man's room and another, in one respect they were all identical: every one contained its 'oak'. This outer door could be bolted on the inside; but bolted or not, Geoffrey found that its being shut indicated to the outside world that the owner was on no account to be disturbed.

Canon Williams' memories go on to deal with what he calls 'Academic Dress and kindred matters.'

Gowns of course were to be worn in all public places between the hours of nine a.m. and one p.m. and after dark. During the summer term dusk was considered as having arrived at nine p.m. It was therefore necessary for a gown to be worn when going to and coming away from the cinema. One was not allowed to smoke when wearing one's gown. An infringement of these rules, when discovered by either of the University policemen, or bull-dogs, Gray (tall and thin) and Plunkett (short and stocky), both patrolling until the 1950's, was reported on the following morning to the Praelector - one of the dons who was responsible for discipline - who would award the appropriate penalty: usually a ten-shilling sconce. No mean sum this in the 'Thirties, when many a man brought home two pounds ten a week, and almost successfully kept a wife and family on it.

Gowns were also to be worn at dinner in Hall, at all lectures, when visiting a don on academic business, and when attending divine service either in the College Chapel or the Cathedral. Undergraduates so dressed were permitted to sit in the Honorary Canons' stalls in the Cathedral at Matins and Evensong.

Gowns were obligatory too when sitting examinations which, being held in June, frequently occurred in hot weather.

If such were the case, the Invigilator would make an announcement before the examination began. This always followed a fixed formula:- 'Gentlemen may remove any garments they wish consistent with decency, provided that they replace their gowns subsequently.' This concession, for obvious reasons, was not extended to the women candidates, and amongst the men there was some speculation about the interpretation of the word 'decency'.

Dark jackets were also obligatory at dinner in Hall. The necessity of dressing for dinner on all occasions had been allowed to lapse after the Great War, but this particular compromise persisted. There was no regulation, Canon Williams noted drily, about the colour of nether garments. The interpretation of what constituted a 'dark' jacket was left to the Senior Man, who if he saw a jacket he determined was 'light' would pass a note to the offender informing him he had been sconced ten shillings. In the absence of the Senior Man, the Senior Scholar presided.

Formal dress, which for students usually meant dinner jacket and black tie, was worn at all evening engagements at which ladies were to be present, unless it was clearly stated on the notice or invitation that 'dress' was optional. This rule even included some all-male gatherings, such as the Visitors' Night's Debate, the College Wine, the Freshers' Concert, and any wine party or evening in a don's house. Subscription Chamber Music Concerts were held in the Miners' Hall, and one attended dressed. At Union Society Debates the President, the Secretary, and the four principal speakers would be dressed, and all would dress for Ladies' Nights and for Inter-Varsity Debates.

Dress was obligatory, of course, for all Balls or Society Dances except the Flannel dance, which was held in the Castle on the last day of the Durham Regatta, in June Week. At the Flannel Dance one wore white trousers, a white cricket-shirt, a blazer, and white socks - but black patent leather dancing shoes. A cricket-shirt being open-neck, a white silk scarf was knotted and tucked inside it. This jaunty costume, only without the scarf and with white plimsolls instead of black patent leathers, was *de rigeur* when punting.

Graduands were required to wear evening dress at Congregations. Since these ceremonies usually began in the early afternoon, it was convenient to dress for luncheon. The soft-fronted dress-shirt, no doubt under American influence, was beginning to insinuate its way into social gatherings, but this garment was regarded by all at Durham as a 'social error'. 'Wristlet watches', as they were known to young Geoffrey and his fellow undergraduates who sported stiff dress cuffs, though decried were usually worn; perhaps because of the expense involved in kitting oneself out with a 'hunter' or 'half-hunter'. White gloves at dances had almost, but not quite, disappeared. There was good reason for continuing this ancient and honourable custom, as the compromise adopted at Durham - and no doubt elsewhere - shows; for the gentleman was obliged to prevent his hot sticky hand from soiling his lady's dress, or clinging like a damp toad to her back, with a ruffled clean white handkerchief. Dress-shirts were the most expensive items in a student's laundry-bill; but human ingenuity enabled some to put off the evil day of laundering by the application to the starched linen of dry stale bread. This formula was likely to have been passed on from generation to generation of undergraduates; or may have found a place in the Mrs Beeton of the day. Made-up bow-ties were universally derided, but almost as universally worn.

Canon Williams moves on to the ever-interesting subject of 'Gyps and Bedders'.

The domestic staff in his day consisted of a Butler, a Cook, housemaids, kitchenmaids, gyps and bedders.

The Butler was a Mr Green who, although he lived in a house in Museum Square - now demolished to make room for Bailey Court - reigned supreme in the Buttery. He was cast in the mould of traditional English butlers, and his dignity and assurance were quite terrifying to undergraduates. He could, however, carve sufficient beef to feed two hundred people during the service and consumption of the soup and fish courses, each slice wafer-thin, at a speed which no mechanical meat-slicer could rival. He presided at his own carving table at the North end of the Hall, and kept the whole company under his serveillance throughout the meal.

The cook was also somewhat traditional, especially in her physical proportions. She had once won a prize in a marmalade-making competition, and any complaint about the food passed on to her by the Secretary of the Junior Common Room was always parried by an acid reminder of this fact.

Geoffrey and his fellow-undergraduates were, however, well-fed.

Inevitably, in those days, the students had more direct and personal contact with the gyps and bedders.

These worthies - for such indeed they were - seemed to regard their profession as a vocation, with the result that the age-range was about as extensive as it could be. Some were reaching a dignified maturity after long and devoted service, and some were mere youths fresh from school. The gyps were males, and the bedders were usually married ladies living in the city.

Both were allotted sets of rooms, often a particular staircase; and the bedders especially would take 'a remotely motherly interest' in 'their gentlemen'. A gyp had to rise early and take to each of his charges an enamel jug which was 'supposed to contain very hot water' for shaving. This he would carry into the bedroom, when he would wake up the occupant and deliver to him the pair of shoes, left outside the door overnight, which again he was 'supposed to have cleaned.' One infers from Canon Williams' 'supposed' that neither of these jobs was always either enthusiastically or efficiently done. The gyp's personal duties done, he would then go to the Hall, to wait on tables for breakfast - as he waited on tables for all the meals of the day.

During the morning he would replenish the coal-scuttle in 'his' rooms. A student was given one large scuttleful of coal a day for his open fire - open fires disappeared in 1950. If the student did need a replenishment of his scuttle, he knew where to obtain it and could help himself, though, says Canon Williams, 'this was unlikely as the allocation was generous.'

This was most certainly not the case in the years just after the Second War, when the scuttles were only partially filled and then with that apology for a fuel which some unconscious Governmental humorist had dubbed 'nutty slack'. Moreover, the coal then was kept behind a grille in one of the corridors of the Keep, and it required both a thin arm and a carelessness about getting pitch black to tease out sufficient lumps.

His job of filling the scuttles done, the gyp would remove the crockery which had been used for the previous night's supper, wash it, and return it to its cupboard; sometime after five o'clock again he would wash up the tea-things.

The bedder's day began even earlier than the gyp's. She would arrive in time to rake out the ashes of the previous day's fire, and light a new one so that 'her' student would find a warm fire blazing in his grate when he staggered, more dead than alive, out of his bedroom. Sometime in the morning she would make his bed and clean his rooms, and replenish the fire, if it needed stoking. During the summer term she would make his fire but not light it. In the late morning she and her colleagues could be seen and heard crossing the courtyard, stridently laughing, their flat Durham vowels echoing wall to stone wall, their shoes clattering on the cobbles, in each one's hands a bag with her students' soiled linen for laundering.

With the returned washing came a bill - a receipt rather, for the laundry was paid for by the Butler out of the gentlemen's battels.

The bedders' day was however not yet done. At six in the evening they were back and, while the students were at dinner, each good lady visited the rooms for which she was responsible, turned down the bed, made up the fire, and in the cold weather put her 'gentlemen's' slippers in front of it, emptied the slop-pail and replenished the ewer and filled the carafe with fresh water.

Down the generations, a shifting army of uncomplaining - well, almost uncomplaining! - servants.

The mention of battels prompts Canon Williams to put down a few facts concerning this important element in student life. It will be remembered that one of Thorp's main objectives had been to discourage that extravagance which was sapping the moral fibre of so many young men at the older universities. A tight rein therefore was kept on students' expenditure on battels.

In Geoffrey's day, nine pounds, and nine pounds only, were allocated to battels on every terminal bill. Beer and cider were the permitted beverages at luncheon and dinner; spirits understandably were not, and neither, curiously, was the eminently more civilised wine. Geoffrey gave his order by signing his name on one of the little pile of tickets placed for the purpose on each table. Castlemen will be interested to learn that beer, in 1935, was sevenpence a pint, and cider threepence a glass.

Students could also buy from the buttery such essentials as tea and coffee, milk and sugar, bread, butter and jam, and cakes and biscuits. When the nine pounds had been used up, 'battels were bust', and no further supplies could be bought on them for the rest of the term. Now was the time for a less impoverished friend to step in, if he would, by allowing his battels to be used in return for ready cash. One was not allowed to add a supplementary sum to one's account: the nine pounds was considered a quite adequate amount for a term. And 'Without extravagances,' Canon

Williams adds, 'it usually was.' If at the end of one term anything was left in the account, that amount was deducted from the nine pounds due the next.

Canon Williams has a lot more to say about that arbiter of student behaviour - the censor.

The three great officers of the College were the Master, the Censor, and the Chaplain. The Master fulfilled a paternal role and was very much a paterfamilias. The Chaplain was responsible for the conduct of the services in the Chapel and was, presumably, available for service in students' spiritual crises. The Bursar's sole contact with those *in statu pupillari* was to see that their fees were paid. The Censor was responsible for the discipline of the College and the morals of the students. His stall in Chapel was the canopied one on the North side, similar to the Master's in the South.

The formidable Dr - later Professor - Claude Abbott was Censor in Geoffrey's time.

He was a tall, elegant gentleman who wore pince-nez spectacles and always spoke as if he were delivering a statement of more than usually weighty importance. He was regular in his habits. At three o'clock precisely every afternoon, in winter or summer, fair weather or foul, he would leave the Castle gate for his 'constitutional'. Thereafter he would vary the route, but if he saw one of the students - perhaps in a rowing-boat in his shirt-sleeves, having discarded his blazer, or not demonstrating sartorial elegance as well as navigational ability in a punt (not standing on the platform to use the punt, for example) - that student would be told of it before the day was over. He was proud of the fact that he was the most regular attender at Chapel, being punctilious in his presence at Evensong once every term! He lived in rooms between the Norman Gallery and the Junction, and outside his door, at the top of the spiral staircase, there was a little table on which was a little book and beside it a pencil.

If on any evening a student expected to go out and did not expect to return before ten o'clock and not after eleven o'clock, he was required to sign his name in this little book before two o'clock that same afternoon. The Castle gate was closed and the doors of Bailey House and the Cowshed (Cosin's Hall) were locked at nine o'clock each day. In the Porter's Lodge, or in the entrance halls of the other two houses, there was also an exercise book in which the students signed their names and put the exact time of their return. Each day the Censor examined these books, and the porters were to see that the entries had been made correctly; and if any student had returned between ten and eleven o'clock not having signed his little book earlier, that student was in trouble. He would be sent for, questioned carefully, and probably sconced. If a student had more than three or four late passes in a week he too would be summoned to give an account of each evening's activity. Attendance at University Society meetings, or visiting friends in other Colleges for the purposes of scholarly collaboration, would be acceptable, but four visits to the cinema would cause a serious dissertation on the importance of not wasting one's time.

Breaches of College discipline were similarly dealt with. Canon Williams recalls how on one occasion towards the end of the Michaelmas term, after a carol service one Sunday evening,

> there was a somewhat raucous rendering of carols - whether using the correct words or a parody I cannot recall - on the part of a group of us who were then living in Bailey House. One of the gyps and his wife, Mr and Mrs Robinson, and their young family of three girls, were also living in the same house, and the children had their slumbers disturbed by this vocal cacophony. Consequently, we were all reported and were summoned to the presence. Dr Abbott pointed out that there was a firm College rule that no musical instruments were allowed to be played after nine o'clock, but, being a just man, he asked if we had anything to say in mitigation of the crime. He was not impressed by our argument that our voices were not musical instruments, and he was even less persuaded when we assured him that in no way could the noise about which we were apprehended be described as musical. We were each sconced ten shillings.

If one wished to stay out after eleven o'clock, and the only time a request to do this would be when a student wished to go to a theatre in Newcastle or attend some Students' Union function there, special permission had to be sought.

The nature of the entertainment had to be stated. A Shakespeare play, a symphony concert, an opera or a ballet might be acceptable, but there was very little hope of being granted a late pass for anything else. More, it was unlikely that such an indulgence would be granted more than once a term. Indeed, the railway timetable would be checked for the last train's time of arrival at Durham, and a quarter of an hour would be allowed in which to make the College from the station. Thus the precise moment of the wanderer's return could be gauged.

Women, of course, were regarded by authority as an occupational hazard of students.

The College, if not monastic, insisted on student celibacy and no ladies were permitted at any time in a student's room without permission of the Censor, and he would only give it if chaperoning was assured. On one occasion I asked permission to have a lady who was a family friend to drink tea with me in my room. Before my request could be accepted I had to say who she was, what was her profession, and how old she was. This last question I could not answer with any precision but I could give an assurance that she was well over thirty years of age. I had to admit that she was unmarried and to indicate which of my friends (male) I would be inviting to meet the lady of something over thirty years of age. Having named one particular friend I was told that under the circumstances, and as Miss So-and-So was a responsible person, no objection would be raised - provided that the lady did not arrive before four and had left by six o'clock . . . I must say that I found it considerably easier to invite - on another occasion - the Principal of Hild's! Generally speaking, however, we were allowed to have 'foursomes' on occasional Sunday afternoons, and . . . the students themselves did not look altogether unfavourably on female invadresses.

Things had clearly improved somewhat since 1909, at the June Sports of which year, it will be remembered, a correspondent complained to the *Journal* that even the presence of a Castleman's aunt was not sufficient security for him to invite two 'sister-students' to the Pavilion for afternoon tea.

Canon Williams adds a perceptive note about the Censor of his day.

Sometimes in an evening Claude would pay a social call on one of the students, and on these occasions he allowed his host to see that in reality he was a kindly, understanding, and possibly a very lonely gentleman.

Canon Williams goes on to describe some 'Customs and Manners in Hall.'

It may not be generally known that, in the years when Geoffrey was up, Hatfield dined in Hall with Castle, this dubious expedient bringing about a considerable saving in expenditure. What follows is worth reading virtually in its entirety.

As the dons assembled for dinner they would gather round the fire-place at High Table until the meal was ready to be served. In recent years the Hall floor had had to be replaced and, when the Master took us who were freshers on a guided tour of the Castle on the first Sunday afternoon of the Michaelmas term, he told us of a controversy which had arisen when this repair had been necessary. Although the College was the owner of the Castle, the Bishop and the Judges of Assize still had certain proprietorial rights. The Master had objected to the restoration of the dais on which High Table stood, because this took away valuable space for dancing on the occasions when Balls were held in the Castle. There were normally four Balls each year, the Freshers' Ball and the Christmas Ball in the Michaelmas term, the Shrovetide Ball before Lent in the Epiphany term, and the June Ball in June Week, when there was also held a Flannel Dance. The Bishop and the Judges wished to keep the historic platform, but the Master, who was a firm protagonist for students' pleasures, conducted his campaign so vigorously that the normal acceptance of the power of the majority vote was made ineffective and a compromise was reached. The dais would not be built, but a large carpet would be woven to replace it, and when required this could be rolled up and allowed to lie alongside the end wall behind a row of chairs which could be placed there to conceal it.

Castlemen therefore also arriving for dinner assembled around or near to the great fireplace with Lord Crewe's arms above it. A huge fire would be blazing in both grates, and the meat-course would be piled in the metal plate-warmer. Hatfield men would be standing behind the benches on which they were to sit - in their places! When the dons moved to their places at High Table, Castlemen did the same, tables being placed for each of the four years in which a man was *in statu pupillari* . Grace would then be said. It was the duty of scholars to read grace for a week at a time, and the weeks were allotted alternately to Hatfield and Castle. When all were at their places, a gyp would approach the scholar, who would stand before High Table, and hand to him the hard-board on which the Grace was printed. Grace having been read, the scholar bowed to the Master - or to whoever was presiding that evening - and returned to his place. Each scholar would only be called upon for this duty three or, at the most, four times in the whole of his three years.

Dinner always consisted of a soup and a fish course. These were followed by a choice between a joint or some other form of meat. A pudding would follow, and sometimes in the Summer term ice-cream would be provided as an extra. Savouries were reserved for those on High Table. At the end of the meal, when the students' tables had been cleared, a decent interval having elapsed, during which it was our belief that the silver cutlery (each piece was hallmarked and engraved with St Cuthbert's cross) was being counted, a message was conveyed to Arthur - the gyp who served High Table - who then advanced to the Master to ask his permission for the junior members to depart. This granted, Arthur signalled to the Butler, who informed the Senior Man that we were released. High Table continued with their meal until they adjourned for coffee and dessert in the Senior Common Room.

Breakfast consisted of porridge or cereal, a main course of bacon and egg, and bread and marmalade to follow. Castlemen could, if they wished, make toast of their bread before the fire. Luncheon consisted of two courses of a pattern so stereotyped that its variations are still remembered: minced beef on Mondays, stew on Tuesdays, fish on Wednesdays, sausages on Thursdays, fish again on Fridays, and cold corned beef on Saturdays. The pudding to follow featured a devastatingly frequent appearance of prunes and rice. Indeed, we were well fed, and a nutritious and healthy diet was provided. On Sundays we dined early (1.15 p.m.) and, as we all finished together, the Master or the Don presiding said a concluding brief grace in Latin - e.g., *'Benedicto benedicatur '*.

The Castle Hall was also the scene of two important ceremonies in a student's life: matriculation and graduation. The former took place in late October or early November, when all Freshmen were summoned to appear in the Hall sometime in the late afternoon to be addressed by the Vice-Chancellor. The station of a student and the nature of an University as well as the high privilege of membership were briefly expressed, and then each man advanced to the Vice-Chancellor and under his gaze signed the statute book, after which the Vice-Chancellor would shake hands, possibly indulge in social intercourse, and raise his square. The graduation ceremony was more formal. The graduands would sit on one side of the Hall and the Visitors on the other. The Dean of each Faculty would plead that appropriate degrees should be conferred on particular persons. At the conclusion of each list, the Chancellor asked the Congregation, 'Is it your will that these graces be conferred?', and on the receipt of the inevitable 'Aye', accompanied by appropriate raising of squares or doctors' caps, he announced, 'These graces are conferred.' Then each student whose name had been read out was escorted by Gray, the senior bull-dog, who took the student's left hand in his right hand, to the Chancellor, who raised his square and shook the graduand's hand. When all the degrees then to be awarded had been conferred, the company moved in procession to the Cathedral to attend Evensong, at which the Graduation Sermon was preached. At other Congregations, when the number of graduands was small, the ceremony would be attended by a representative number of members, the event would take place in Cosin's Library, and the ceremony would last only a few minutes.

Apart from these ceremonial occasions and the University Balls, certain other social events would take place in the Hall. Notable amongst these was the Freshers' Concert, when each Freshman was obliged to provide an item for the programme. I well remember one excruciating occasion when a man not endowed with a pleasant singing voice or a well-trained technique, mouthed his way through all the verses of 'The Lost Chord'. Dons were present, so audience reaction was restrained. Then there were the College Literary and Debating Society's annual Visitors' Night Debate; the June Week Concert, when an eminent musical artiste was commissioned to perform; and the College Wine, which was an excellent wine party to which students were permitted to invite a friend (male) from another college.

As the Censor was usually the only don to be in to breakfast on a Sunday morning, he would frequently invite three or four students to join him on High Table.

On the days when the Balls were held, students were provided with a packed cold collation for their dinner from the Buttery, and High Table was served in the Senior Common Room.

On the occasions when a sporting team had won a cup or trophy, a 'Floreat' was held after the pudding at dinner. The cup, much decorated with ribbands and silks, was ceremonially brought in having been filled with punch, and presented to the Master. He would stand, as would the man sitting on either side of him, take the cup, proclaim *'Floreat Collegium'*, and pass it to his left; when the next but one on the left would stand and the one on the Master's right would sit. The new middle man of the three standing would then cry *'Floreat Collegium'*, and drink, and this would be repeated until every member of the College present had drunk from the trophy. Gyps were on hand to replenish the punch as required - which was fairly frequently.

Canon Williams passes on to the Junior Common Room - 'not a large room, but one adequate for our needs.' This was so because it was not until 1935 that those members of the College who were *in statu pupillari*, and those included fourth-year students doing a postgraduate course, exceeded fifty in number; and that figure was not reached again until after the Second World War.

Certain features about the JCR of Geoffrey's day are worthy of mention.

The room of course had an open grate, round which a number of leather arm-chairs was deployed in a semi-circle. These chairs were strictly reserved for graduates; although a third-year student could sit in one if all the graduates in the room were comfortably accommodated. The chances of a Freshman's having a comfortable chair in the JCR for any length of time in his first year were quite remote.

Canon Williams confirms that the hierarchical structure of College life was still very evident in his day; for 'it was a grave social misdemeanour for a Freshman to invite a senior to drink tea or coffee in his rooms until that senior student had first established social contact by inviting the Freshman concerned.'

Such social divisions as existed were extended, quite sensibly, to the division of labour:

> The second year students were usually expected to do manual work in connection with the preparations for College events. It was they who saw to the decoration of the Castle for the June Ball. Strings of electric lights (fairy lights) were abjured. Tallow night-lights were placed in glass jars - saved and provided by the cook, and having originally contained meat products - and these were placed along the castellated walls and the edges of the grass plots in the courtyard and in Fellows' Garden. There were also wooden rafts cut to resemble the leaves of a water-lily, with a metal-petalled flower in the midst to contain a similar night-light. There were also iron arches from which these candles could be suspended. The collection down the years of these meat-paste jars had amounted to several hundred, and each year they had to be washed and got ready. When these lights were lit the effect was utterly enchanting.

The JCR meetings were held under the chairmanship of the Senior Man, who was appointed by the Master. The Master also appointed the Chapel Clerk, who fulfilled in the Chapel the function of a sacristan, in making all the necessary preparations for Communion services and compiling rotas for the reading of the lessons at Morning Prayers and Evensong. Only the JCR Secretary was appointed by the members.

College Societies such as the Literary and Debating Society held their meetings in the JCR, but the more exclusive College Clubs such as the Read and Weed met in the President's room or - by permission - over a meal in a local hotel.

Canon Williams is critical of little in the College of his day; but he is scathing about the system that operated until very much later of entrusting to the housemaids the task of acting as guide to visitors to the Castle - entrance fee: sixpence!

They had learnt the rigmarole without any apparent comprehension, and any student in the JCR on any afternoon would have his meditations rudely and frequently interrupted by the sound of a high-pitched voice, half-reciting, half-singing, and with a total absence of variation of punctuation or pitch: 'This - is - the - Norman - Chapel - built - by - William - the - Conqueror - in - 1072 - this - way - ladies - and - gentlemen - please . . .'

Curiously, at meetings of the JCR cigarettes were provided *ad lib*, and the cost divided equally between the members. It appeared later on battels. Also 'there were very few students who did not smoke at that time.' Of those who were non-smokers, many took to smoking in self-defence, because the atmosphere in the JCR at the end of a meeting 'resembled a huge tangled skein of wool.'

The Freshers' Debate was, in his day as well as later, 'a kind of initiation rag'. But 'the President and Secretary of the Literary and Debating Society, as well as the four principal speakers, were in dinner jackets, the others wearing blazers.'

The motion chosen was always of a frivolous nature, such as 'Work is the curse of the drinking classes' or 'We're here because we're not all there.' The proposers and opposers of the motion were Freshmen selected by the President, but all the Freshers were expected to make a contribution from the floor if not from the table. Each was submitted to a barrage of heckling given as much to try his patience as to test his wit. This usually induced a situation where the speaker was almost rendered unable to voice anything of the speech he had carefully prepared in total ignorance of the nature of the 'Debate'. When the uproar became uncontrollable and the President's cries of 'Order! Order!' went totally unheeded, the President adjourned the sitting, and sweeping with him the Secretary and the four speakers, left the room for some unspecified part of the Castle - it might be the Norman Gallery or the Chapel stairs. In due course a deputation of one or two was sent to find the offended party, present to the President a humble apology, and beg him to return and resume the debate. This was, of course, accepted - and the uproar continued as before.

The business meetings in the JCR which Geoffrey attended concerned themselves with such matters as which newspapers and periodicals should be taken in the Common Room, complaints about lack of support for various sports and fixtures, and complaints about the food coupled with wildly optimistic suggestions for improving it. Frequently the Senior Man would be asked to convey resolutions passed by the JCR to the Master, but, Canon Williams noted,

> there was rarely any serious conflict of opinion, and the 'us-and-them' attitude of students to staff which became rather more common in the post-war years was almost totally absent. There may have been complaints about certain particulars of College and University discipline, but in the main they were accepted as part of the tradition.'

Canon Williams moves on to 'Scholars and Commoners'.

Although the Bidding Prayer always used by the preacher at Matins on Sunday mornings in the Cathedral during term contained, after the prayer for all Universities, Colleges and Schools, the words, 'and here in Durham ye shall pray especially for the Chancellor and all Proctors, Doctors, Masters and Scholars,' in the day-to-day life of the College or University very little, if any, attention was paid to a student's status. Scholars had a slightly different gown and were allowed to take nine books at a time out of the University Library instead of the regulation five for other students. On the debit side, scholars were only allowed to break five days a term instead of the commoners' nine.

As far as 'Keeping term' was concerned, Canon Williams remembers that each lecturer called the roll before delivering his lecture, always addressing the students as Mr or Miss. When Canon Quick was lecturing, and the class was large, one of the bull-dogs had the list and ticked the students' names as they entered the room.

Lectures began at nine. In some cases a lecture would be given at 5.15. The students were given five minutes' grace before being marked absent; but the lecturer was given ten. If the lecturer were late, the class would study their watches carefully until the ten minutes' grace was up, when would follow a split-second departure. Alas for young Geoffrey, this fortunate experience happened only once in all his three years.

At the end of each term, each student would receive a certificate to say that he had kept term. If a commoner had missed more than five days, such a certificate would not be forthcoming. Nine of these certificates had to be produced for inspection before a first degree could be conferred. Those men who were reading for an honours degree in Theology, or a diploma in Theology, or were in the Divinity group of third-year students reading for a general degree, were also required to produce at least one certificate to say that they had attended a course of six lectures in Pastoral Theology. These were delivered at weekly intervals during the Lent Term by a distinguished visiting lecturer. Frequently these lectures were subsequently published in book form. Canon Peter Green's best-selling *Man of God* was one such publication.

When it came to sport, the Science students, through having to spend some of their afternoons working in the laboratories, were inevitably disadvantaged. Things were made worse of course by the smallness of the student population of the day, which meant that opportunities for playing games were inevitably curtailed. Rowing, too, took up almost all the students' spare time, so that 'to maintain the Colleges' participation in Association and Rugby football, fives and hockey, most of the athletically inclined would have to devote themselves to all four types of sporting activity.'

There was not much tutorial work in Geoffrey's day, and very little indeed of individual tuition. Not every Don would return work submitted at a personal interview. Interestingly, Castlemen received the results of their Collections at a private interview with the Master in the Senior Common Room - 'with or without any comments he chose to make.'

As is to be expected, Canon Williams has a lot to say about 'The Chapel'.

Two services were held on each weekday during term. When the University was first founded, for some years, until the number of Colleges increased, each with its own chapel, all the students were required to assemble in the Galilee Chapel for morning prayers, which took the form of an abbreviated version of Matins. This form of service came to be known as 'Galilee Prayers', and the books were still being used in the Tunstal Chapel just before the Second World War. It was held at a quarter to nine. Evensong was sung - without choir - every weekday at half past six. There was an Organ Scholar, whose duty it was to play at these evening services. One of the Psalms for the day was sung, as were the Canticles, and one hymn took the place of the Anthem. The lessons were read by students: Freshmen the first lesson, seniors the second, according to a rota drawn up by the Chapel Clerk. The Chaplain was responsible for saying the Office and taking the Prayers.

The Holy Communion was celebrated every Sunday at 8 o'clock and on the Red-Letter Saints' Days at half past seven. The Chapel Clerk, sometime on the previous evening, would go to the Octagon Room, where the wine and bread and vessels were kept in a cupboard, and prepare for the next day's service. This included cutting small cubes of bread from a specially baked loaf and arranging them on a patten in groups of ten cubes.

On two Sunday evenings in each term there would be a service of Evensong in the Chapel at which a sermon would be preached either by the Master from his stall or by a visiting clergyman from the lectern.

Canon Williams cannot recall either the Chaplain's preaching a sermon or the Master's celebrating Holy Communion. Canon How, it will be remembered, was the last Master of Castle to be in Orders.

Attendance at all these services was voluntary, and there was quite a high proportion of Geoffrey's contemporaries who never put in an appearance. Things had not improved by 1949, when the then Chaplain, the Rev J.C. Wallis, complained in *Castellum* that, 'on the whole the attendance is most disappointing.'

The College branch of the SCM regularly arranged for Compline to be said every Friday evening at half past nine, and a College Carol Service was arranged by students towards the end of the Michaelmas Term. The Durham Colleges' SCM also arranged a rota of students to take mid-day prayers in Hatfield Chapel on Tuesdays, Wednesdays and Thursdays from three minutes past one to ten past, luncheon being served in all College Halls at 1.15. The Dean and Chapter also agreed to let the SCM organise the preaching of a University Sermon in the Cathedral on a Sunday evening in January. The first dignitary to preach this sermon was Dean Inge of St Paul's, then a household name, and known generally throughout the kingdom as 'The Gloomy Dean' or, alternatively, as 'A Pillar of the

Church and two columns of the Evening Standard.'

Canon Williams marches more merrily on to 'Clubs and Societies'. Among these was the Pure Science Society, which was popular because some of its meetings took the form of excursions to individual concerns. A visit to a brewery or a sweet manufactory could be guaranteed to increase membership.

Somewhat surprisingly, students in the immediate pre-War, as in the immediate post-War, years were not politically motivated. There were political clubs young Geoffrey could join, the Labour and Conservative Clubs; but their membership was small, and their activities consequently restricted. Perhaps the most effective was the League of Nations Union, 'which had the distinction of having Dr E.G. Pace, the Praelector no less, as its Chairman.' This branch from time to time held meetings 'of a political nature' which were often quite well attended. They were sporadic rather than regular, and no doubt prompted by one of the numerous crises of the inter-war years for, as Canon Williams points out,

> During our period there was the Spanish Civil War; the Italian Abyssinian Campaign, leading to the Hoare-Laval proposals (which led to a telegram being sent from one meeting); the Austrian Anschluss ; and the Occupation of the Rhineland by Germany.

Most interestingly:

> Far from the students of the 'Thirties - as we frequently read and hear being typical of those in another place - being dissatisfied with our present capitalist system and looking towards a communist dissolution, in Durham they were more busily arguing about the relative dangers of Communism and Fascism, and whether Russia or Germany constituted the greater menace to world peace.

By far the most thriving society in the University was the SCM. Of course this was composed mainly of Anglicans, although a small but nonetheless vigorous Methodist Society existed as a sub-section within it. Each College had its own branch and, as we have seen, its members arranged meetings and sometimes liturgical activities in the Colleges. The Durham Colleges' SCM had a lively executive Committee, which arranged a missionary weekend as well as other events. Once a term too the SCM held a large evening meeting at which a celebrity was the speaker. At one of these the young Geoffrey heard William Temple, later Archbishop of Canterbury but then Archbishop of York. Let the Canon tell what follows in his own words.

On that occasion I was the President of the Durham Colleges' SCM. Canon Quick had offered to provide hospitality for the Archbishop, but then he was informed that His Grace would be coming by train (third class) and that he would arrive at a quarter before three o'clock in the afternoon to speak at the meeting which had been arranged for a quarter past five. Canon Quick said that I would have to entertain him to tea as he would not be able to do so. This information filled me with alarm, and I did not advertise the tea-party which had been forced upon me. I ordered a taxi to take me to the station, and I am sure the garage proprietor in New Elvet who ran a taxi service thought it was for some student who was trying to impress his girl-friend, for he provided me with the most decrepit vehicle in his rank. Now everyone in the country at that time knew what the Archbishop of York looked like, with his ever-gaitered legs, his rotund figure, his boyish, open, smiling face, and his constant companion - a furled umbrella. He was a gift to all newspaper caricaturists. As soon as this familiar figure stepped onto the platform even the porters recognised him, as did the taxi-driver. In those days, at least in Durham, railway porters and taxi-drivers knew how to address an Archbishop as 'Your Grace.'

We arrived on Palace Green a few seconds before three o'clock and, as the taxi turned into the Castle barbican, Professor Abbott was approaching the Gatehouse from the Courtyard, as punctually as ever setting out for his afternoon constitutional, pince-nez superiorly clipped to his nose, silver-topped walking-stick in his hand. It soon became quite clear that the taxi and the Censor would meet in the somewhat narrow strictures of the archway. Professor Abbott did not yield to intruding taxicabs, and taxi-drivers conveying the Archbishop of York did not give way to Professors of English. Rapid speculation on my part resulted in a diminution of attention to the prelate's conversation. Excitement mounted, and the seconds required for a motor-vehicle to cover the distance from the gate to the Gatehouse extended into what seemed minutes. The taxi, being rather more powerful, was victorious, and the Censor was forced to stretch himself flat against the Porter's door.

Dr Abbott's face was purple with annoyance and it was tinged with not a little surprise. But when he recognised the other occupant of the cab, for the first and only time in the four years I spent in the Castle, I saw the Censor's jaw drop. The taxi sped on its way, swung around the oval lawn, and drew up at Hall steps (my rooms were on the top floor of Hall Stairs). I jumped out of the vehicle, helped His Grace to alight, and gave the driver his fare. Stealing a glance - I hoped inadvertently - towards the Gatehouse, I saw Claude still open-mouthed with astonishment.

Trying to give the impression that I was in the habit of entertaining establishment figures, I escorted the Archbishop into the Castle and up the stairs.

There is a tailpiece to this story. Some weeks later the King and Queen were visiting Durham on their post-coronation tour of the provincial towns. They were due to arrive at the station in the Royal Train at ten o'clock in the forenoon and, having fulfilled a host of engagements in the area, were scheduled to leave the station at five o'clock in the afternoon. I was alone in my room the previous evening, doing some work, when I heard a single knock on my door. The visitor did not - as was usual - forthwith enter. He did come in, in answer to my invitation, and reveal himself to be Dr Abbott. He civilly refused my invitation to sit down, apologised for the interruption, and said he wished to make an enquiry. 'I would like to see their Majesties tomorrow,' he said, 'but I do not wish to stand in the crowds which will be on the street. I wonder if you would be so kind as to tell me the hour at which they will be coming to drink tea with you?'

The SCM held another memorable function.

Every Summer Term the SCM organised 'The Framwellgate Tea'. Framwellgate was a most appalling slum which reached from Framwellgate Bridge along the left bank of the river and up the hill to where St Goderic's Church still stands. As part of the slum clearance campaign of the 'Thirties, of which Fathers Morse Boycott and Basil Jellicoe at Summertown were pioneers, these mean dwellings were all destroyed in 1938. Until that time the 'Tea' was held every year. SCM reps would collect money from the students - a generous response was almost universal - and through the parochial clergy invitations were issued to all the Framwellgate children: about two hundred and fifty in all. On the Saturday afternoon of the 'Tea' they would repair to a field, on which a sports day was organised. After spending superfluous energy on such events as three-legged, potato, and egg-and-spoon races, every child would receive a cake-carton provided by Lyon's Café (no connection with Joseph of that name) containing a packed lunch. The crockery and tea urns from St Margaret's and St Nicholas' parish halls were used to serve tea.

The afternoon of the Framwellgate Tea was the only time in the year when those who had been indulging in sporting activities yielded precedence in the bathrooms, and to the early supply of hot water, to those who had not. It was in the general interest of the College that body parasites which the SCM members had caught from their temporary charges should have the speediest possible disposal.

Canon Williams rather deprecatingly refers to another Christian Society, 'less vigorous than the SCM' - the Durham Inter-Collegiate Christian Union - DICCU.

This attracted sincere young Christians of a certain brand of Churchmanship, who used to meet in a house in Sadler Street. The strains of revivalist choruses would be heard percolating through their windows; but what other activities transpired was, to me, something of a mystery.

It seems that, despite this aberrant behaviour, most members of DICCU were also paid-up members of the SCM.

The Societies to which virtually all students belonged were the Men's Union, on Palace Green, and the Women's Union, in the Bailey. Alas, 'never the twain did meet'. For even the guests at the Ladies' Night Debate at the Men's Union were invited through the Colleges rather than through the Women's Union.

The Men's Union premises consisted of a Committee Room, a Debating

Chamber, a Reading Room, and a large coffee bar where light meals were served. A plate of egg-and-chips, or sausage-and-chips, could be bought there, as well as sandwiches, biscuits and cakes. No alcoholic drinks were obtainable; but cigarettes were sold. These rooms were of course subsequently absorbed into the University Library, when the Union Society moved temporarily into Pemberton.

It cost young Geoffrey seven and six a term to belong to the Union. He had to fork out five shillings for a ticket for the June Ball and the other Balls, though a student's ticket for the Chamber Concerts in the Miners' Hall set him back only half a crown. A Union membership card was valid at all other University Unions in the country; and after twelve termly payments a life membership card was issued. Canon Williams still carries his, along with his driving licence and bank cards.

The University Dramatic Society produced an annual play either in the Assembly Rooms in the Bailey or in Neville's Cross College - now New College. Charles Morgan's *The Flashing Stream*, Eliot's *Murder in the Cathedral*, an appropriate choice for Durham, and *King Lear* were for Geoffrey memorable productions.

The Assembly Rooms had been used as the headquarters of the OTC. Most curiously, in view of the virtual certainty of a second European war, and also of the big guns on the staff who were the mainstay of the Corps, the OTC 'had been disbanded some years before 1935.' Whether because of lack of support or 'deliberate suppression', Canon Williams did not know.

In addition to the University Balls, two Societies a year were permitted to hold a Ball - a Dance, rather - in Lecture Room Five, situated then 'upstairs in the building adjacent to and immediately south of Bishop Cosin's Library.' This was the examination school for the University, and it was also often used for meetings such as that addressed by the Archbishop of York. This of course has also long since been incorporated into the Library.

Societies often met too in Lecture Room Six, which became part of the Music Department.

Sometimes a Society would arrange one of those delightful occasions known as a *Thé dansant*. These were held in an annexe to the *Dunelm Hotel*. Though a popular feature of the 'Thirties almost everywhere else, they were not really cottoned on to in Durham.

Supper meetings were occasionally held in the upstairs room of the Fulling Mill, by the Wear - then known as the *Museum Café*. This was a popular student resort for fairly substantial high teas, especially on Sundays when supper in Hall was both cold and frugal. The enterprising proprietor had petitioned the Dean and Chapter for permission to apply for a dancing licence; but this was refused on the ambiguous ground that 'the banks were very dark.' The *Victory Café*, which was - but is no longer - in Sadler Street, was also happy to hire out an upstairs room for meetings. There was no charge; the profit came with the purchase price of the food and drink taken.

Canon Williams is as revealing about his next subject, 'Students and Dons', as about everything else.

The smallness of the University in those pre-War years sounds quite idyllic. The eight Colleges together mustered, in young Geoffrey's day, scarcely more than five hundred. Consequently, every College had all its students in residence as well as some of the teaching staff. Each was therefore a close and compact community, resembling nothing so much as a tight-knit family; and although its structure was hierarchic, teaching staff, students and domestic staff knew one another well and, as the Canon says, 'somehow managed to live together as friends.'

The dons entertained the students in many and various ways. The first taste of such hospitality actually greeted the Fresher on his arrival at the College, when he found in his pigeon-hole in the Lodge an invitation from the Master and Mrs How to take tea with them in the Senate Room the following afternoon. All the Freshmen accordingly gravitated there, to stand overcome by the place's elegance, before being greeted by Mrs How. In time, others came along to introduce themselves: the Chaplain and his wife, the Bursar and Mrs Macfarlane-Grieve, the Censor, other dons living in College, and Miss Diana Stringer, Mrs How's companion. This last lady was always introduced as 'Miss Stringer', for 'Christian names were only used by contemporaries who had reached between themselves a certain condition of intimacy.' All the women students, in Geoffrey's time, were addressed by their male counterparts as 'Miss So-and-So.'

At the Master's 'Tea' every guest was supplied with a plate, a cup of tea in its saucer, and a knife and a napkin, but not with a chair or a place at a table. This presented a diabolical obstacle course for young men who, three months previously, had been mere schoolboys. Sandwiches were handed round first, and later scones and cakes. Mrs How would then press meringues on her guests, declaring that it was almost obligatory for them to take one, since all young men were in possession of a sweet tooth.

Meringues when devoured under these conditions have a tendency to explode and scatter sugary shrapnel in all directions. They also possess a malevolent attribute of smearing cream in inelegant streaks over the cheeks, nose and chin.

The Censor's custom of inviting a few students at a time to breakfast with him in Hall on Sunday mornings has already been mentioned.

There would also be invitations to tea in the homes of various dons, when the students would meet and get to know their families and play with their children.

A custom that will fill today's readers with surprise is that of the evening party. Dons and their wives and students were invited to these, the ladies providing partners for the men as far as they would go round. Thereafter, horribly, men were paired with men. There was lavish party fare in the dining room, with 'wild games' to follow: treasure-hunts and Murder among them.

The young and blushful Geoffrey was present at one of these when Mrs How, introducing a treasure hunt, gaily announced: 'You can go anywhere in the house and look everywhere except in my drawers.'

The ensuing pregnant silence was broken by the Master saying, 'What did you say, my dear?' On hearing a reiteration of the invitation he muttered in an expressionless voice, 'I thought that's what you said.'

Amongst the most pleasant of these evening functions were the Master's wines, when he entertained a group of second and third-year men and graduates to dessert in the Senate Room.

Enjoyable as these were, with the candelabra illuminating the room, and bathing the table and the silver in a soft radiance and casting ghostly shadows on the tapestries, they too had their snares and hazards.

For a gentleman is distinguished from other mortals by his ability to pare, prepare and eat a fruit without the use of any divinely appointed tools such as fingers. In short, with a dessert knife and fork.

A slice of pineapple is the easiest of all to despatch. Apples can usually be managed, but ripe pears are often elusive; and oranges present
all kinds of dangers, not the least being the squirting of projectiles of
juice into one's neighbour's eye.

The other snare lay in wait for the man sitting on the Censor's left. Dr
Abbott, it was darkly said, would wait spider-like for the port to arrive
before his neighbour at risk, then request that he 'pass the port'. 'If he did
it in the common-sense way, and not despatch it in its interminable career
around the table, he would earn a humiliating rebuke which would
include a reference to the student's questionable origins. Fortunately for
young Geoffrey and his friends, those who 'had passed that way before'
issued timely warnings to those who came after; and so he and they were
spared the dire fate of the socially ignorant whose solecism offended the
Censor's shell-like ears.

Students would receive invitations to dine with certain dons and,
although this was much less usual, students so invited could issue an invitation to their host to drink tea in their rooms. It is a comment on the desperate loneliness of the academic life that 'One gained the impression that
such advances, when they were made, were welcomed.'

Canon Williams passes, with nice logic, from Dons to Drink.

As has already been mentioned, a student in Castle was permitted to
drink beer or cider with his luncheon or dinner. Provided that outward
decorum were preserved, no limit was imposed on the quantity consumed,
save that of the student's own pocket. At the Christmas Dinner, but at no
other time, one could order a bottle of port. No alcohol was permitted in a
student's rooms; this was a rule generally accepted and obeyed.

No student was allowed, without permission from the Censor, to enter
licensed premises within five miles of Palace Green, and (Catch 22) no student was allowed to take himself off to any place more than five miles from
Palace Green. These two rules were largely ignored. Geoffrey and his
friends would take an afternoon's walk along the river to Finchale Abbey
without once thinking of the five-mile limit; and a Saturday afternoon trip
by train or bus to Roker, Whitley Bay or Newcastle would be undertaken
without ever asking formal permission.

As regards entering licensed premises, it was generally assumed that
Plunkett and Gray, the two 'bulldogs', would restrict their beat to the actu-

al city, so that a student felt fairly confident when entering a public house outside its confines. Some pubs of course were more highly favoured than others: the *Rose Tree* at Shincliffe was one such, although Gray had been known to pay a surprise visit there on one occasion. The *Wellington* at Neville's Cross was another.

In Durham itself circumspection was required. The *Shakespeare* gained a certain popularity because of its possession of a discreet back door leading into Moatside Lane. A warning that the incorruptible Gray was on the prowl, when passed to the rooms within, caused a precipitate exodus. Plunkett however could be squared by the honest gift of a pint from a student he had apprehended - provided that the behavioural decencies were observed. The *Waterloo*, now part of *The Royal County*, was also popular. The *Three Tuns*, in those days an old-fashioned tavern, boasted a labyrinth of small rooms where the dangers of detection might be risked.

In pre-war as in post-war days, The Castle had the reputation of being the hardest-drinking College in the University. This having been said, Geoffrey found very little real drunkenness - and what there was was sporadic.

Such a subject as Drink leads Canon Williams ineluctably to that of Women.

Despite the rather ostentatious monasticism of the Colleges, romance flourished. Whispered conversations could be conducted across the Library tables. Also, most of the Societies catered for a mixed clientèle; visits to the dark ecstasies of the cinema could be arranged; and coffee in the morning and tea in the afternoon could be taken in perfumed company at Carrick's - 'the rather refined restaurant'. Country walks were then, as they always have been, good for the health and for the susceptible heart. It was, of course, considered forward for a lady to visit a public house. It was proper for a man to escort his partner in the Last Waltz to her home after the Ball was over. Because lock-up at the women's Colleges was a quarter of an hour after the conclusion of a Ball, the ladies from Mary's were popular partners for this romantic and sentimental dance; but after Neville's Cross ladies, at their Principal's insistence, took to hiring a bus to take them home, and this was parked right outside the Library on Palace Green, Neville's Cross ladies showed a jump in popularity.

There was always a host and hostess at the Society Dances and the Balls; these were usually the head of a College and his wife, a Cathedral dignitary and his wife, or a professor and his. One introduced oneself on arriving. Most people present knew one another, and no inhibitions were placed in the way of a gentleman's asking any lady present for a dance. Interestingly, guests were not restricted to the University, and many elderly gentry from the County attended the June Ball, sat under the stained glass windows in the Hall, waited for the gardens to be illuminated, and walked gently around them before climbing into their motors and driving, or being driven, to their country homes.

The five Balls could be considered the highlights of the social life of the College. At them, the Senior Common Room was used as a 'sitting out' room, while Tunstal's Gallery provided a promenade, and this 'sitting out' room provided the opportunity for romantic interludes. An extra Ball was put on in 1937, to celebrate the Coronation of King George V1 and Queen Elizabeth.

The previous year the June Ball had been under threat, for George V had died on the first day of the Epiphany Term and, following protocol, the Court was plunged into a year's mourning. In the Cathedral the red cushions in the choir stalls were covered with black crape, and those members of the Chapter who were King's Chaplains (they were the Dean, Canon Quick, and the Archdeacon of Auckland, A.E.J. Rawlinson) abandoned their Popish scarlet for Puritan black cassocks with white cuffs six inches deep. The new King, Edward V111, promptly curtailed the anachronistic mourning period to six months; but the June Ball still fell within the University's Ban. The argument that the palace had decreed that national mourning should last no longer than the funeral had no effect on the University.

Eventually, following a deputation from the Students' Representative Council, and the expostulations of many senior members of the University, the inevitable English compromise was reached: the June Ball could be held - but colours were not to be worn! To the evening-suited men, of course, the absurd edict made no difference; but the ladies were hard hit. Matrons were required to wear black with, if they so wished, silver trimmings; spinsters and young brides must put on white. The colour bar also meant, of course, that no jewelry could be worn which had coloured gems; and so the ladies were restricted to diamonds! Before this memorable Ball therefore, the ladies descended like the Assyrians on Woolworths. But it was memorable too, to young Geoffrey, for another quality than the bizarre: its ghostly sparkle and glitter made that Ball seem one long dream-like scene out of some wistful enchanted ballet.

Canon Williams remembers that the Durham ladies of those days had no hesitation about going to Balls in borrowed plumes: 'we saw the same dresses at different Balls - but not always on the same ladies.'

The band was often a student band.

The heights to which the authorities soared - say rather, the depths which the authorities plumbed - in their ceaseless struggle to enforce the moral law strike one now as richly comic. A high-spot of the social year was the SCM Concert, which raised money both for the SCM's London headquarters and for what is now called 'the third world'. This was usual-ly held in Neville's Cross Hall, and took the form of a variety show with music, dancing and sketches. In 1938 a sketch was chosen which called for two players - one male and one female. The man was Castle's Gordon Berriman, later the College's Chaplain, and later still a Canon. None fore-saw the difficulties that would arise when it came to the performers' rehearsing their parts. He could not go to her rooms, which were in Mary's; she could not go to his, which were in Castle. He could not enter the Women's Union; she could not enter the Men's. Carricks was closed in the evening. And as it was winter, the hours of daylight were few. The two were reduced to finding a street-lamp and standing beneath it, like Lili Marlene and her lover; but there were few street-lamps on the peninsula which gave any light worthy of the name, and to see their scripts the two had to stand in dangerous proximity. In no time at all the bulldogs moved the two on from what was palpably unhealthy loitering; while on the approach of familiar figures - and what figures in the Durham of those days were not familiar? - they were forced to move on again.

Despite all this, the canon records with some satisfaction, 'friendships were formed, courtships proceeded, troths were plighted and - subse-quently - marriages were solemnised.'

Indeed, a middle-aged lady who is a graduate of another University told me recently that she had been warned off Durham by being told that if she went there she would find herself married to a vicar.

Canon Williams concludes with a look at the relationship between Town and Gown.

Before the second World War, fraternisation between town and gown was not encouraged. The attitude which prompted this segregation seemed to some to be symbolised by the rule forbidding members of the University to stand about in the Market Place. But, as Canon Williams points out, this rule must almost certainly have been applied for the students' own protection. In those days Durham had its own Alsatia in the shape of the Framwellgate slum; and the times were times of mass unemployment, poverty, and resentment of those who apparently had the fruits of this world to enjoy by those who certainly had not.

The Market Place had traditionally been a forum for political propagandists. Meetings there could, and often did, turn nasty. Students 'represented a different order of humanity', as of course did everything that was represented by Palace Green. On one occasion the Dean himself was nearly thrown into the river. On another young Geoffrey himself was accosted on Framwellgate Bridge by

a cloth-capped, collarless individual who aggressively tugged at my gown sleeve and, in a disagreeable voice and with a shining look of hatred in his eye, demanded that I go back to my bloody college.

Rag Week brought the two disparate worlds temporarily together. Despite the resentment and the downright hatred of some, when the students made their house-to-house collections for the hospital in the neighbouring villages and towns, they were greeted with warmth and a truly amazing generosity. Geoffrey found that it was in the suburban residential areas that receptions were frigid and donations niggardly. For all that, few from the Town went along to the Palace Theatre (now demolished) on any of the three last days of Rag Week, where the Rag Revue was performed twice nightly.

Colonel Macfarlane-Grieve provided an important link between these two worlds, being involved with the Durham Lads' Club. On becoming Master, he recruited a number of Castlemen to help in the running of it. Geoffrey was one of these dutiful volunteers, becoming - but an ignominious once only - a timekeeper (one totally ignorant of the rules) at a boxing match between the town lads and Durham School, in the School's gymnasium.

In the week before the Michaelmas term there was a student mission of a week's duration to three of the parishes in Sunderland. This, like so many other good works, was organised by the ubiquitous SCM. About a dozen students stayed in houses in the parishes, visiting schools and clubs, and holding street-corner meetings during the day and preaching at mission services in the evening. It is comforting to know that these Christians were not thrown wholly unprepared among the wolves, for they were trained for this savage Circus contest in the year preceding by the vicar of Monkwearmouth, the Reverend W. Stannard.

Let us leave Canon Williams to have, as is his priestly right, one very last word about that perennial human hobby - Sin.

Ladies who lived in the town were not looked upon at all with favour. If a bulldog saw a male student walking with a female companion who was not a student, he would pluck the sleeve of that student's gown and ask if he knew the lady. This happened on one occasion when a student was taking his sister to catch her train after a visit to Durham. It may be that the basic human right is the right to sin; but it was not easy to exercise it in one particular in those not-so-far-off days.

CHAPTER 15

The Rule of The Colonels

Colonel Slater, writing in the 1954 *Castellum* of Macfarlane-Grieve's last days as Master, recalled how, during the Castlemen's Reunion in April, one old Castleman had remarked to him, with a glance at his predecessor, 'You'll have a hard job to follow him.'

Nearly all of Macfarlane-Grieve's active working life had been spent in the service of the University of Durham, and especially of University College. Those bare facts tell little to those who did not know him about the man who underlies them.

Angus Alexander Macfarlane-Grieve was born in 1891, the third son of W.A. Macfarlane-Grieve, of Impington Park, Cambridge, and Edenhall in Roxburghshire. He went to the Perse School, Cambridge, from where he went up to University College, graduating with Honours in Mathematics in 1913, despite a distinguished career as a College and University oarsman, and his becoming President of the Boat Club in his final year.

After graduating he was briefly in residence as a tutor, before being commissioned in 1914 in the Highland Light Infantry. While in France he obtained a regular commission in the Second Battalion the Seaforth Highlanders. By 1918 he was Acting Lieutenant-Colonel, and wearing the M.C. and the Italian *Croce di Valore*. In 1923 he retired from the Army with the substantive rank of Major and returned to Durham as 'Lecturer in Military Subjects'.

In 1929 Macfarlane-Grieve married Sarah St Osyth, second daughter of the Reverend George Margoliouth, an artist and lecturer at St Hild's.

Made Bursar of the College first, he was appointed Master in 1939 - the first Master of University College not to be in Holy Orders. His already failing sight could hardly have made the task of running the College through the Second World War easy, but added to the present disruption and the future uncertainties, he was, from 1940 until 1949, Master of Hatfield as well. He became Sub-Warden of the Durham Colleges from 1948 to 1953, the right-hand man of the Warden, then Dr (later, Sir) James Duff.

Always a sportsman, 'Mac' was for many years prominent in the Durham University Athletic Union, and Chairman of the Regatta Committee. After the War, having sympathetically helped steer Hatfield back to its rightful place as an independent College, he founded the Durham Castlemen's Society. After the advent of women - the Durham Castle Society.

On succeeding his brother in the family estate at Edenhall, he gave up the Mastership - with, I have no doubt, a heavy heart - and withdrew to the Scottish Borders, where he interested himself in farming and forestry, and to establishing his two sons as farmers in Dumfriesshire.

Castlemen who attended Reunions after he had left will remember with added poignancy the chant rising up, year after year after dinner 'Mac . . . Mac . . . Mac . . .'. When would follow a few gentle words.

Macfarlane-Grieve was Durham.

It's surprising how little of the man - indeed how little of any of the dons - we undergraduates of his time knew. It was widely believed that he was a History graduate, and that he lectured, once in a blue moon, in Military History; but nobody whom I or anybody else knew had ever heard him teach. Certainly very few gave him credit for scholarship; and it is perhaps easy to see why: for 'Mac' was sensitive and self-effacing, hiding his private self behind his virtually impenetrable pebble lenses. Slow to reply to one, his voice, when he did, was gentle, low, modulated. All of him, I think, belied a holder of those two battle honours, or his military rank, as it belied the scholarly mind that put Mathematics to one side for what scornful academics might well call 'a dilettante interest' in what he believed were things of value.

He wrote, as has been said earlier on, his *History of Durham Rowing*. In the same year as this came out, 1922, he published an article in the *Durham University Journal* on the *Treatise of Military Discipline* by Lieutenant-General Humphrey Bland, a manual first published in 1727. In March 1928, in the thick of a controversy over the proper timing for the celebration of the University's centenary in the forthcoming decade, he published in the *Journal* an article, quoting first sources, entitled 'The Centenary of the University: 1832 or 1837.' The matter touched him deeply.

Can there be any doubt that the passing of the Act of 1832 founded the University? How could a Staff be appointed, students come into residence in 1833, eight scholarships be endowed, if the University were not founded? Who would come into residence to read for degrees if there were any doubt as to the power of the University to confer degrees at the end of their course of study? True, there were no degrees conferred until 1837, but none of the students qualified by residence to take a degree until 1837. In neither the Act of 1832 nor the Charter of 1837 is the power of conferring degrees specifically mentioned. The name University surely carries with it that privilege.

It would be as reasonable for a man to celebrate his birthday on the anniversary of his christening, as for the University to celebrate its Centenary in 1937 instead of 1932.

Macfarlane-Grieve also published in the *DUJ*, over the period 1929 to 1932, a selection of letters: 'The Thorp Correspondence Concerning The Foundation of the University.' A year or so earlier he had unearthed the invaluable old Bursar's Book, or 'Waste Book', as Luke Ripley had called it, and part of this he published in the March 1925 issue of the *Journal* under the title 'University College in 1833.' On a lower note, if one may put it that way, are two Boating Songs (*DUJ*, June 1914 and March 1920). The earlier one was 'Arranged from *Edite, Bibite* in the *Kommersbuch*, by A.A. Macfarlane-Grieve, Esq.', though the words are by one H.St.G. - a frequent publisher of verse in the same source. The later one is wholly Macfarlane-Grieve's, words and music. They are included in the Appendix.

Of interest too is an article he wrote for the twelfth number of *Castellum*, 1959. Much of what he says about his time up at Castle, as an undergraduate that is, will be already familiar, but some new lights are thrown on already familiar features and people. There is little doubt, I think, that Macfarlane-Grieve's traditionalist, indeed paternalist approach to the College stems from his inheritance: those peaceful Edwardian days, halcyon days indeed, of the turn of the century: the Belle Époque.

When I came up to Castle in 1910 nobody dreamed of change and indeed nobody wanted it, and Durham was a happy little backwater ruled by men who saw no future for Durham but as a cheap alternative to the two older residential Universities. Indeed all the emphasis was on cheapness and Durham's motto seemed to be 'We may not be first class, but we are cheap.' In the College prospectus it was stated that the expenses in Durham amounted to about £100 a year but that many undergraduates had passed through the College on £20. Poor fellows!

The Durham Division numbered little over 200 and consisted of the Castle, Hatfield and the Unattached and the newly founded St Chad's and St John's. The Castle and Hatfield dominated the place and Hatfield was a degree cheaper than the Castle. It had candles instead of oil lamps and margarine instead of butter. Castle High Table dressed for Hall but Hatfield did not.

On Henry Gee and Lowe he is interesting. Did he, one wonders, model his own Mastership on that of Gee?

Dr H. Gee presided over the College as Master and an excellent Master he was. Sympathetic and kindly, he knew all about his men. He had a fund contributed by himself and some friends out of which he helped any undergraduate in need, a great boon in the days when there were no grants in aid by local authorities for the ordinary student. Like most of the staff he was a clergyman but he was one of the few Durham dons who were known outside Durham and he was Chaplain to the King.

When he became Master in 1902 there was no resident College Tutor . . . the following year Gee appointed W.D. Lowe as College Tutor under the Title of Junior Censor and as the Senate would not find the money to pay him, Gee paid him himself. Lowe was a grand fellow . . . He could easily have moved on to a more responsible post elsewhere but preferred to work in a small College where his influence was to have an incalculable and lasting effect. And he did not receive great encouragement in the Division as he was appointed by the Master, for independent action by a College was not to be encouraged . . .

'Mac' has of course something to say about rowing. Readers born into a more sceptical age will find the following of interest.

The Castle won the Pickard-Cambridge Cup in my first term but were disqualified for going on the wrong side of the last buoy.

Hatfield took the Cup so the College subscribed for consolation pewters for the disqualified crew and as far as I remember the cox got one. We took our rowing very seriously and it had been the custom for the crews to attend Chapel formally the evening before the race; this the cox had failed to do and the inference was obvious.

Of Lowe again:

Lowe was the Castle coach and the mainspring of the rowing, spending every afternoon on the river bank coaching one or more crews. The dons in turn used to give a training breakfast in the Senior Common Room and the night before the race Lowe entertained the crews to port and dessert in his room; when successful the crews held a Wine in one of the large rooms of the Keep to which Lowe was invited.

We have already been introduced by Canon Geoffrey Williams to Mr Green, the College Butler, and to Mrs Chilvers, the marmalade-making cook. Now hear Macfarlane-Grieve on the culinary couple:

The most important man in the Castle was R.J. Green, the Butler. A capable and strong-minded man, he had the complete confidence of the College Authorities which he justified by saving them all trouble on the domestic side. He was not altogether popular among undergraduates, one of whom described him as 'a portly product of beef and beer', but a drink had a mollifying effect on him and on the whole he used his influence fairly. His imposing figure in a tail coat added the right touch of dignity to Hall which was a good deal more formal then. We were required to wear dark jackets and stiff white collars, and turned-up trousers were frowned upon. Lunch on the other hand was more informal as the dons had lunch in their own rooms.

We saw little of the Master who usually dined in Hall once a week unless there were guests, but his influence was strong. He was a stickler for convention and we were severely reprimanded when we went out in a punt on the river on Sunday in a College blazer. He was equally strict with the College servants, and Mrs Chilvers, the cook, was admonished for walking out on Sunday wearing a hat trimmed with flowers, which was particularly reprehensible in the case of the Castle cook. Incidentally, Mrs Chilvers had never been married but her position in the Castle required the courtesy title.

Of the very vestigial relationships between the sexes, Macfarlane-Grieve wrote:

> Dances were not fashionable in Durham and it required some determination on the part of the men to make the acquaintance of any of the few women students in residence. To begin with, no male student was supposed to speak with one during lecture hours on Palace Green, and were he sufficiently bold to invite one to tea in his room he had to invite the Principal too. I think on the whole, however, we were in those days less flirtatiously inclined and more studious or sports minded according to our temperaments than later generations.

'Durham' in 1910, of course, included in its ambience Newcastle.

> There was very much of a family feeling in the Durham Division, everyone knew everyone else and the Medicals and Armstrong College in Newcastle were regarded as somewhat uninhibited in their outlook on University life. Our contact with them was in sport and the OTC, which was in fact very good for both of us as we were inclined to look down upon each other for different reasons. No doubt Durham was somewhat overweighted with budding young clergymen, some with a rather narrow outlook, and some of us used to take pleasure in shocking them and pulling their legs, not altogether to their detriment, I hope.

Macfarlane-Grieve was a Scholar of the College reading Mathematics; but in those days Honours men had to take during their first year all the Classics and Theology in the Pass Course as well as their Honours subjects. Thus at the end of his second year he was examined in Fisher's 'Theistic and Christian Belief' and on a Gospel in Greek.

I said earlier that Macfarlane-Grieve was 'self-effacing.' He was, I think, and as some of the above extracts show, a man of simple beliefs; simple tastes. Let him, in conclusion, speak for himself:

We were quite content with our tin baths and oil lamps and old-fashioned furniture. Perhaps the most enjoyable memory of College life in those days is sitting down to tea before a roasting coal fire after an afternoon on the river with two or three friends to share it and a pile of toasted tea-cakes on the hearth.

The impressions made by an older man on young impressionable men wholly dependent on him tell us often a good deal more than any number of 'salient facts' about his career. 'Mac', to his young men, was an institution. He had his eccentricities. He walked his spaniels sockless; walked bare-ankle deep in yellow daffodils over the Keep mound in Durham's late Spring. His impenetrable pebble-lenses removed him from any really effectual personal contact; but it was known that he would forgive a fellow Castleman anything - or almost anything. It was believed too that to row was the surest way to his heart. It would be truer to say that to be a loyal Castleman was the true key to his unassuming heart.

Graham Geoghegan, who later became Librarian of Reading University Education Library, told of him the following:

We were celebrating the fag end of an Aidan's maiden's twenty-first in my room in Bailey House. Having spent the evening at the *County* we were pretty high flown. We were making a hell of a row, and girls were everywhere, though it was well towards midnight. Then Hatfield's Censor, who was losing his beauty sleep, rang up our Censor, Dr Gregory, to complain, and he came bustling along to put a stop to the merriment. Nobody recognised him, as he pushed open the door, for the wine and the candlelight and the smoke and the crush and the euphoria of youth which haloed us all. So, 'Come on in!' I struggled to him through the throng. And I thrust a *Newcastle Brown* into his outstretched palm.

The very next day I had to appear before the Master. He sat there in his study scribbling his signature on one sheet of paper after another. He didn't look up. At last I had to splinter the silence. 'Master,' I croaked, cravenly pleading, 'I know I've broken College rules . . . 'And fell silent before that raised impassive masklike face.

His eyes, what little I could see of them behind the pebble-lenses, clouded over with mystification. Then at last the dawn broke, and in its uncertain light the lenses seemed to me to sparkle. 'Oh yes, I remember. Well, Geoghegan, College rules are made to be broken . . .'

There followed a long pause, before he leaned forward, shook his neat grey seal's head, and added: 'You see, the trouble is, it was a Hatfield man who complained!'

It surprises one that such a man could be heavy-handed. The Minutes of the Junior Common Room chronicle an Extraordinary Meeting held on Friday 10 December 1943 - halfway this through the Second World War.

The Senior Man [E.R. Mercer] explained the cause of the meeting, held only 19 hours after the last. The College had been astounded, disturbed and greatly shocked by a notice which the Censor had posted only that morning. This informed the College that owing to the behaviour after dinner last night the whole College was to be gated that night from 7 p.m. onwards. The Censor emphasised that everyone must remain in their [sic] rooms, and that noone in Castle should be allowed to go to the dance [the Christmas Ball].

The Senior Man said that he had seen the Master, who appeared to be intractable. The Master took a serious view of the fact that a) certain Castlemen had erected the road block on Prebends' Bridge, and b) certain members of the College had visited the Common Rooms of all the other Colleges and sung carols. Apparently he had received protests from the Dean and Chapter, and the Principals of the Women's Colleges.

The Committee expressed the JCR's disquiet to the Censor and Master.

The meeting was adjourned, and reconvened at 4.15.

The Master to some extent mitigated the penalty. 1) He said that the more serious offence was the erecting of the road block on Prebends' Bridge. As he had been assured that this was the work of a certain enthusiastic half dozen who had just finished finals, and was entirely separate from the carol-singing episode, he proposed that if these gentlemen would own up they would be gated for the night. 2) As it now appeared that the carol-singing was undertaken only by some 50% of the College, he proposed to sconce these gentlemen only, provided they owned up and gave their word of honour they were unconnected with the affair of Prebends' Bridge. These latter gentlemen and the rest of the College would be free to go to the dance.

It is suitable to add here that noone had been asked yet to own up - the penalty was inflicted without the College having been consulted at all, and the Master had been under the impression that the College had been in the affair *en masse*.

There was a positive queue waiting upon the instant to confess, and the Senior Man took a list of those gentlemen concerned.

It is pleasant to record that the dance proved a highly successful one, 'with everyone in an extremely good humour.'

By 1947, only four years later, such high-handed measures to enforce discipline would never have been contemplated by a Master, let alone tolerated by such sinners.

On his retirement in 1953 the College - old Castlemen too, of course, were invited to subscribe - presented Macfarlane-Grieve with a crayon portrait of himself by the artist John Wheatley - Macfarlane-Grieve himself begrudged the expense of an oil portrait - and with a gold wristlet watch. The portrait, a splendid likeness, hangs of course in Castle. Touchingly, at the Macfarlane-Grieves' farewell dinner, Mrs Macfarlane-Grieve when thanking the College for her bouquet said that, though she had been associated with the Castle since the day of her marriage in 1929, this was the first time for her to have dined in Hall!

In this same year a certain amount of change, sometimes even of real progress, was effected. One must remember that during the War little or nothing could be done save maintain a holding operation, and indeed for some five or six years after the war was over the stranglehold of economic stringency inhibited any serious reform. Now the University Grants Committee gave a grant of £16,500 for carrying out a scheme, devised by Mr Elgey, for building new domestic staff quarters on two new floor levels, constructed underneath the old silver pantry and adjacent to the west Courtyard. This freed the former servants' quarters to be completely remodelled to form five new single bed-sitters for students, opening off the back of Hall Stairs. Work was also about to begin on converting the silver pantry and staff dining room adjoining the Hall on the west side into a servery and wash-up, with access directly through a widened entrance into the Hall. This promised that warm meals would, when the work was completed, be served warm. The College still owned Abbey House, and a further grant of £2,200 enabled some new rooms and what was described as 'a sumptuous new bathroom block' to be created from the House's dilapidated basement cellars.

From this, the first real post-War construction programme, one can see that the outstanding need for the College was felt to be single rooms; and it was a sad side-effect of the great increase in numbers, from which every difficulty seemed to spring - students resident in 1953/4 mustered 248 - that nobody, not even a third-year man, could now be guaranteed a single room in Durham.

The great achievement of Macfarlane-Grieve's last years was however the restoration of the Norman Chapel - one of the earliest and most complete pieces of early Norman work in the country, and dated to within a few years of 1072. It presented, to pre-1950 generations of Castlemen, a picture of dilapidation and decay: was become but a convenient passageway to the Keep; a mere means of access to the JCR; on occasions even a cloak-room, a cycle-shed and a general store-room. Restoring it to its former splendour cost £10,000, the money coming from a bequest under the will of Mr John Wilson Lowthian, which the Council of the Durham Colleges put to the restoration fund; from another generous gift of the Pilgrim Trust; and from various smaller donations.

One of the main problems facing the restorers was the appalling dampness of the building, the floor being fifteen to sixteen feet below the level of the ground outside. As a consequence the sandstone walls and columns and the basaltic stones of the floor were badly eroded. Hot water pipes were now laid under the floor to damp-proof it, keep the columns dry, and guard the soft sandstone from further disintegration. The two old steps at the east end, which were thought to have been added some time after the building of the Chapel, were removed and a small dais put in their place to take 'an altar of the Laudian type.'

An alternative route had now to be made, of course, from the Courtyard to the Keep and the JCR, and this was provided by excavating a passage under the Tunstal Chapel to connect with the Keep stairs and give an entrance to the JCR on the right of the fireplace. Inside the Chapel, concealed lighting showed the richly ornamented capitals to their best advantage. Oak furniture, an altar, five benches and two prayer desks, were given by the Warden of the Durham Colleges, Sir James Duff, in memory of the RAF Cadets who died in the Second World War.

On a smaller scale, another ecclesiastical advance was made, with the addition of a vestry to the Tunstal Chapel, which was constructed in the same year above the Keep stairway. This was made possible through a gift from Macfarlane-Grieve; the Old Master's arms are to be found on the vestry door.

But the first cracks had begun to appear in the traditional facade. 'Impassioned' declamations were to be heard in JCR over the wearing of gowns after dusk. Gowns, inevitably, would go. Meanwhile another old tradition, the *Floreat*, was horribly eroded. Numbers having become so great, the ceremony, so it was claimed, 'lasted far too long and thereby lost much of its spontaneity and enthusiasm'. In a grey shadowing of its old splendour, the Arthurian Cup now went only to High Table, the Senior Man, the Secretary and the winning team.

Even the Literary and Debating Society showed signs of falling on evil days. A report in the 1955 *Castellum* lamented that the interest of Castlemen in the Visitors' Night Debate seemed to have decreased rapidly over the past few years, so much so that consideration was even being given to the possibility of holding the 1955 debate in the Union Debating Hall in - informal dress!

Much of this lack of interest stemmed, of course, from the difficulty of getting speakers of stature up to Durham. It was a simple question of logistics. The Freshers' Debate retained its ancient popularity with, in 1954, 140 attending, 'of whom 248 voted for the motion [That the House would never dream of it], and 248 against, with 248 abstentions. But the Visitors Night Debate presented the organisers in those pre-Inter-City Flyer days with an impossible situation - unless those pressured into speaking were local worthies.

Things had been exactly the same five years earlier when the present writer was Secretary. Of the twenty or so well-known names invited to speak on the motion 'That Fanaticism is essential to Success', all declined, most with a cursory postcard or note, but some confessing outright that Durham was far too far for them to attend in person. In the end, 1950 had to make do with Dean Alington speaking for the motion, and the Warden, Sir James Duff, speaking against. The quite phenomenal success of 1950, as far as the Literary and Debating Society was concerned, was the appearance of the remarkable Dorothy L. Sayers, who gave a talk on Dante, 'The City of Dis', which received all but a standing ovation. This most memorable evening was however only made possible because Dorothy L. Sayers was in Durham to receive an honorary D.Litt.

It seems to have taken the President and Secretary of the 'Lit and Deb Soc' an inordinate time to realise that Durham, unlike Oxford and Cambridge, suffered from the crippling disease of distance. One must assume also that the prestige of the two older universities played a considerable, though perhaps not preponderant, role in swaying prospective speakers against making the journey to the Durham debating chamber. In 1947, for instance, T.S. Eliot was invited - only to decline! By the following year the message had still not sunk in, since the President and Secretary, at the initial meeting to decide the programme for the year, said they would 'try to obtain Mr Churchill and Mr J.B. Priestley.' Mr Roy Arnold countered that he might secure Mr Eden, or (he being a Labour Party supporter) Mr Attlee's private secretary.

Some few things remained however - if only for the time. Mr 'Joe' Bryce, the Bursar's clerk, celebrated twenty-five years' service with the College and was presented, at the Christmas Dinner, with what can only be called the century's greatest anachronism: 'a Queen Anne table lighter'. The Castle Wine persisted, as did Castle Day. And the Read and Weed was in full puff; though its earlier aura of secrecy had been obliterated in the egalitarian post-War dawn. Now it went public, if not full frontal.

Mr J.S. Morland delivered a paper entitled 'Dark Interlude', being a study of witchcraft in the Middle Ages . . . Thomas Sharp's book *Cathedral City* was reviewed by Mr G.H. Hunt . . . Mr Ward read a paper entitled 'Chivalry: Actuality or Ideal of Mediaeval Society' . . . Mr W.R. Howell . . . gave a biographical sketch of Auguste Renoir [and] an interesting discussion followed on the relative merits of the Impressionist and Classical Compositionist schools of painting . . . in 19th century France . . . 'The Natural History of the Honey Bee' was the subject of a talk by Mr T.L. Goodfellow . . . [and] 'The Christian and Biblical view of history outlined in the light of and in contrast to the secular views associated with the ancient Greek philosophers, the Western Liberalists, Hegel and Marx, and contemporary historians like Fisher,' was the subject of a provocative talk given by Mr R.B. Jackson, [while] at the Annual Visitors' Night Meeting, Mr M.M. Derhalli, one of the members of the College SCR, gave a . . . paper on the 'Cultural Problem in the Near East.'

The following year, 1955, saw the surfacing of the same old problems of the lack of single rooms, the decrepitude of College furniture, the dinginess of the Castle's decoration, and the perpetual shortage of money contingent upon the College's being spread over two mediaeval castles and four separate outlying buildings around Palace Green. Now for the first time there was talk of the College's hiring itself out for residential courses and other similar functions, to try to make ends meet; and inevitably the Catch 22 situation arose: in order to make the College attractive to such courses both the furnishings and 'the plumbing' would have to be taken in hand.

Meanwhile, Mutabilitie continued to wreak her deadly handiwork. The Castle lost its Fives Courts in Fellows Garden to the Library. And to the Library went also Lecture Room 5, where Castlemen, and others, had waltzed and fox-trotted their partners time out of mind before walking them 'home' across the echoing green.

At Lumley Castle too the long drive between the sheep-patched fields was tarmacked. Gone now was the old rutted track which gave the romantic undergraduate trudging up it the blest illusion that he had stepped back into the Antony Watteau world of Vanbrugh. And this is as good a time as any to say what has to be said about that place of incomparable beauty, Lumley.

The story begins with the return, after demobilisation, of Leonard Slater, to take up again his post of lecturer in charge of Geography. This was in January 1946, and he and Mrs Slater were given rooms in Castle. Later in the same term however he was called in by James Duff to be told of 'a new project' - to take into University College Lumley Castle, the family seat of Sir Roger Lumley, who in a very short while was to be Earl of Scarbrough. From the point of view of the University, the proposed extension of the College's accommodation was timely, if not ideal (Lumley being just outside Chester-le-Street, seven long miles out of Durham), for a bulge in student applications was expected owing to the government's Further Education and Training Scheme. In the words of James Duff, 'four or five dozen.' From the point of view of the owner, it was ideal. Handing over Lumley Castle to the University meant that an application could be submitted for a licence for steel, necessary to make the castle structurally sound; and to obtain other materials in short supply, such as piping to extend the very small existing central heating system to cover virtually the whole building, thus making almost all of it available for use. The rent paid by the University was to be a peppercorn one only; but by the usual ingenious tax disarrangement, the capital cost of conversion and development for College use was to be recovered by the Earl of Scarbrough over twenty or thirty years.

The Colonel moved into Lumley in the summer of 1946, and Mrs Slater moved in in the September, before the castle was in any way ready for civilised habitation, there being for instance no hot water but the pittance pourable from kettles. Local girls were averse to coming to work there, on account of the local tradition that the castle entertained a ghost - in this case Lily of Lumley. The first two maids who dared venture to come did so only on condition that they shared the same room. An intrepid married couple, Mr and Mrs Mitchell, were not put off, however, and were appointed steward and housekeeper respectively. As well as no hot water, there was also no electric light, and the candles without doubt did as much as anything to encourage the fears among the servant girls of the ghostly Lily. By October however forty-five rooms had been made ready for students, and about twelve staff, eight of them heroic residents, had been appointed.

In a couple more years the old stables were converted into students' rooms, while a previously unused tower was tortured into making another six. Thus by 1948-9 Lumley provided accommodation for seventy-five students.

In the tower rooms - some housed half a dozen places; some eight - flimsy partitions about eight feet high separated a vast rectangular space into smaller rectangles, each of which was a student bedroom. Their occupants had to make their hazardous way down stone spiral staircases to find the lavatories and washbasins with running water. Studies were further down again, and provided reading rooms for four, six or eight.

The author of all these 'woes', though woes they certainly were not to those undergraduates fortunate enough to live there, giving his account of his time as Vice-Master in charge of Lumley, writes somewhat apologetically of all this: 'tolerance was the order of the day . . . Lumley was a good deal better than barracks . . .'

But those happy enough to have lived at Lumley remember it very differently; remember it as one of the most moving experiences of their lives. It was indeed a close-knit community which lived there; so close-knit indeed that a real fear came to exist in those who were *Durham* Castlemen that Lumley was becoming a place apart, with a *genius loci* all its own.

If Durham had its magnificent Great Hall, Lumley had its own Baron's Hall, smaller of course but exquisite in its proportions, with marble busts of Victoria and some of her Ministers perched high up on the high white walls. There was a bar. There was table tennis. And there was also the nucleus of a library. On the first floor, to which one mounted by a flight of elegant stairs on the right or by another exactly symmetrical on the left, one took coffee after dinner. Standing there on the blue carpet, under the towering white walls, one might be forgiven cocking one's sudden ear to hear the rustle of a stiff petticoat, the click of an unfurled fan. And no Lumley Man will ever forget the Pillared Hall, low-ceilinged, intimate as one would never imagine stone could be - the embrasured sitting-out room at the paradise's 'Lumley Dances'.

Only Lumley's distance from Durham, and its inevitable severance from the Castle itself, made for criticism. Lumley men travelled to Durham every day to their lectures in the departments, each being presented with a free bus ticket giving him a hundred and twenty journeys per term in either direction. To ease life, an early morning bus left the bottom of the drive at half past eight.

Of course administratively, the use of Lumley, involving as it did duplication of both housekeeping and maintenance staff, made University College grossly uneconomic; that despite this Lumley ran until 1969 is sufficient testimony to both its success and its popularity. Part of this success was of course due to its homogeneity: like the Castle itself, it formed a family. The same could never be said of the 'outhouses' which had for far too long housed Castlemen: Abbey House, Cosin's Hall, Bailey House, Owengate, Parson's Field House, and the digs scattered over the city to which hapless teaching certificate students were exiled.

The answer to the whole problem of student accommodation, and the subsidiary problem of preserving the College as an entity, lay only in rebuilding, especially in the rebuilding of Owengate, standing as it did next door to the Castle; and it was to this objective that the new Master turned his attention.

One can say, I think, that this period of the College's history was a coming to terms with, and a coping with, the changing face of the University - and therefore that of the College. For over a century Durham had been a small northern university, so small sometimes that the normal social and sporting functions associated with a university were in grave jeopardy;

and while it did draw students from other parts of the kingdom, it was to the north that it really looked for its undergraduates. Post-war Britain changed this, and changed it radically. The RAF Cadets who flocked to it at the start of the war came from everywhere; and those students who came to Durham after the war under the Government's Further Education and Training Scheme came from everywhere. To cope with these extra numbers places had to be found, and, certainly in the new brash and demanding post-war climate, what amenities there were had to be brought drastically up to scratch. More, to cope with the increased and increasing financial burden of running a College like University College, recourse had to be had to vacation lettings: to cashing in on the new pastime of traipsing all over the country - indeed all over the world - to conferences both business and academic. And logic pointed out very clearly that conferences would not come to Castle unless the amenities found there were at least on a par with those found everywhere else. These parallel advances, in population and in plumbing, took the University from being the small self-contained unit it had for so long been, to being a close runner in popularity to the two older Universities, and made University College one of the most sought-after Colleges among prospective undergraduates. This understood, the growth, indeed the transformation, of the University and the College can be easily understood.

Since he had run Lumley so successfully, 'Len' Slater was, not surprisingly, the front runner to take over the Mastership from Macfarlane-Grieve; yet he was, by his own account, a surprised and none too consenting victim.

The story of his apotheosis is an interesting one. As a part-time teacher in the Geography Department, and now a Reader, he had academic ambitions that inevitably came into conflict with the day-to-day running of a College, as Lumley itself showed him. Durham *academia* therefore called him. He bought a plot of land on Quarry Heads Lane and set about planning a house. A lively lot of students gave a new zest to life in the Geography Department. And now, by 1953, a second son had arrived. As for Lumley, it had expanded to its full 75-student capacity. Now, if ever, was the time to go; and Colonel Slater was on the edge of resigning the Vice-Mastership, to engage in research and try for a Chair. There was a lot in favour of his choosing an academic career: he had been External Examiner for Edinburgh; he was on national committees in both the

Institute of British Geographers and the British Association for the Advancement of Science; and he had already been asked whether he would be interested in applying for a Chair in Glasgow.

Then the blow fell - if one can call such a happy chance a blow. James Duff told him that Angus Macfarlane-Grieve was proposing to retire early in order to teach his two sons how to farm in Scotland, and asked him to consider running for the Mastership. Aghast, Len Slater set before the Warden his academic plans. Duff countered that in his opinion the Durham Geography Department would not grow sufficiently for it ever to be able to offer him a Chair; but in any case, the Mastership of University College was more important - so important indeed that there was no question of his being able to combine the two posts. His Readership would have to be given up.

Duff won the day.

One of the more interesting developments in Colonel Slater's earlier years was the transformation of the Undercroft to what he himself rightly described as 'one of the most distinctive and characterful JCR's in the United Kingdom.' The Undercroft, as he inherited it, was divided in two by fairly recently bricked-up arches. One half had a cracked concrete floor and was a tangle of wires for the electricity, and a refinery of pipes for the central heating, above. The other half was a wood store, left over from the days when kindling was used in quantity for the students' fires, and a repository for discarded furniture. The Master, who had been trained as a surveyor, surmised that the floors on both sides were very likely level, so that were the arches only to be opened out the two rooms could be made one. Prolonged argument with 'the Authorities' finally carried the day; their further contention that the place would be inadequately ventilated was countered by the Master's proposal to glaze the small embrasures at Courtyard level, put a staircase up through the thick wall to the servery, and make another door into what was called 'the tunnel'.

Had this happy transformation of the Undercroft been foreshadowed, one wonders, as early as 1951, when the ever- imaginative Boat Club used it for its December Dinner, a banquet attended by the new Dean, Dr Wilde, and Macfarlane-Grieve? It was certainly the first time it had been used in decades; and the Boatmen had to clear the place out themselves. After this Kierkegaardian 'leap in the dark' it was used only sporadically, until Len Slater made it into the JCR of all JCR's.

The gallery in the Great Hall had always been an eyesore. The floor of this was now levelled, and an access door made to lead to it from Hall Stairs, while of the arms and armour which had long been propped nonchalantly against the wall, some were now decently housed there while others were transferred to new quarters in the Tunstal Gallery.

The Lowe Library was also transferred from its old quarters on Garden Stairs to larger premises adjacent to Hall Stairs; a spiral staircase was built in to lead up to a low gallery and, further on, to a room on Hall Stairs which for generations had been occupied by the Librarian.

One change of the time totally unconnected with the physical requirements of students was the abolition of Assizes, which came about through the Streatfield reform of the administration of justice, so that, for good or ill, judges no longer came to stay in the Castle.

The Bishop's Room however continues to be used by the Bishop from time to time, but *O tempora mutantur!* that humbled man is now constrained to ask the College if 'on a certain time, on a certain day, it would be convenient if he might use his room.'

In fulfilment of that aforementioned aim of providing single accommodation for every student, changes were made to the sets in the Keep and the Junction. Early on in Colonel Slater's Mastership, the Keep and Junction rooms were re-partitioned to increase the number of rooms. For a time each of the sets in the Keep (a large sitting-room with an adjoining small bedroom) housed three. One student used the small bedroom as a single bed-sitter; the other two shared the large room as a double bed-sitting-room. 'It was,' Colonel Slater writes cryptically in his memoir of his years in office, 'asking for trouble, and we got it.' As a result of whatever problems the system gave rise to, these large rooms were subdivided to make two single bed-sitters out of each. Single bed-sitters now became the 'norm' in Castle, as they were in every modern College in Durham.

This period of expansion also took in, most happily, a bigger wine-cellar under the Lowe Library.

Further developments during this period were those at Owengate and Bailey Court. The Moatside Lane development was completed after Colonel Slater's time, though it had been planned many years before. The pressing need for these developments was, of course, the large increase in the numbers applying for places at University College; but there was also the numbing requirement that the College become financially sound, something which could be achieved only by adding to its present complement another sixty to seventy student places.

There is an interesting aside in Colonel Slater's memoir relating to the continuing problem of financing the Castle as the heart of University College. The Masters of the new Colleges being aggrieved at the subsidies which, in one form or another, were going to maintain the Castle, there was in the 'Fifties a quite serious proposal to make the Castle the administrative centre of the University, the argument being that, this being effected, the money frittered away on running the Castle would more productively be spent on offices, typewriters, Tipp-Ex, concertina-files, computer back-up, and all the other jungle paraphernalia of bureaucracy. Thus at a stroke would disappear the single cause of envy and disaffection among College heads. This at once debilitating and wildly optimistic proposal was thankfully exoceted at once when the Old Shire Hall became vacant - it being already accustomed to such mundane uses as offices and officers require.

The administration of University College inevitably changed. No longer the sparse, if not Spartan, establishment of one part-time Tutor, one part-time Bursar, one Finance Clerk, one girl Secretary and a Master; but something altogether new and strange. This to cope with a University College worlds removed from that envisaged, and almost single-handedly run, by Charles Thorp: a College which, in 1958, at the beginning of the boom in Durham's popularity, numbered 277 students, of whom 219 were undergraduates, and of whose 58 graduates no fewer than 30 were holders of Research Awards. A College for which, in this year, there were 1,800 enquiries for application forms, and 1,500 of those forms returned - all for the mere 75 vacancies to be filled.

In 1958 a bronze tablet commemorating the work of old deaf Professor Heawood, who twenty-five years before had done much to raise the money for the Castle's preservation, was fixed to the panelling of the Hall near to the doorway of the Black Staircase. He had been a mathematician of genius who had written a treatise on the mathematics of colour. And the College welcomed as its new Chaplain Geoffrey Griffith, who came into the Church from Industry, and was, so we learned much later, a footballer of some renown.

To the horror of some, the JCR adopted a new Castle tie; with but one brave abstention discarding the old model of white stripes on a maroon background in favour of one which consisted of black crosses and gold mitres (two motifs from the Castle badge) on maroon. With a sanguineness which seems to have seeped through from a long-lost pre-Darwinian world, Hunter Davies, the then Senior Man, wrote: 'It [the change] is unlikely to be treated as a precedent, and there is little danger of other Castle traditions being altered.'

After all, the Read and Weed was still going strong. Two old Minute Books, very recently discovered and covering the years 1922 to 1926 and 1929 to 1939 shed some honourable light on its past history.

Not altogether surprisingly, during the 'Twenties the muscular Boat Club seems to have secured a monopoly of the Read and Weed's members - one remembers that Castlemen then numbered a mere handful, all of whom were expected to do everything. The numbers of the Club were then limited to ten, and they met deliciously for breakfast on Sunday mornings in a room at the top of the Keep.

Previous to 1922 the Read and Weed, 'along with all the other College Clubs', had for unspecified reasons been dissolved by Dr Gee. One would dearly like to know the reason for such a draconian measure, but of course one never will. It was resuscitated in 1922, only to die within the hour, but was resurrected again in 1929. In 1940 it fell - with France; to surface in January 1947, with a new constitution which limited membership to eight, to be elected by secret ballot. Under the new regime, horizons were clearly expanded beyond the frowsting over dramatic texts, the lectures on 'The Ideal State as Described in Plato's Republic', and the puffing of lethal cigarettes and noisy suckings of recalcitrant pipes; for the final meeting of the year was a punting outing at the end of the Easter Term, for which the gods bequeathed the eight Tribunes fine weather.

But despite Hunter Davies' sanguineness links with the past were being steadily broken. In 1959 one of those two 'Varsity policemen who had bade Gordon Berriman and his fellow Thespian to 'move along there!' retired: Jack Gray, who had been University Bedel since 1930, and who, in that awesome capacity, had carried the Mace at every Congregation and every official University ceremony. To the surprise, no doubt, of the many who had trembled before him, it came out that he had long served as President of the Durham Colleges' Golf Club. To commemorate P.C.Gray's twenty-eight years' service the University presented a silver cup, known forevermore as the Jack Gray Trophy, to be held by the Durham University

Athletic Union and competed for annually between teams composed of both staff and students from the Durham Colleges, King's and the Medical School.

Though links with the past, however tenuous, however frail, were still being forged (Freshers' Coffee for instance was hauled squealing back into life; together with Castle Wine - small victories these), the Freshers' Debate was soon brought under the ban; for a most horribly pious reference to this ancient institution in the *Castellum* of 1959 declared that

> The form of the Freshers' Debate in previous years has been regarded by many members of the College and by Officers of the Society as rather distasteful and unworthy of a student community. An attempt was made this year to convert the event into something more worthwhile, but what must surely be a minority faction of the audience made this attempt extremely difficult if not entirely fruitless. Short of abandoning the Debate altogether, there is little that can be done except to impress on members the infantile nature of much of the humour that has in recent years become typical of the Debate. It is to be hoped that constant reminders will eventually convert the event into what it should be: a frivolous debate whose wit would be a credit to the College and a good introduction for Freshers into the true nature of student life.

Perhaps the Freshmen had been unsavoury as well as unseemly; and the new Chaplain had not sufficiently thrashed his whip. Yet ways other than this draconian one had always existed to modify pernicious behaviour.

Christmas Dinner even was deprived of much of its charm by the exclusion of Lumley men from it, on the grounds of space. Rumour had it that this was but a specious manoeuvre to strip from the tables some of the camouflage from which Castlemen had been wont to snipe at High Table - one Dr Atkin having been struck the year before by a quarter of a pound of margarine.

But Freshers' Coffee and Freshers' Wine still promised well, looking back for inspiration as they did to an age that provided for itself its own entertainment.

For the first:
Freshers' Coffee (16th November, 1959):-

1) Sketches by Bob Earnshaw, Malcolm Thompson, Bill Darwin and Co., including a fashion parade and a travesty of 'Look Back in Anger.'

2) Songs from Schumann's 'Dichterliebe', sung by David Ingall.

3) Piano solos by John Peace.

4) Ballads by Paddy Roberts, realised by Roger Mills and Robin Walter.

And for the second:
Castle Wine 10th March, 1960:-

1) More sketches from the same combine, including an exposure of University interview technique and the première of a pantrymime, 'Harleyquinade', in which Malcolm Thompson performed most movingly the Dance of the Dying Duck.

2) Piano pieces by Milhaud, played by John Peace.

3) An oboe sonata by Loellet, played by Malcolm Turner.

4) Unprepared impromptus by the College Scouts.

5) Piano duets by Dr Atkin and Mr David Barlow (Lecturer in Music at King's). These proved the most popular items of the evening, executed as they were with all the loving musicianship that can make the overtures 'Zampa', 'The Marriage of Figaro' and 'Poet and Peasant' sound alike . .

But this seeming health of Castle Wine was all too illusory, like the last upsurge of energy of the flushed consumptive; for in a year or two K. Spyer, reporting on the JCR for *Castellum* lamented that 'Castle Wine has for the last two years been replaced by party-dances in accordance with the general trend to replace the sophisticated humour of the cabaret with the vibrant beat of the rock group.' And saddest of all to relate, the insidious foe television - to the Hasidic Jews 'the open sewer in the sitting-room' - threatened even Freshers' Coffee. The report in 1964's *Castellum* began: 'Freshers' Coffee seemed likely in spite of Z-Cars . . .'

1960 saw a rather charming instance of *deja vu*, for the new Lowe Library, now splendidly equipped with leather chairs embossed with gilt College crests, was opened by that same Miss D. Lowe, the sister of W.D. Lowe, who in February 1926 had carried out the initial opening ceremony. It saw also the death of the Lowe Librarian, Dr J.V. Whitworth, who had first joined the Senior Common Room in 1948 and who had been Lowe Librarian since 1951. A convivial man, 'Jimmy' Whitworth bade fair to become, had he lived, one of that dwindling band of Durham eccentrics: in the words of a more spacious age - 'large as life and twice as natural.'

One cannot say that *deja vu* marked the Queen's lunching in the Castle during her visit on 27 May, except at the very longest remove, for the last monarch to dine there was that execrable dullard James the First of England and Sixth of Scotland, who braved the north at the start of the seventeenth century. Queen Elizabeth having expressed a gracious wish that members of the College would lunch with her, as it were, the members as graciously did so in their gowns and best suits.

The account of the Queen's visit in the *Castellum* of 1960 jogged the memory of a Castleman, F.H.T. Cartwright, who had been up from 1897 to 1899, and who quaveringly wondered

> Was it in 1897 or 1898 when the then Prince of Wales came and was shown round? He did not stay for lunch but had a glass of the College port which he pronounced very good. I believe we paid 3/6 a bottle for it in those days. As he was driven off to lunch with the Dean we tried to hang on to the carriage but the escort of mounted police tried to stop our rag and one at least of us was rather badly damaged.

I can tell him - though of course now he knows! - it was 1898. For on that memorable visit of the Great Peacemaker, smelling of 'Skittles' Walters's patchouli and prime Havana cigars, the following delightful encounter took place:

> When the Prince of Wales was taken into the Norman Gallery, on the occasion of his last visit to the Castle, he expressed a wish to see

one of the students' rooms. A door stood open, and the Master invited him to enter. Unfortunately, a Lady of the Bedchamber was concealed behind the door, endeavouring to get a look at His Royal Highness. The Prince courteously raised his hat, and said, 'A lady-student, I presume?' 'Get along, your Royal Highness,' said the Lady of the Bedchamber, 'we don't take lady-students at University College, though there's no knowing what we may come to.'[1]

The eleven o'clock curfew went in 1961. The gate, long shut at eleven and opened by the Lodge-keeper for a late fee, was kept open till midnight, the College undertaking to pay the portresses for their extra hour of wakefulness. Perhaps this momentous change was what lay behind the hugely increased popularity of Castle, which in this year received over 2,600 applications for only 72 places.

And, two years later, women were allowed as guests in Hall.

Readers will certainly remember Canon Geoffrey Williams' quoting from the little booklet he was sent by Dr How, on his applying for information about scholarships to Castle, and will recall the somewhat florid description of the College contained in it. The writer was Sydney Walton, who died in 1963, aged 82. While the prose-style of his contribution to the College booklet might not have been to the more sophisticated taste of the young Geoffrey, betraying as it does a too too great familiarity with the boys' books of G.A. Henty, it showed a man only too moved by the laying-on of hands by that *genius loci* who has touched some few in this place. If only on that account, he deserves a mention in these pages.

Sydney Walton, who was born in Frosterley in Durham, was a journalist. To his credit, he studied at evening classes to get to the University; and coming to this College the hard and not the soft way, he had the most passionate commitment to the place.

Macfarlane-Grieve wrote of him in the 1964 *Castellum* :

The death of Sydney Walton has removed not only a remarkable man but a true friend of University College. He himself said that he regarded his years of residence in the Castle as the inspiration of his life and he never stayed in the Castle without paying a visit to his old room in the Norman Gallery. He was proud of being a graduate of the College and was not afraid of saying so. In the 1920's when the Castle was in danger of collapse he did what he could as a publicist to raise money for its preservation. He never lost an opportunity of singing the praises of Durham and its Castle and Cathedral.

It is not necessary to mention in detail the many ways in which Sydney Walton showed his love for his College. I received a letter from him three days before his death in which he expressed a longing to be back in the Castle once more 'The Cathedral bells ringing in my ears.' He was the most loyal and devoted of old Castlemen.

1964 saw too the departure, but not to the Elysian Fields, of the Vice-Master, Dr W.A. (Willie) Prowse, who migrated from Lumley to the new College, Van Mildert.

There were other changes too. The Owengate site came 'on tap'. The Minstrels' Gallery came into use for Luncheon. And following the experiment of the previous year, ladies were now able to dine at High Table on any Wednesday and at Low Tables on Mondays, Wednesdays and Sundays. Over three thousand young hopefuls applied for the seventy-five places at Castle; and for the first time the total membership of the College exceeded three hundred. With the erection of the new SRC building, Dunelm House, at the east end of Kingsgate Bridge, Castle could once more almost call its Hall its own, without being called upon to be hosts to every SRC Ball; but, such are the vagaries of Fortune's Wheel, it was almost simultaneously discovered that the Hall's acoustics could scarcely be bettered for concerts, and the demands that the College play host to players of Bach and Bartok, of Poulenc and Prokofiev, grew apace. While for the 'muddied oafs and flannelled fools' (not my words, reader, but Tennyson's) the new Maiden Castle Sports Hall and Playing Fields were opened by one who emerged from out the Celtic twilights: D.C.T. Rowlands, Captain of the Welsh Rugby Union XV and member of the National Council for Sport.

Aggrieved members of this College who feel I have long neglected sport will be relieved to read now that the Sports Hall cost £110,000 - in this year, 1994, about £550,000. It has an indoor area of 13,500 square feet, and is equipped to provide facilities for basketball, netball, tennis, cricket, golf, indoor football, indoor athletics, trampolining, table tennis, gymnastics, badminton. volleyball, weight training, physical training, judo and - alas - boxing; and it has spectator accommodation for 250 and twenty changing rooms. As to the Playing Field, which cost a trifling £20,000, its area of 40 acres provides grounds for three Rugby pitches, four Association Football pitches, three hockey pitches, two cricket squares, and one full-size hard-surfaced Athletics track.

1965 saw Authority in once again a hard-featured light for, disapproving of the riotous assemblies which Christmas Dinners in some Colleges had become, the Dinners were banned for the foreseeable future in every one of them. This at a time when Castle Wine, being considered no longer 'a viable affair', was amalgamated with Freshers' Coffee to create Freshers' Wine; and the once venerable Literary and Debating Society prepared to celebrate in 1966 its tenth year of hibernation.

The following year saw another break with the past with the end of battels, it being considered in the frenetic 'Sixties that the time spent by the College office and the JCR in operating the system quite failed to justify its existence. The Lit. and Deb. Soc. made one last throw to avoid extinction, and produced in Castle Hall, though to a pitiful audience, *The Hollow Crown*. At the end of the year no new President was elected as noone was prepared to stand.

At least the College, like the other Colleges, was spared the spectacles that were enacted in 1967-8 in Universities throughout the world, when protests, marches, sit-ins, lock-outs, strikes and demonstrations were as daily fare as toast and marmalade; and the names Danny the Red and Tariq Ali were on everybody's lips. One wonders whether it was to disarm those who muttered abuse against privilege that an invitation was issued to all graduates of more than one year's standing to feel themselves free to join High Table.

The shadow too was falling black on Lumley. Faced with the imminent departure of University College from the castle, Lord Scarbrough was preparing in 1970 to lease it to the 'Institute of European Studies', the brain-child of a number of 'conjoined' American universities. It was a deal however which never materialised; and when 1970 arrived Lumley was left empty, unfurnished and silent - until a restaurateur with an eye to its uniqueness took it over and staged in it weekly mediaeval banquets.

If generations of Castlemen knew, and wrote, some rhapsodically and some acerbically, of Green the old Butler, so later generations of Castlemen carried - and still carry! - around with them the ikon of their as venerable Portress, Mrs Shaw.

A pillar of the Castle, Mrs Shaw. As Iron a Lady, in her domaine, as any prime minister in hers. As indeed she had to be; for how else survive unscathed thirty generations of undergraduates, wily, feckless, glib, predatory, unprincipled, for whom the days were always those of wine and roses, and the nights the unwearying renewals of old passions? On how many balmy nights was her name bawled on the sweet night air from the River Bank over to Durham School? And always with a hint of nostalgia:

> 'Oh who will ring the Castle bell, Castle bell,
> When we are far away?'

She was succeeded by her daughter Cicely.

The Shaws, John and May, with their two daughters, Cicely and Jessie, and their three sons, came to live in the Lodge in 1938. Heart disease had forced John Shaw, who had been chauffeur to Mr Merrett, the City Surveyor, to give up driving. To him the job of Gate-keeper at the Castle must have seemed ideal; but his tenure of it was woefully short. Within the year Mr Shaw died, leaving his son Gibson to take over the Lodge. Then came the War; and Gibson was called up. And his redoubtable mother took over, to rule the Lodge, and the latecomers, for nearly thirty years. While she officially retired in 1967, in her later years her duties had been taken over more and more by Cicely, who now succeeded her as Portress. To both of them the College was their life; for Cicely went into the Buttery on leaving school in 1942, and helped her mother out in the Lodge.

Cicely, interviewed by *Castellum* in 1987, a full twenty years after her mother's retirement, said of the Portress's duties:

> The hours are long - but not so long as when my mother was alive. Then we worked seven days a week with no time off. Now I work from seven to eight in the morning, and from twelve to one when the Porter [an addition on Cicely's appointment] has his lunch, then from five until midnight Monday to Friday. Saturday I work from seven to eight, and then I'm off for the rest of the day; but Sunday is from seven in the morning till twelve at night during term time.

Unsocial hours indeed!

The Lodge in 1938, when the Shaws arrived - to stay fifty years - could be forgiven for being thought untouched during the previous fifty.

In the Lodge here I have a living-room and kitchenette and bathroom, and there are three bedrooms across the way upstairs. When we first came here the present bathroom was the Porter's bedroom, and we could not all be expected to sleep in that. When my mother came for interview the cobwebs upstairs went from the top to the bottom. Mr Potts, the previous porter, had only one daughter and ours was a family of five, so they cleared out the bedrooms upstairs; but we didn't have a bathroom, and when there was nobody in we could use the Bishop's or the Senate Room bathroom.

The latter pages of a history of this kind are always in danger of developing into a doom-ridden catalogue of change and decay. It is as well therefore to tell here, instead of at the time of their conception, of some of the post-war changes that enlivened the workaday life of toiling Castlemen.

Castle Informal, a distinctly post-war innovation, proved an annual success. A later development, which shows that evolution very occasionally manages to bring about some improvement, was the introduction into it of a theme: in 1967 this was Alice in Wonderland. Castle Formal was another innovation of the same year, made possible by the reduction in the number of University functions held in the Castle owing to the completion of the new Students' Union building. Castle Day bloomed like the flowers themselves in Mrs Slater's Festival of Flowers at the Castle in 1969. And a dashing account of the 1970 Castle Day shows the sophistication which time had brought to this once sober, rather '*thé dansante*' function.

take lunch in the Great Hall, add a pinch of afternoon tea, a dash of sideshows, round it off with a buffet in the Undercroft and heat well with an excellent dance, the whole lubricated by an assortment of alcoholic beverages, and the result is a very successful day. Innovations this year included a marquee on the Courtyard lawn, the Esh Colliery Silver Band, sideshows in the Fellows' Garden, and a formal dance with a band . . .

The pseudo-sophistication seeping out of television seems to have affected Freshers' Wine as well as so much else. An undergraduate, Peter McM. Tinlin, began his account of the Freshers' Wine of 1970 with a not-unfamiliar lament:

The opportunity of contributing in some small way towards the entertainment at Freshers' Wine aroused little enthusiasm in the Freshmen of 1970. Some disapproved of the whole idea, and were offended by the extra 1s. 6d. extorted from them so ruthlessly. Some didn't want to make fools of themselves and some obviously thought that their superior talents would be wasted on something so petty.

Enough however did turn up to make the evening memorable for those concerned. Peter McM. Tinlin's account of the proceedings makes good reading.

Wine was of the usual quality, and the small amount of cheese which actually found its way into stomachs, rather than on to floor, chairs, walls and performers, was generally appreciated. Unfortunately, wine and silence are difficult to keep together for any length of time, and an excellent classical guitar recital by Mr Jim Valentine was heard only by those in the front row.

Mr J.C. Richardson then baffled the audience with his amazing powers of prestidigitation, and continued for the rest of the evening making wine disappear.

An excellent natural talent, which should certainly go far in music halls throughout the nation, was displayed by Mr Dave Cross, who gave a vigorous unaccompanied performance of 'Hole in the Ground'. Then the Dave Cross Gargling Quartet gave such a moving rendering of 'God Save the Queen' that the closest listeners constantly appeared to be wiping the tears from their faces.

For the next, unprecedented, act, two courageous ladies from St Aidan's College, Miss Annelise Fjortoft and Miss Priscilla Brereton, appeared in almost authentic Edwardian dress before the all-male audience. When the noisy reception was stilled, with harmonium accompaniment and a swishing of petticoats, these two sweet young things danced and sang 'Don't Dilly Dally on the Way'. The applause was tumultuous, and the gallant young ladies fled from the clutching hands.

Mr Johnny Soars, later to distinguish himself by throwing eggs across Palace Green, drank a pint of beer while standing on his head, and challenged anyone in the audience to better his time . . .

The evening ended in much mirth, with a trouserless M.J.J. Nicholson singing loyal Castle songs to an admiring audience.

At some time in the late 'Sixties, perhaps under the Organ Scholar of '68 to '70, Christopher Mahon, a Castle Choir seems to have been started. It bore little resemblance to the old Choral Society of pre-War and earlier, nineteenth century, days. Readers will remember the somewhat eclectic programmes that were then given. The Choir, true no doubt to its name, exercised its musicianship on English Cathedral Music, in 1970 voyaging even into the Avalon mists of Llandaff to sing the daily offices in the Cathedral. Their liturgical singing of Byrd's Five-Part Mass at the Ash Wednesday Eucharist in the Chapel looked to be becoming a tradition. In the Easter term, accompanied by the University Music Group, they gave a performance in the Great Hall of Handel's four Coronation Anthems. In the Chapel they sang a Folk Mass on Ascension Day; and a Eucharist according to the 1549 liturgy, which employed Merbeck's original plainsong setting for the new English rite, was sung by three 'clerks'. Outside the Castle again, the Choir ventured into the Prison to sing evensong, sang Communion services at St Hild's and, on the invitation of our old acquaintance the Rev Gordon Berriman, at St Hilda's, South Shields; and broadcast Christmas music on BBC Radio Durham.

And the Thorp Club, a graduates' club which had been founded in 1960, simply for coffee-drinking and the reading of intellectual newspapers, and which was housed in a small room in the Norman Gallery, flourished like the green bay tree with an annual dinner, a Club Tie, and the most aesthetic line in furnishings. This amiable club, so appropriately named after the College's Founder, seems to have been remarkably successful socially. In 1967, for instance, it rather greedily held two annual dinners, one in the Senate Room and one in the *City Hotel*; threw a Sherry Party before all three College functions; and formed a Thorp Association Football Club.

The Thorp Club was successful clearly because it was a homogeneous unit and, moreover, occupied single premises. The same could not be said of the rest of the College during this period; and the Master's perpetual complaint throughout these transitional years was that the distribution of the College over a number of separate establishments (even after the abandonment of Bailey House and Cosin's Hall) made for a growing strain on the College's corporate feeling. In 1968, for instance, undergraduates were dispersed over the Castle, Parson's Field House, Abbey House, Owengate, a few additional rooms in the Bailey, and a handful of 'Durham Rooms.' These last were the rather dubious expedient of 'digs' without board, but costing the same in fees as rooms in College.

Was it, one wonders, in an endeavour to pull these separate strands of the undergraduate body together that a Joint Meeting of Common Rooms was instituted in 1967, and that the Senior Man and Secretary of the JCR were, in 1969, made co-opted members of the Governing Body? One would like to think so, but at the same time one suspects that some of the rationale behind these two somewhat radical proceedings was the greater independence demanded by students as a right. In contrast to previous generations of undergraduates, a disturbing number now regularly petitioned to be allowed to live outside College, in rooms in the town. Similarly, those who lived in College found the nightly locking of the Castle Gate irksome, and compared unfavourably the restriction of their freedom with the licence allowed by the newer Colleges which were built on wholly open lines. The solution to this latter grievance was found in abandoning the traditional 'Gate' and issuing every undergraduate with a key for a Yale lock newly affixed to the wicket.

If Castlemen wanted to be out, the upper echelons of society at large wanted to be in; and the College took advantage of this yearning among the 'executive classes' for 'something different' by throwing open the State Rooms to bed-and-breakfast.

Other links with the past snapped. Both 'Willie' Prowse and Macfarlane-Grieve lamented in 1969 the passing of 'the quiet man', Charles Sands, who came into College as a gyp in 1902, to retire as Senior Gyp in '48. Willie Prowse caught in a sentence the essence both of the man and of the College in which, on the other side of the wire, he had spent his life:

> The college of his young and middle life was small   enough for everyone to know everyone else - the sense of family was remarkably strong and friendship was commoner than prosperity for all of us. Charles Sands knew and liked us, and we liked him. For forty-six years he saw young people grow up and less young people grow older.

While Macfarlane-Grieve wrote:

Charles was one of the most modest and retiring of men and a faithful servant of the College, in whose service he spent his life. His quiet voice and kindly manner . . .

'In whose service he spent his life . . .' A fitting obituary that for its writer, who so soon followed him -

Macfarlane-Grieve: 1910-1913; Master of this College 1939-1953.

And in the tragic 'Sixties died too Mrs. Shaw: 'I have never seen,' wrote the Master, 'so many Christmas cards in a small household than in the Lodge.'

Lumley was left for ever; and the Mitchells, Steward and Housekeeper there since its inception, went to Newcastle.

Joe Bryce, Bursar's Clerk Extraordinary, retired after 41 years.

And the Maddisons, Caterer and Housekeeper at the Castle since they abandoned Hatfield for higher things in 1960, went into retirement. One has only to read the eulogies of their meals in the Senior Man's and the Thorp Club Secretary's reports, and the accounts of the Reunion Dinners, during the years they were up, to appreciate the changes that had come about since the war: those days of rabbit, and meat pies, and fish, and rabbit, and . . .

In order to counterbalance the dangerous fragmentation, the College did make a first giant stride towards centralisation. Bailey Court, between the back of Cosin's Hall and North Bailey, was built, and provided close on 120 rooms, including three dons' sets. Furthermore, the saving resulting from the abandonment of Lumley made the balancing of the College's books no longer seem an impossibility.

Competition being always a spur, the need to match the other and newer Colleges in the provision of creature comforts made for a steady extension throughout the Castle of modern 'plumbing'. Little by little, wash-basins, shaving-points and electric sockets made their brash appearance in every room; while in 1970 the old benches in Hall were sent down, to be replaced by chairs upholstered in College maroon.

Noone though in those early 'Seventies rightly interpreted the omens that were there for all to see. Though the new College, Collingwood, that was to go up by 1973, was to be 'mixed'; and Van Mildert was proposing to admit 25 per cent women, the Master could write, in the 1971 *Castellum*: 'There has been no suggestion that University College shall become mixed. On the contrary there has been a tacit assumption that we shall not . . .'

1972 at least saw cause for celebration, for it was nine hundred years since the start of the building of Durham Castle. A number of ideas for celebrating this noncentenary were discussed, but only one materialised: a Grand Celebration Ball.

This, the biggest event of its kind that the College had ever hosted, sold some 600 double tickets. A marquee was erected in the centre of the Courtyard for supper; and another, with a dance-floor, covered the tennis court in the Fellows' Garden. Covered ways connected the pair of them to the Hall and other parts of the College. Dance Bands and 'Groups' played for the dancing; chamber music and madrigals delectated the Tunstal Gallery; a barbecue of sausages and roast pork made savoury the North Terrace; cartoon films went on show in the Norman Gallery; and a disco concertinaed the walls of the Undercroft.

Alas, the same year saw the discontinuance of the old Assizes. The Castle's State Rooms therefore needed no longer to be made available for the Judges; and so, weighed down with their new responsibilities for maintaining them, the College Authorities thought it timely to have their contents valued for insurance purposes. The result was fairly pleasing: the contents of the State Rooms, including the pictures in the Castle, were valued at £137,000, and the silver at £24,000.

Sic manet gloria mundi

---

1)   *Durham University Journal*, February, 1898

CHAPTER 16

INTERLUDUM

Change had come to University College barely perceptibly during the long period from its foundation to the end of the Second World War. With the onset of the now almost universally execrated 'Sixties change accelerated; towards the end of Colonel Slater's long rule the College showed with every passing year a new face, one scarcely recognisable by those who had known it when it, and the world which in many respects it mirrored, had been held fast in the mould of tradition. This is therefore a fitting place to mark a phenomenon not peculiar to this College but inseparable from places like it: the coming together in such a place, under the invisible tutelage of its *genius loci*, of kindred spirits.

The men who were up at this College have left few records of close comradeship, since such things belong not to history but to the unspoken ephemera of things. But one gathers, here and there, from nostalgic letters, from nostalgic reminiscences, that such friendships were a potent force in the shaping of the lives of those who enjoyed them: outlasting the all too few years in the Keep, in the Junction, up Hall Stairs or in the Norman Gallery; outlasting the years of getting and spending; friendships persisting, in the best of cases, even unto death.

One will never know whether in every year there exist such close fellowships. Perhaps not. In my own year, the Class of '47, one never properly came into being. Yet two years later, so powerful a grouping came together as to form a generative force that could be felt at every level of Old Student life - particularly at Reunions.

Is it that, in all such instances, one man binds a whole body of men together? Certainly in the latter case one man held a very large group together - men of his own year, and men of contingent years both before and after: Ralph Appleton. It may well be so; for those with such loving, and lovable, natures act as magnets do, pulling towards them the not altogether disparate elements which otherwise would spin directionless away.

A similar group to ours, which those of us who frequented Reunions got

296

to know well, belonged to a vintage much much earlier. Almost all these were priests. And because they represent that half of the equation without which no man-made thing of stone and mortar, however beautiful, however inspiring, can be said really to exist, they will have their place here.

First, two bachelors. Canon William Purdon - 'Bumble' to his friends - who was up from 1920 to 1923: a cherubic, happy man, high-church and high-principled; and H.C.H. Francis (1911-13, and 1921-2), whose mild, rather fussy schoolmasterish exterior belied his having been commissioned in the Great War in the Royal Scots. Then two married priests: Vic Hill (1921-23) and Bernard Goodwins (1920-23), and *Times* journalist Reginald Easthope (1922-26), a trio who sported to the last at Reunions the maroon blazers they had worn in the 'Twenties.

Vic Hill, turbulent priest of Matfen, and soldier in the Church Army before he soldiered in earnest in the Montgomeryshire Yeomanry and the Camel Corps, and flew 'kites' of wire and plywood in the Royal Flying Corps, was a man of great wit. Was it he, I wonder, was the linch-pin that kept all his friends together? One story will give the essence of the man.

Shortly after retiring to Keswick in 1957 he went to Carlisle, and was soon browsing in a bookshop. A big man, whose scarf inside his overcoat hid his clerical collar, came up and said:

'I don't know you! Are you in this diocese?'

'I've just retired to Keswick from the diocese of Newcastle,' replied Vic Hill.

'And have you written to the Bishop asking permission to officiate in this diocese?'

'Yes I have,' said Vic, adding, 'but the old buffer hasn't replied yet.'

'I am he,' bassooned Bishop Bloomer.

Bernard Goodwins gave out a divine benignity. Tall, handsome, a priestly enjoyer of life and its humours, a man easily touched by beauty, he was, in his own way, a poet. This is what he wrote after the 1972 Reunion, when he recollected in tranquillity the marvellous experience; and this too conveys, as no words of mine can, the yearning essence of the man:

I shall never see its like again.
Vic Hill can vouch for what it was -
for he was in the room next door,
part of the Chaplain's suite.
Vic and I were getting ready for
the eight-thirty service in Chapel,
when looking through my bedroom window,
I shouted for Vic to come and see,
what I shall never see again - or he.
A perfect, brilliant, rainbow -
framing the dull brick viaduct,
and the city roofs below -
both ends touching down;
one beyond the Prebends Bridge,
the other to the right of the Station.
And while we watched this wondrous sight,
a train passed gently over,
with a royal blue engine (or was it Palatinate?)
drawing six, or was it seven cream coaches?
'We could only stand and stare,'
without a brush of camel's hair,
and neither of us paint - do you?

And last of this trio, Reginald Easthope, Journalist Extraordinary: dignified, eccentrically elegant, with white hair and white pointed diabolic
beard, and curling upturned moustaches after the old Kaiser's fashion. A
lover of magenta shirts, which brought back to him the Palatinate purple
of his sportive youth, and of flowery ties, which made up, year following
year, his Reunion uniform.

These are not all. For there were Tommy Corden and Frank Chase,
inseparable Canons both, and Geoffrey Williams, Canon of Blackburn, all
three of a later vintage, that of the early and mid 'Thirties.

And closer to home, and to this writer - Ralph Appleton, and Ridley
Coats and Mike Pulling and . . . and Len and Harry and Derek and John
and John. . .

But the reader of this book will have his own names; for these are the
College as you, and you alone, in your inestimable good fortune, know it.

Chapter 17

GREEN BURSTING FIGS AND CHIAN WINE

The departure of Len Slater coincided with the onset of a period of even more enormously accelerated change than the College had known hitherto, one which saw the College quite metamorphosed from the homogeneous, close-knit, even monastic family it had remained until the end of the Second World War, to the coeducational assemblage that an increasingly inchoate society dictated should be the 'norm'.

It is significant that the retiring Master, in his Letter written for the 1973 *Castellum*, spoke still, and nostalgically, of the College fabric; for in the main, as we have seen, it was the fabric which had occupied so much of the thought and the energies of the two Masters who had ruled the College in the post-War period.

An apologetic reference in this, the twentieth and last of such Letters of Mr Slater (for he had long abandoned the title 'Colonel'), would have raised many a quizzical eyebrow among the College's tutors of forty years before. The italics are mine:

> The dais in the Hall for High Table, part of the large platform used annually for Congregation, was retained experimentally for a term and its continued use later agreed. *It is certainly not intended to indicate hierarchy* but it does improve the appearance of the Hall from both ends . . .

For once, aesthetic considerations were allowed to outweigh the levelling influence of the Brave New Bedlam, as the New Age was proving itself to be.

The five years during which Dr D.W. McDowall presided over the College's Treasury as Master are so singularly sparing in interest as to be passed over with the speed that events in the 'Sixties and 'Seventies generally merit. Dr McDowall, a numismatist and civil servant in the UGC (Universities Grants Commission), arrived in 1973, and left in 1978 to become Assistant Director of the Polytechnic of North london . . . an institution with 'twice as many students as the whole of the University of Durham . . .'[1]

The year 1979 saw a new Master appointed: Edward Salthouse, an Electrical Engineer from Belfast, who had served an apprenticeship with Harland and Wolff, and who was Reader in Engineering Science.

By now the College had grown to a size unimagined, perhaps unimaginable, by Archdeacon Thorp. There were now 330 residential places, an increase of 60 over the past five years; and accommodation for the extra number would not have been possible without the opening of Moatside Court, which ensured that all Castlemen would now live within easy walking distance of their Castle.

It was the increase in the number of Castlemen, as well as outside inflationary pressures and, one assumes, the accelerated tempo of life, which brought about, in 1976, what the Senior Man of the time (Vince Hesketh) described as 'one of the most radical changes in day to day [sic] college life . . . the shift from waitress-served to self-service meals.'[2] 'This much feared move,' he continued, 'from the traditional meal system was greeted with less hostility than many anticipated . . . Many prefer the speed and flexibility of self-service.'

Certainly the most important event of any in succeeding years was the 150th Anniversary of the University - that is, of the College, which took place in 1982.

Cast your mind back now, reader, to Verdant Green, on whose 'fast' friend Larkyns' walls simpered those delicious *au naturel* 'pets of the ballet', and to Tom Brown's elegant-mannered friend Drysdale, who sported on his walls those greatest of dancers Taglioni and Cerrito. For Fortune's Wheel was now come full-circle: that most perfect of all the arts was given at long last its rightful place in Academe; and stuffy scions of ancient Houses and fulsome and inglorious politicians alike were passed over, in the hunt for a new Chancellor, in favour of the beautiful and blessed Margot Fonteyn. Her Installation took place in the Cathedral in Anniversary Year: the most beautiful and most talented Chancellor ever to preside over any University.

Of her fresh choosing were the artists who were presented, on this occasion, with Honorary Degrees: Malcolm Arnold, Kiri Te Kanawa, *in absentia* the benign and courtly John Betjeman, and 'Madame' herself (to her dancers) - the very great Ninette de Valois.

There were Open Days at the 150th Anniversary, Fun Runs, and open-air performances of a mediaeval Mystery Play. And there was an Anniversary Ball so magical that we Old Castlemen who danced at it were whirled back to the June Balls of our sequined and glorious youth. Guests arriving were met in a moth-heavy Courtyard with glasses of 'Bubbly', and mediaeval music whose shawms and rebecs and six-holed pipes and citoles and hautboys were thrummed and tootled by a suitably attiréd ensemble; while in the Hall, later, dances were danced to the music of the Army Air Force Band. And Old Castlemen, in the strength of their youth, threw a boozy party afterwards in the Dons' Set, up Hall Stairs.

By 1985 it had become clear to the Governing Body that, in obedience to that most fundamental law governing life on this planet, Adapt or Die , the College must admit women. Obliquely as the Pythoness the Master, in his Letter for the 1985 *Castellum*, said:

> to all of us involved with running the College it has been quite clear for some time that for the future well-being of Castle it [the admission of women] is essential.'

The fact of the matter was that many men were now, in this most curious of ages, being deterred from applying for a single-sex college; and (dare it be said? and what did it mean?) those who were applying were 'not such as we would have wished to apply.'

So in two years came the biggest break of all with the old traditions: the entry into College of its first women - forty-nine of them.

This surely is the right and proper, indeed the only, place to stop. Others, in days to come,

> Still nursing the unconquerable hope
> Still clutching the inviolable shade

can take up pen and chart the continuing history of our College; I, for my part, must hove to, where those shy traffickers the dark Iberians come, and there on the beach undo my corded bales.

---

1)   *Castellum*, 1979
2)   *Castellum*, 1977

APPENDIX

The Durham University Song.

WORDS BY W. D. LOWE, M.A. (*Univ.*).

MUSIC BY JOHN H. BATTEN, MUS.B. (*Hatf.*).

With vigour.

1. Up, com-rades, let us sing, Mak - ing the old halls ring With Dur-ham's praise;
2. Hail to thee, Northern light, Burn as a bea-con bright, Ne - ver to wane;

Grey Dur-ham, thou hast stood Tow'r - ing o'er Wear's flood From an - - - cient days.
Gold - en has been thy past, Long may it ev - er last, Mo - ther of men.

CHORUS.

Te, mat-er, de - cor-et Pro - pri - a glo - ri - a: Sit e - a-dem ti - bi For - tu - na aur - e - a.

(ENTERED AT STATIONERS' HALL).

BOATING SONG.

FOR MEN'S VOICES.

Composed by Captain A. A. Macfarlane-Grieve, M.C.

Words by H. St. G.

The cedar boat is the boat for me,
   Sing hey, Sing ho.
The cedar boat of a seasoned tree,
With a clean cut bow and running free,
And varnished as just such a craft should be.
   Sing hey, Sing ho.

This joy that is mine is shared by you,
   Sing hey, Sing ho.
In the riggers taut and the rowlocks true,
In the scrunching blade through a swirl of blue,
And the slide and swing of a rattling crew,
   Sing hey, Sing ho.

The long swing down and the sharp drive back,
   Sing hey, Sing ho,
With muscle and sinew stretched on the rack,
While Fortune frowns and your chance looks black,
Then the quickening spurt till the others crack.
   Sing hey, Sing ho.

And these are the joys men don't regret,
   Sing hey, Sing ho.
And these are the fights we think of yet
Where each of us owed the rest a debt,
And the debt was paid and we can't forget.
   Sing hey, Sing ho.

Supplement to The Durham University Journal, March, 1920.

For Men's Voices.

Arranged from Edite, Bibite in the Kommersbuch by A. A. Macfarlane-Grieve, Esq.

Plaudite, remiges,
   Gaudio grandi,
"Floreat nobilis
   Ars remigandi."

Hearty boat-songs to-night,
Echoed with will and might,
After the keen delight
   Of a stern race.
Sing along, swing along,
Training behind us,
But as fit every whit next term shall find us.

Long as our river flows,
Rowing tradition grows,
Meting out fame to those
   Great oars of old.
Sing along, swing along,
Clean off the feather,
Drive it strong, keep it long, pulling together.

And when in later life
Troubles and sordid strife
Through your whole world are rife,
   Hope to the end.
Sing along, swing along,
With your old ardour,
Share the work, never shirk, finish the harder.

So let us honour pay
To those who day by day
Trained in whole-hearted way,
   Summer despite.
Sing along, swing along,
Muscles all glowing,
Laud and applaud the Sport, 'Varsity Rowing.

Plaudite, remiges,
   Gaudio grandi,
"Floreat nobilis
   Ars remigandi."

H. ST. G.

INDEX